LIONS' PAWS

The Story of Famous Hands

BY NELLIE SIMMONS MEIER

PREFACE BY DR. WILLIAM BENHAM
INTRODUCTION BY MEREDITH NICHOLSON

NEW YORK *Barrows Mussey* PUBLISHER

"Length of days is in her right hand; and in her left hand riches and honour."

Proverbs, Ch. III, vs. 16.

TO RUTH

Whose intelligent interest and helpful criticism have inspired my application and concentration—hence this book.

NOTE: The prints of the hands have been reduced except those of the following: *Helen Hayes, Lynn Fontanne, John Erskine, Elbert Hubbard, Elsie De Wolfe, Susan B. Anthony, Jane Addams.*

Introduction

Palmistry should not be confused with fortune-telling, table-tipping, ouija-board writing, forecasting by means of coffee-grounds or like media. It has many centuries of discussion and belief behind it. It was known to the Chinese long before the Christian era; the Egyptians and the Greeks were not without belief in it. It has survived the contumely of modern skepticism; it has acquired dignity and substance. The introduction of the fingerprint into criminology called attention anew to the individuality of the hand. If nature has been at pains to place so irrefutably the clue to man's identity in the finger tips, why should not the great mother of us all have mapped in our palms traits and tendencies indicative of distinct personalities?

The practice of palmistry as a parlor pastime touches only the superficial aspects of what deserves recognition as a science. It affords me great pleasure to say of the author of this book that, in the many years I have known her as my interesting and delightful fellow-citizen, she has been a diligent student of all the arts. She has made of palmistry something more than a fad, and I venture to say that no one has ever carried the study of it further or to a higher plane. She is, in the fullest sense, a cultivated woman. Such a remark will seem unnecessary and possibly a trifle patronizing to Mrs. Meier's wide circle of friends in America and in Europe; but I should like to make it clear that this book is a serious contribution to a fascinating field of research and exegesis, and that it deserves acceptance as the most interesting, comprehensive and credible work yet produced on the subject by a conscientious and enlightened investigator.

MEREDITH NICHOLSON.

Preface

It has been my pleasure to know Mrs. Nellie Simmons Meier for many years, and to know her as a lady of refinement and culture devoting much of her time to a scientific study of hands. Many who have consulted her have written and told me of the constructive character of her workmanship, and the helpfulness her hand analyses have been to them.

She is one of the few who realize the responsibility devolving upon those who make hand analysis a serious profession. Through the frequent correspondence which has passed between us, covering a number of years, I have had occasion to know that she has, and is, devoting herself to a truly scientific interpretation of what the hands reveal. Her work in this field has had a militant influence in bringing to important people in all walks of life a real appreciation that hand analysis for vocational purposes is a science, not a pastime.

Her work as I know it is based upon sound principles, properly coordinated. I have, therefore, looked forward with keen anticipation to the publishing of "Lions' Paws."

Wm G. Benham

Dr. William G. Benham.

Contents

Chapter 23

He Who Walks Alone

William Fortune
Walt Disney
Charles Holman-Black
Marie, Grand Duchess of Russia
Quill Jones
Ishbel, Countess of Aberdeen

PAGE 154

Chapter 1: *Let Us Shake Hands*

For two hours I had been sitting opposite Lawrence Tibbett reading one of the most difficult palms ever spread for my inspection. The time for the interview had long since gone by. The telephone kept ringing—Tibbett was overdue at another engagement, but he refused to budge.

"It's so true it is almost uncanny," he said. "Please go right on."

It was very arduous work. Hands like Tibbett's are no open book, they are more like a cross-word puzzle. The mounts or cushions of his hands are developed to a point where they must dominate the hand reading. The lines are secondary in importance. Anyone who possesses such hands will do well to regard his machinery for living in the light of a high powered auto which he is purchasing at great cost, of which, therefore, he wishes to take excellent care. To reach the end of the journey without disaster requires the greatest intelligence as well as the greatest caution. For hands like Lawrence Tibbett's mean life on a road full of hairpin curves.

There is a wide stretch between the thumbs and the fingers—Danger—the owner is all too likely to reason, "I know what I am doing," and go off half-cocked.

A spendthrift of life, in time, energy and money, especially if his affections are involved, Tibbett drives down the road with a reckless disregard of the petty details he hates. But although he hates them, they are not beyond his power to control. His left thumb, only fairly flexible, shows that he can put the brakes upon himself. The first and second phalanges of the thumb, which represent will power and logic respectively, are pretty well balanced, but there is a thickness of the joints which means stubborness—he can if he will, but will he? Together with his smooth fingers, these joints show a nature that fairly leaps forward when opposed. In the driving seat his first reaction to an obstacle in his path is to get over it or around it without slowing up sufficiently to consider it.

Tibbett's first fingers show him to be just, merciful, and to have a real feeling for the under dog. The pointed tips reveal how quickly he can see—all that he wants to see.

In the long nail phalange of the middle finger is shown an understanding of the finer or higher things of life, and the square tip also reveals that he reasons from a practical basis upon metaphysical problems. This phalange also indicates that, while he is interested in theories and idealistic propaganda of others from a common sense point of view, he is

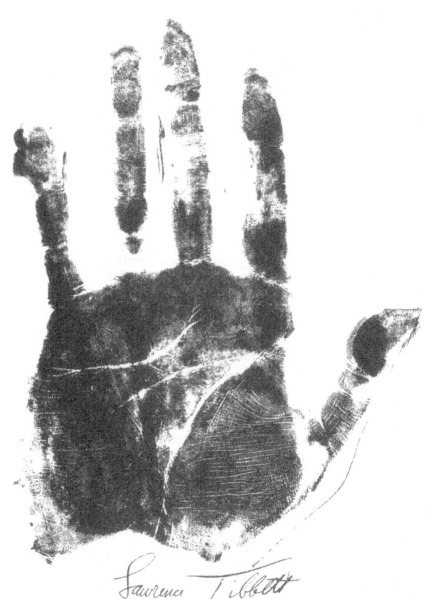

Lawrence Tibbett
April 12/31 — New York City

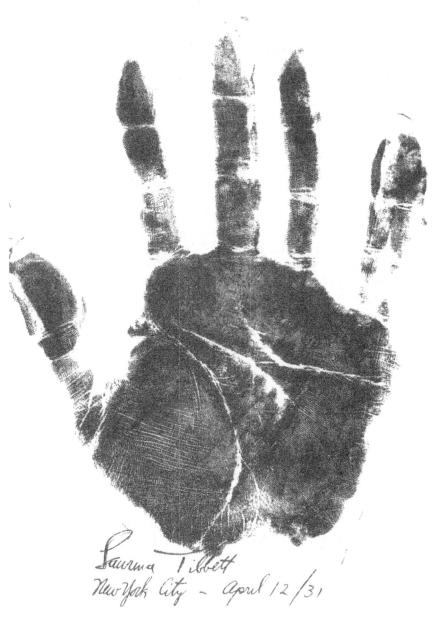

Lawrence Tibbett
New York City — April 12/31

cautious in avoiding the criticism or ridicule which might come from being classed with fanatics. This caution is his emergency brake which he can use in the driving of his car of life.

The nail phalanges of his third fingers mark desire for truth and sincerity in art as well as in living. The second phalanges show a love of color expressed as actual color or through the arts. His gift of expression lies in his fourth fingers. And in the stretch between the third and fourth fingers lies a lightning-like rapidily of thought and of action.

But the mounts!

They are huge, filling the hand, dwarfing the lines. Venus, the base of the thumb, fairly shouts of the fire, the passion, the ardor, the love of life that animate the man. Here is Tibbett's high powered engine, here is the motor which will generate the power for the long and arduous up-hill drive towards artistic perfection. It is a good engine, capable of speed, and constructed so that it will stand up under wear and tear. The distance from the second joint of the thumb to where the line of life encircles it shows an enormous vitality.

Fuel to the engine is supplied by two mounts, the one under the forefinger, Jupiter, which tells of Tibbett's love of approbation and pride in achievement, and the lower part of the Mount of the Moon, opposite Venus at the base of the palm, which shows a powerful imagination.

With this high powered engine, well fueled with pride, approbation and imagination, Lawrence Tibbett would be unable to keep his car upon the road at all except for two safe-guards which have a very large development. The middle phalange of Saturn, indicating wisdom and prudence, is the balance wheel. Tibbett can, at will, weigh his thought and action, consider his course and alter it. The lack of flexibility in the thumb helps to the same end. But the mount of Saturn, under the second finger, holds a secret. There is revealed a grave and sober side to this gifted man, a side shown to hardly anyone, and which only a very few of his friends would believe possible. So far it has given depth to such characterizations as that of The Emperor Jones. In the future—but I do not forecast. I am willing, however, to state that brilliant as has been Lawrence Tibbett's career, his potentialities have not been nearly realized. He can—again, if he will—make his life and work a bigger finger production than it is at this day.

Lawrence Tibbett's hands were, so far as I can reckon, about the twenty thousandth pair I have inspected and read for their owners. For thirty-five years I have been studying and examining hands.

Long, long ago, when I was a girl I found that to be one of the leaders I must acquire what a later generation dubbed "a line." I was no prettier, no better dancer, no more intelligent than the girls about, and there were many, many girls. I just had to do *something*. I began to study palmistry. As soon as it was known that I could read hands I was in demand. All my young friends (and many of their parents and grandparents) wanted their hands analyzed. I worked willingly; I served an apprenticeship at church bazaars and charity entertainments. If I danced less at a party, it was from no lack of attention. Instead there was a waiting line, pleading for favors. Was I popular? I was.

This new study brought an entirely unsuspected reward. I found after reading many, many hands that I was actually telling the truth. I knew that whereof I spoke. Some reader may now lift a skeptical eyebrow. Very well, you Doubting Thomas, let us journey back into Time, a long way back, and visit no less a personage than Aristotle. In the year 350 B.C. we find that great philosopher engaged in writing a work to be known to posterity, even to this day, as "Aristotle's Masterpiece." And in this Masterpiece there is one complete chapter—

"Of Palmistry, showing the various
judgments drawn from the hand."

At the conclusion of the chapter appears this verse:

"Thus he that Nature rightly understands,
May from each Line imprinted in his Hands,
His future Fate and Fortune come to know,
And what Path it is his Feet shall go.
His Secret Inclinations he may see,
And to what Vice he shall addicted be
To th' End that when he looks into his Hand,
He may upon his Guard the better stand;
And turn his wandering Steps another way:
When e'er he finds he does from Virtue stray."

I strongly suspect that the translator originated the verse. But it appears as a part of the "Masterpiece," first published in English in London in 1878. All through the centuries since Aristotle, hands have been studied, and as I went through those centuries with the sages who have believed in hands, I too became a serious student and reader of hands. I anticipate the question—For money? Have I ever been a professional reader? Yes. After some years of popularity I suffered from too great a demand upon my time. I could not appear anywhere, socially, at clubs, even on the street, without having at least one pair of palms stretched inquiringly to me. All sorts of people sought me out. In self-defence I put a charge upon my services. As I had other resources I have always put every cent of this money into a fund which is shared by those who need it; it has never been mine except in trust. The fee has increased with the years, but not a day passes without several requests for appointments. I cannot begin to accede to them all. I am a professional reader of character through scientific palmistry.

To know people through their hands requires certain definite, technical information. In a book of this size it is impossible to give all the rules, but it is quite possible to give a brief outline of them which will enable the reader to master the major points, and so to understand the readings of the Lions' paws which are included in this volume.

To begin: Let us shake hands!

You have given me a firm, even pressure, and I know at once that you are likely to be a person to whom I would go in an emergency, whom I could rely upon in a crisis, and who, I feel, would be as ready with active help as with words of advice.

Leslie Howard shakes hands in just that way. When, at the request of his managers, he was brought to me at my hotel in Hollywood, and we shook hands, he gave me a firm, equable grasp—in which I read an inborn courtesy which acknowledged without words that he considered himself to be receiving a favor. He did not question my ability; he assumed it. Until he proved otherwise, I was as able in my profession as he was in his. It was the handshake of a man who gave all others in the world an even break. Howard always gives the other fellow a fair chance.

But perhaps you have not responded with a firm even pressure. Instead you have laid your hand limply in mine and have not pressed mine at all. You give out as little as you can, perhaps nothing. This may be due to timidity, secretiveness, or to the fact that you are a negative character.

But suppose that you have done neither of these. You have grasped my hand hard, so hard that it has hurt, and I sigh with relief when my numbed fingers are released. You are a cordial person. You have strong likes and dislikes and if you had happened not to like me, you probably would not have shaken hands at all.

And last, you may have met my hand in totally different fashion. You may have extended your fingertips in a perfunctory handshake. You make little impression upon me, and I make little upon you. In so presenting the tips of your fingers you have definitely erected a wall between us, usually a wall of caste, which can be entered only through a door of equality, as you see equality.

In the handshake then, is the first index to character, and these four types are those usually encountered. The first, the even handshake, usually is that of a person who has a palm which tapers either at the wrist or at the base of the fingers. The other end of the palm is likely to be square or broad. Such a palm is indicative of finesse and tact. Leslie Howard's hand carried these in addition to sureness of personality and cordiality; in fact, Leslie Howard had a delightful quality of handshake that is comparable to the delightful quality of his acting.

After the handshake comes the difference in the two hands. In the ordinary right handed person the left hand shows natural characteristics, the right, the acquired ones. If the person is left handed the reverse is true.

Consider the two thumbs. Together they are the index to what is to be made of life. Lines or mounts or fingers cannot begin to compare in significance with thumbs. When the thumbs are weak, that is small, set low in the hands, and are pointed and decidedly easy to bend back, their owner will avoid being a failure only by a miracle. Usually persons with weak thumbs have, as well, weak chins—that is, chins that recede. Thumbs that are very flexible, that bend back easily and have a wide stretch between the thumb and first finger, belong to people who are affable, who adapt themselves with ease to others and to whatever their surroundings happen to be.

If they are good story tellers they do not spoil their story by sticking closely to facts. They are good mixers, the joy of any hostess. When their friends have learned to season their tales with a liberal sprinkling of salt they offer delightful entertainment. This variety of flexible thumb may be counterbalanced somewhat by the nail phalange. If it is longer, or as long, as the second phalange of the thumb, the lucky owner will have the ability to check his exaggerations and to stick nearer to truths. But if the thumbs are flexible and have a wide stretch, and the nail phalange is short and very pointed, the owners will be found fickle, disloyal, fully capable of arguing always in their own favor and of sacrificing those who have done the most for them, to their selfish interests. Unfortunately our memories can supply many illustrations.

The opposite type of thumb, those with the nail phalanges very long, rather flat and square on the end, with the thumbs themselves very stiff, almost bending in rather than out, and set close to the hand, belong to secretive people, who are narrow and opinionated in their views and outlook. They rarely express an opinion, but pride themselves on being consistent in their views. They say—or even think—a thing and stick to it. They have few, if any, intimate friends and are quite sufficient unto themselves. They are self-contained people who view with suspicion an affable advance from a stranger. They usually hold the mental query, "What are they after?" They look after their own interests first, but with those looked after. they are safe to deal with and will then take care of yours.

Ideal thumbs reach nearly, if not quite, to the middle joint of the first finger. The two phalanges are almost equal, slightly flexible and slightly rounded. Their owners are decisive, but open to reason. They are open minded, fair in judgment, generous, truthful and loyal.

Tom Taggart, Democratic leader. the man who gave to America the knowledge of the healing waters of French Lick, had ideal thumbs. Taggart had a personality so warm, so delightful, that the colored people in Indiana would cross the street "jes to shake hands with Ma'ss Taggart," even when they were on their way to vote "Republican." Taggart was all that his ideal thumbs and the great cushions of his palms proclaimed him, a royal giver, a royal liver.

To read thumbs one must experiment with many hands until the terms "flexibility" and "stiffness" are fully plain. But it is worth while. By their thumbs more than by any line, mount or finger, shall ye know them.

Chapter 2: *Study These Paws*

It is impossible to chart a handshake or to picture flexibility of thumbs. But many of the remaining characteristics of hands can be diagrammed. Directions for hand reading usually illustrate the various mounts, lines and joints by offering a stiff waxen-looking model. Instead, I offer you the paws of a living Lion, a man who is well known to you through an intimate radio talk each evening—the hands of Lowell Thomas.

I owe to Mr. Thomas not only permission to use his hands, but acquaintance with many other Lions who run through these pages.

Upon the prints of Lowell Thomas's hands are marked the lines and mounts and the identifying names of the finger joints. We are not yet ready to read the hands. As they are to be our guides of the reading of all hands, we shall examine them first in impersonal fashion and then make a specific analysis.

Look at the marks upon the fingers. The three divisions made by the joints are called "phalanges," the first or nail phalange, the second or middle phalange between the first and second joints, and the third phalange next to the palm of the hand. The shape and length of fingers speaks of general characteristics. Short fingers that are smooth through their entire length are those of a person who is quick to grasp generalities, and who is impatient of detail. Knotted short fingers belong to a person who is accurate in details and who will not accept a general statement or conclusion unless it is based upon satisfactory proof.

These characteristics may be modified by the length of all the fingers or of a single finger, and by the shape of the tips or of a particular finger tip, so that it is wiser to consider each finger separately. Hands in which all the fingers are of one type or shape are rare.

A pointed or tapering first finger usually belongs to a man or woman who is quick to grasp an idea and who is receptive of new impressions.

A moderately pointed tip of the second finger marks the natural optimist, he who looks upon the bright side of the present and confidently expects better things to come. If unusually pointed, the owner lives lightly, may be frivolous, gossipy, and is likely to be irresponsible. To this light living individual sorrows are evanescent and make little impression. Such folks are honey sippers, avoiding care and forgetting anything disagreeable, but they are often charming companions since they can find a glimmer of sunshine and play in its warmth.

A pointed third finger accompanies a direct relation to the beauty of life. Its possessor will love the ideal behind life or art, and will appreciate

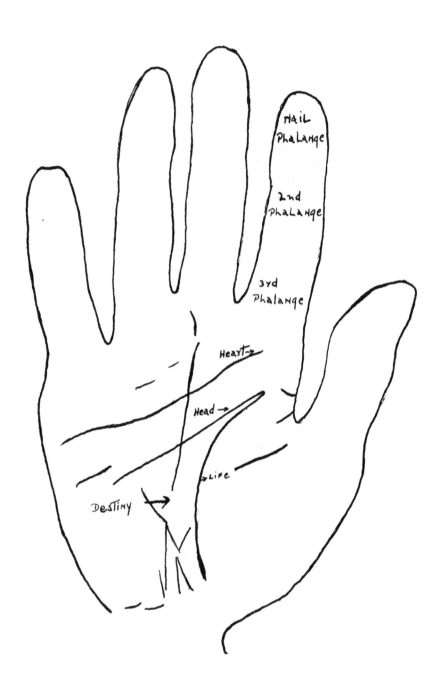

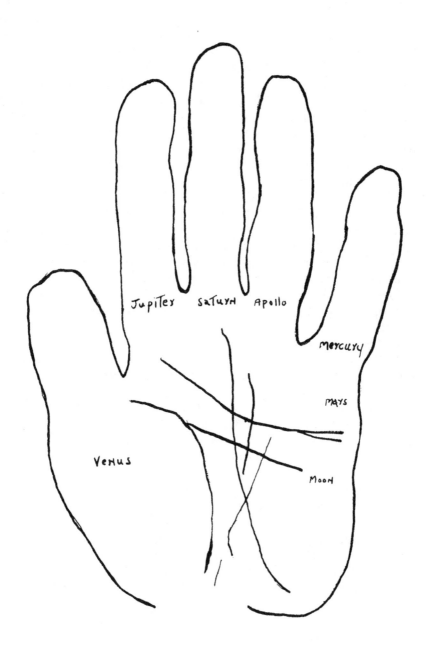

it more through delicacy of detail than breadth or depth of conception.

A pointed fourth finger belongs to a quick witted owner who has the gift of words. He is good at repartee and may be eloquent on occasion.

Square tipped fingers belong to those of very different traits. A square tipped first finger denotes a man who is slow to accept the new; he has to be shown, and more than that, he wants to think it over. He is not likely to blaze a trail but will travel in the safe, beaten track. A square tipped second finger shows an appreciation of the sunshine of life because its owner sees clearly the shadows. A square tipped third finger reveals one who demands reason and a use for things. Fads, fancies and whimsicalities are uninteresting to him. A square tip on a little finger indicates that its owner could present facts based on knowledge of his subject convincingly, and where the finger is short he will express his thoughts better in writing than in conversation.

The third type of finger tip, the spatulate which is the square tip that flares at each side of the nail phalange, marks another variety of human beings.

Spatulate tips on first fingers are the property of very few people. But they exist. Their owners are extremists in thought and action. Religious fanatics have spatulate first finger tips. To gain their ends in business or achieve success in an undertaking the unlucky possessors of such tips will employ methods that will react with boomerang effect and cause their defeat.

A spatulate tip on the second finger shows a nature physically and mentally restless, one eager to adventure in the new. The explorer, the inventor, the research worker delving into the secrets of the universe, have such finger tips.

A spatulate third finger means that the owner has individuality. A worker in creative art, not a dreamer. His gifts are peculiarly a product of his personality. As an artist, unsigned pictures are easily recognized as his work; as an actor or orator, he employs a technique that cannot be imitated; as a musician, he makes the work of a composer his very own as he renders it. He creates as he interprets.

A spatulate fourth finger tip belongs to a quick, active person who is likely to be explosive in speech and action. When it accompanies a spatulated second finger tip, and the owner is an investigator in scientific fields, it will lead him to fame as a discoverer.

Now we are ready to look at the hands of Lowell Thomas and to read his fingers. In a completed reading these finger tips are related to lines, mounts, and to each other. But even with the simple information which

24

I have given here, it is quite possible to discover certain facts about Mr. Thomas.

As a whole, his fingers are shorter than the palm of the hand. This at once places Lowell Thomas in the ranks of practical people. His first finger, which is comparatively short, discloses a certain dislike of executive responsibility; he has powers in this direction but, emotionally, he does not respond to them. The nail phalanges on all the fingers are long. If he believes it necessary for him to accept executive responsibility, his conscientious qualities force him to such action. The quickness of thought and action indicated in the wide flare between the third and fourth fingers and the diplomacy shown in the length of the little finger, as well as the gift of language revealed by its pointed tip, all these enable him to show or teach others how to carry out his ideas successfully.

Take the fingers separately. The rather square tip of the first finger shows that Mr. Thomas will listen to suggestion but will think it over before he acts upon it.

The second finger has a rather spatulate tip. He wants to know what is around the corner and he will assume a risk to gain that knowledge.

The square tip of the third fingers shows that the practical or useful side of art productions appeal to Mr. Thomas more than the mystical or metaphysical. He requires a reason for the existence of various phases of creative art. Lines of use as well as beauty, as shown in architecture, constructive engineering or the building of ships, etc., would be the things in which he would find intelligent interest. He is not interested in the modernistic pictures which, to the public, may mean anything or nothing. Music to him means rhythm and melody, and not the attempt of composers to place a musical interpretation on practical work.

The fourth finger is square tipped. He does not like to speak extemporaneously, he works better when he writes his talks out first. Also, he tells the truth as he sees and understands it.

The impressions shown are marked as to the lines and mounts of Mr. Thomas's hands. For clearness the mounts are marked in the right hand and the lines in the left. Remember that these are impressions, and that therefore, just as reflected in a mirror, the right hand is shown on the left and the left hand on the right. In all readings the left hand on a normally right handed person shows natural characteristics, and the right hand shows developed characteristics. In a normally left handed person these are reversed; the right hand shows the natural characteristics and the left, the developed ones.

Look at the right hand—so labelled. You will see seven mounts, clearly indicated, together with their names, Jupiter below the first finger, Saturn below the second, Apollo below the third, and Mercury below the fourth. The mount of Venus is really the third phalanx of the thumb. Directly across the palm is the mount of the Moon and above it the seventh mount, upper Mars.

If these mounts or cushions are developed, that is, full and rounded, or on the contrary undeveloped, that is flat and almost hollow, they tell certain truths about their possessors. But, as always, these are modified by other characteristics shown in the thumbs, fingers and lines.

When the mount of Jupiter rises high, the owner is said to be a Jupiterian. If the finger above it is long, he is ambitious and may be a leader. He is apt to be self-confident, sometimes vain. But he is always warm hearted. If the finger is short, he lacks initiative. He wants approbation but he fears to risk in order to attain.

Under the second finger is the mount of Saturn. If Saturn is very full, and the second finger is long with the other fingers inclined to lean towards it, the owner is a Saturnian. He is inclined to take himself and others seriously, often too seriously. If his second finger carries a pointed tip he will have more of an optimistic outlook, and incidentally is less likely to remain unmarried. For decided Saturnians are averse to ties. They rebel against being held. But if they do marry they may be counted on to make loyal husbands and wives. In business the Saturnian is a hard worker who builds slowly.

When the mount of Apollo, under the third finger, rises high, the owner is healthy, vigorous, possesses considerable versatility, and is often brilliant. He has a decided liking for the beautiful and the artistic. A star on the mount of Apollo, which marks the end of a line rising in the base of the palm, together with a long well developed third finger, slightly longer than the second finger, marks the potential genius.

The full mount of Mercury—under the fourth finger—is often possessed by rather short, rather dark, active persons who are restless both physically and mentally and are often nervous. The Mercurian wants change of scene, change of events and change of associates. He seeks a mate early in life, falls in love with a person of his own age and usually of his own type. The male Mercurian likes women who are full of go and life, and who present a smart appearance.

Palmistry does not recognize the marriage tie. It is aware of affections and of passions, but it has no relation to a legal or a religious ceremony. The Mercurian wants to be proud of the woman he loves, and if he is a father he is devoted to his children.

He is ingenious in finding ways in which to make money. Usually he makes money readily, but unless his hand shows checks, such as a cautious joining of the head and life lines, he is apt to spend money as fast as he makes it. He possesses shrewdness, can make others work for him and has a good deal of diplomacy.

The mount at the base of the thumb is the mount of Venus. When Venus is developed, its possessor is likely to possess charm, sympathy and tenderness, and to combine these with susceptibility to the attractions of the opposite sex. If the head line is well marked and the thumb stiff, the emotions will be controlled but will nevertheless be strong. But if there is a full mount of Venus and a very pointed second finger, beware! The possessor will be fickle, flirtatious, irresponsible in affection.

The mount of the Moon directly across the palm opposite Venus, indicates, when developed, that the possessor is imaginative and has an understanding of the problems of others. The more developed the mount, the more intense are these qualities.

One last mount, that of upper Mars, directly above the mount of the Moon. Well developed, this means courage and coolness in dealing with danger.

And now we may return to the hands of Lowell Thomas and make our second reading through their mounts.

The outstanding and most interesting mount on his hands is that of the Moon. It contains a whorl like a finger print. This indicates an intuition I term the sixth sense. In a writer it denotes the quality of human interest throughout his work; in a singer we find what we call the heart quality in his voice; in a musician we speak of his wonderful touch. The work of artist or sculptor who possesses this mark is best described in Richard Realf's poem "Indirection."

> "Back of the canvas that glows
> The painter is hinted and hidden;
> Into the statue that breathes
> The soul of the sculptor is bidden."

In the hands of Lowell Thomas, it is called "personality plus."

The mount of Venus, normally developed and firm, shows vitality and energy. The charm of its possessor lies in affection and sympathy, as well as a desire to please others, rather than in sex appeal, and susceptibility is well guarded.

The upper mount of Mars, well developed, tells of Mr. Thomas's coolness in danger. Directly beneath this is a development which indicates that he accepts unavoidable circumstances equably. He is not a grouch or whiner. He has considerable aggression which his strong will holds in

27

check. He does not know when he is whipped. A definite project is but deferred and not given up.

The mount under Jupiter, the first finger, together with the length of that finger shows his willingness to work, but a preference for being a member of, rather than a boss of an expedition.

The mount of Saturn and the finger draw Jupiter and Apollo, that is, these fingers lean towards Saturn. Lowell Thomas has ambition and stability which is tempered by judgment. He is not a true Saturnian and does not take life too seriously although he is practical enough to tackle it in direct common sense fashion.

The mount of Apollo is high, showing a wide interest in practical efforts of others such as inventions, experiments, etc., and also that Mr. Thomas has considerable versatility in personal creative ability.

Mercury is very full. Mr. Thomas is decidedly a Mercurian. Of all the mounts this is the dominating one. Look back at the paragraph describing a Mercurian and apply it in full to Lowell Thomas. There is one exception. The cautious joining of his head and life line which checks his spending propensities is much better developed in the right hand than in the left. Mr. Thomas has deliberately held himself in restraint, curbing his tendency to recklessness.

Chapter 3: *Their Very Claws Have Meaning*

The question on the lips of almost everyone who comes to me for a hand reading is, "How long does my life line say that I am going to live?" Almost everyone knows his life line, that line which rises on the thumb side of the palm somewhat below the finger of Jupiter, rounds the mount of Venus and ends somewhere toward the base of the palm. It is popularly supposed that its length decides how long its owner will stay in this life. But the life line does not tell that. In its length, depth and clearness it does tell how long you are *likely* to live. But rarely does it tell more. If the life line is long, clear, unbroken, and rounds out well into the palm, its owner has a very good chance at long life. If the line is broken, interfered with by cross lines, chained, the owner suffers the usual illnesses and accidents and interferences with life that are the common lot. When there is a second line running parallel or nearly parallel to the life line on the side that is next to the thumb, the fortunate possessor has protection. His recuperative faculties are good; he can fight illness and ill-fortune with a good chance of a successful outcome. Many persons who live to a ripe old age possess life lines badly broken. But they possess also thumbs which tell of a strong will, hearts that are good, serviceable engines, and the hand reader knows that with these two a man many outlive another who has a long, clear life line but has no will power or who possesses a weak heart.

The head line runs across the palm usually just above the middle. If the line is deep and clear it shows mental concentration. If the line is short, this concentration is limited, the possessor has what we call a single-track mind. If the line is long, he is an authority on a few things but he knows something of many. Usually this line is very different in the two hands and is somewhat difficult to read, as developed abilities in the right-hand head line must be compared with the natural gifts shown in the line in the left hand. If the head line is closely joined to the life line at its beginning on the side of the palm above the thumb, its owner is a man who is over-cautious, and who needs to be taught independence and self-reliance, especially if it is joined quite a little. If the space between the life and head line is moderate, the owner is independent and self-reliant. As the space becomes wider this increases to a point of self-approval and self-love which ends in recklessness, a flaunting of the personality, an overbearing quality.

The heart line rises in various places in the palm, and upon the location of its rise is determined the reading. If the heart line, which is the first well marked line running across the upper part of the palm, starts under Jupiter, the first finger, its possessor combines ambition and desire for leadership through the affections. He is apt to be jealous, proud, easily wounded by those he loves. In seeking a mate he is influenced by social position as well as affection.

If the heart line rises below and between the first and second fingers, its owner is prone to idealize the one he loves. When he awakens from his illusion he is likely to lose sight of those traits which are worth while in the object of his affections. But he has strong affections and is dependable and constant.

When the heart line starts under Saturn, the second finger, desire rather than love will rule the life of the possessor unless he applies the forces of will and intellect to check his natural tendencies. If the line is much chained or looped its owner has heart trouble or is a sensualist. People possessing such heart lines are always seeking new mates. They keep the divorce courts busy. They mate at the call of the flesh and of propinquity, and when desire is gratified, they tire. If they are able to discipline themselves and to seek a mate who will offer them companionship through mutual interests, they make good partners because they are interested in love and passion.

The fourth line to be studied is variously called the line of Fate or Destiny, or the Success line, or the Financial line. It springs from the base of the palm at about the middle and runs up the hand ending in various locations. If at its base it starts from or joins or runs close to the life line, its possessor has been pretty well tied down to home ties or duties during the early part of life, bound to follow the wishes of those over him rather than his own. This would be a condition common to all children, but I am referring to early manhood. A free Success line which starts upward with no joinings belongs to a person who started out upon his career with few if any ties. If the Success line is near the mount of the Moon, it tells of a man who owes his success or start in great measure to outside influences, rather than to his own seeking and his own power. When the line is crossed and broken by other lines, changes in life in various ways are indicated. When the line rises clear and unbroken to Saturn (which is rare) the lucky owner is assured money throughout life. He will never starve, and he will be fairly comfortable, provided his head line is clear. If the Success line is cut by a variety of lines, ill health or poor judgment has interfered greatly with Success. When a fainter line springs from the success line, or springs from the palm and travels parallel to it for a time, it tells of assistance, through affection or outside aid. Squares forming across the Success line show preservation in time of defeats or disasters which would otherwise crush or baffle the personality.

The fifth line, that of Apollo, which is the line of ability, is varied in the extreme. In many hands it does not appear at all. This does not mean that such persons have no ability, but that their abilities are shown in other developments of the hand. If the line of Apollo is present it rises from the upper part of the mount of the Moon or even above that in the palm and mounts toward Apollo, sometimes reaching that mount, sometimes stopping short. It is often called the line of brilliancy, which is a mistake as many people who have this line in their palms are far from brilliant. It does, however, indicate that the owner has far more ability to start with than the average man possesses. If he recognizes and develops his potentialities he will make a success in life. The length of this line is its most significant factor. A long line rising from the top of the mount of the Moon shows that its possessor has imagination to add to the power to express himself. If the line rises above this in the palm and comes from the mount of Mars, he will never allow himself to become discouraged, and abilities properly directed will in the end achieve success and reputation. The ability line may spring from the life line and show that physical activity is necessary to reach the goal, or from the head line and indicate success through mental ability. Or it may start between the heart and head line on the percussion of the palm. The term "percussion" in palmistry defines that part of the palm running from under the finger of Mercury, the fourth finger, down to the base, and rounding over towards the outside of the hand. If the line of Apollo starts on this part of the hand between the heart and head line its owner will make a success that is due to public fancy, or it may come from "beyond waters" that is abroad, from some country other than the owner's dwelling place.

Let us return to the hands of Lowell Thomas and read them through the lines. The life and head lines are clearly joined for some distance. Mr. Thomas is slow in action and overly cautious. He is anxious to give full value for everything for which he receives credit, money or the admiration of others. He wants above all things to play fair, and this anxiety results in a diffidence at heart; he is afraid that he may not "deliver the goods" or accomplish what others expect from him.

His is a good, clear, deep line without any particular variations. The head line is straight, showing common sense and power of analysis and investigation. This is lucky, for Mr. Thomas's long nail phalange on the second finger, Saturn, tells that he can be almost a fanatic in upholding what he believes to be the rights of others. Balanced by the head line characteristics, as well as the well-developed second joint of the finger

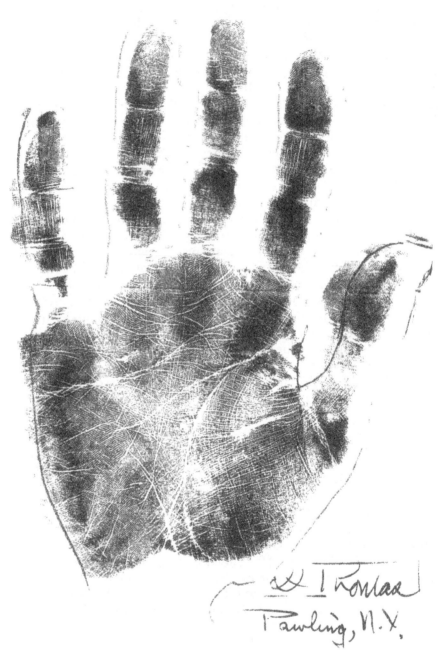

Norman Vincent Peale
Pawling, N.Y.

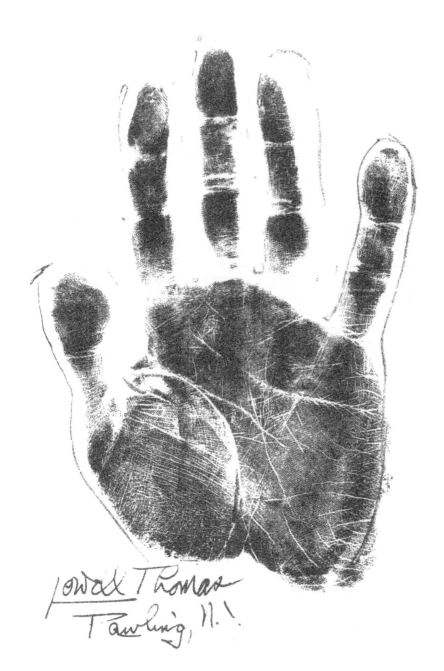

Lowell Thomas
Pawling, N.Y.

Saturn, he will not allow his emotions to hold sway until he has applied his mental faculties towards some solution of the problem which appeals to him. The heart line, starting between Jupiter and Saturn, shows that he idealizes those he loves. Physically he has a strong heart. The line also shows that in early life he was dominated by his affections, but that some shock to them called into play his mental powers which are now in the ascendancy.

The most significant thing in Lowell Thomas's hand, when the lines are being read, is the big square which is on the plain of Mars in the center of the hand. The lines of life and success and the head line run through it. It tells of preservation from fatality in war through a personal enemy, or of danger that threatened life. It records a mental shock which has had a lasting effect and marks the preservation of the line of success which would otherwise have been wiped out. The ability line is present and shows versatility and a healthy vigor.

The impressions of hands shown here cannot tell of the qualities which are indicated by the reverse sides, particularly those indicated by the nails. For a long time it has been a popular fancy that long finger nails are the hallmark of the aristocrat and that the short, square nail is that of the proletariat. This idea came into being doubtless through the art reproduction emphasizing physical beauty. Caste would be a curious matter if we clung to this idea.

Long nails indicate amiability, dislike of stirring up a fuss, and their owners will, outwardly at least, yield a point rather than argue about it. Often they will sacrifice their own wishes and desires to avoid unpleasantness. Long nails will always be found on the hand of a visionary person, but owners of long nails are not always visionary. That depends also upon the shape and consistency of the palm.

Moderately long nails, as wide as they are long, square at the tips and base are usually found on the hand of those who demaned facts. In dealing with such persons one is unwise to remark "I think"—to be believed, one must know. Such nails are found upon the hands of attorneys who are noted for their skill in examining witnesses.

The nail that is broader than it is long will be found on the hands of those who are irritable, argumentative, sarcastic, critical of others. If their fingers are smooth they have, fortunately for them, a quick sense of humor which will act as a soothing salve in curbing the antagonism they are likely to arouse in others.

You will have to take my word for it that if these hands of Lowell Thomas could be reversed, you would at once see that his nails are of this short, broad type. He is capable of mental irritability, but the diplomacy evidenced in his long fourth finger enables him to keep this under cover. Even when he cannot keep it under cover, his quick keen sense of humor, shown in the shape of the nails, prevents him from being of the snapping turtle type of human being, and limits his irritation. His nails and the cushions of his finger tips show Lowell Thomas to be very sensitive to criticism when that criticism is unfavorable, and especially when it is unmerited. He is likely to become introspective and irritable when he does not succeed by the use of his diplomacy and humor in guarding against unfair censure.

Mr. Thomas's handshake is also out of the picture. I have experienced it a number of times, and it is always the same. It is much like that of Leslie Howard, except that Lowell Thomas has a much firmer hand. It is a warm, cordial, sincere clasp which puts you at once at your ease. This man is not only going to give you a square deal, but he is going to like you if he can—and he does not find liking people a difficult task.

For the complete reading of Lowell Thomas's hands go back over the characteristics of his thumbs, fingers, mounts, lines, nails and handshake. A hand reader must consider all these things and relate them.

There are other hand lines, and as the readings of our Lions' Paws progress you will be able to add them to those that have been considered in this chapter. By this time we have probably set that diffidence of Lowell Thomas at work demanding of him why his hands should fill two chapters and serve as a model. He is a nice Lion, but we must spare him and hasten on!

Chapter 4: *Kings of Make Believe*

If you were to call upon me today, stretch out your hands for inspection and demand, "Tell me, can I succeed upon the stage or screen," in all probability I could not reply. That is one of the two questions concerning a career which I am most frequently asked. Young men and young women want to be actors.

The second career question, "Can I be a writer?" is put to me by people of all ages. These are two almost universal desires. Nine-tenths of the educated fraction of the human race want to succeed as actors or writers.

In a few instances hands have such positive indications of abilities and of the health and mentality to develop such abilities, that I can honestly assure the owners that they will make a success of any occupation to which they feel drawn. Others show "diversities" of gifts and the necessary ability to develop those gifts. But their success will depend upon opportunity plus hard work. Even very great Lions may have become Lions because of the conditions of their own lives or of their own times, rather than because of their native ability or the struggle they have made.

Of the eight Lions we meet in this chapter there is just one development of hands that is common to all, with one hundred per cent average. They all have fingers which are smooth, if not all the way, at least to the second joints. This means that they all possess inspirational qualities. Given the opening—the time, the place—without conscious thought or even especial training they can take advantage of the opportunity and leap to conclusion.

Some of them actually visualize all that they are to do, while others possess an instinctive knowledge of methods to be applied to objective consciousness.

There are other qualities common to most of them, but just this one is common to all.

Look at the hands of that dainty, exquisite captivating little Lioness, Helen Hayes. Miss Hayes's stage manager, the veteran William Seymour, who was directing her in "The Sub-Deb" in Indianapolis in 1921, asked me to read her hand. Helen Hayes, he felt, had something—something worth while to give her audiences. Her charming little hands bore him out. Her palms slope towards the wrist, the skin is satiny, of exceedingly fine texture, and these together with her nicely placed but rather short fingers, show quick, inspirational, mental grasp, such as she applies to her character delineations. On the mount of the Moon is the whorl, which in Lowell Thomas means personality plus. In Helen Hayes's hands it means the sixth sense, the ability to project a character portrayal, the spark of genius.

How hard she had worked to develop that spark was even then shown in the differences between her two hands. Her left thumb is decidedly flexible, although the nail phalange, will, and the second phalange, logic, are well balanced. The thumb in her right hand is stiff. Inclined naturally to use her will power by fits and starts, she has applied reason to her methods of work, and her mental muscles of perseverance and concentration are well developed. She is a quick worker; the spread between thumb and fingers, and between all the fingers shows her instant reaction to opportunity. The shortness and smoothness of her fingers tell of her ability to rid herself of all unnecessary details. The tips of her fingers have diversified endings. These with the smoothness of the fingers show that she can submerge her own personality and enter into that of the character she impersonates.

Contrast her "Paws," if such hands can be called paws, with those of another actress to whom the adjectives I have used to describe Helen Hayes, "dainty, exquisite and captivating," apply equally well. Who among us who ever heard that breathless heart-touching appeal,

"Do you believe in fairies?"

would deny them to Maude Adams? Lost to us, her public, for many years, 1932 brought her back in a joyous revival of "The Merchant of Venice," and the next winter the radio brought to us that wisful, poignant voice in scenes from "The Little Minister," "Rosemary," "Secrets" and "Peter Pan." Maude Adams and Helen Hayes were both young women when I first read their hands, which means that I read Maude Adams' hands before Miss Hayes had begun her work. Miss Adams was full of curiosity and interest as to the possibilities of her hands. She was then playing with John Drew in "Rosemary" and the zenith of her career was yet to come. The sixth sense, the vital spark leading to genius, is in her hand. But there is no flexibility in either thumb; both are stiff. Maude Adams was never a mixer in any sense of the word. The first phalange of her thumb is longer than the second; her will is stronger than her sense of logic and she can be stubborn as a mule—think of the years in which she could not be induced to come from her retirement! In her dramatic work no one could sway her from her conception of a role. A significant difference in the two women is show in development of the mount of Venus. Helen Hayes has a fully developed mount. Her head dominates her affections and passions, but they are a pulsing, powerful part of her and she sublimates them in her

35

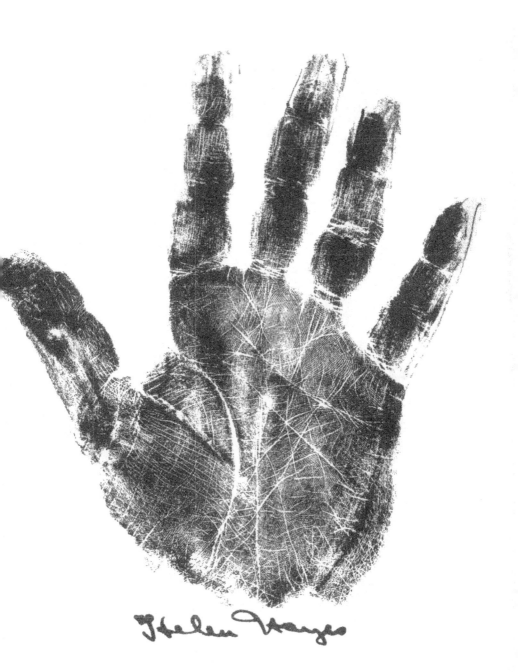

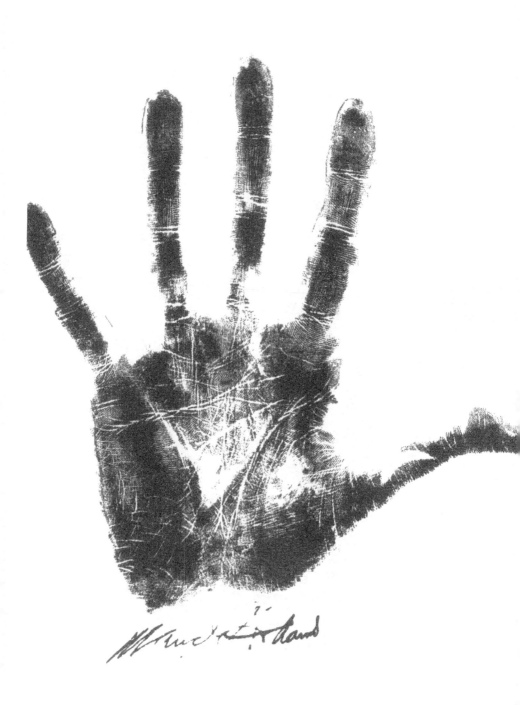

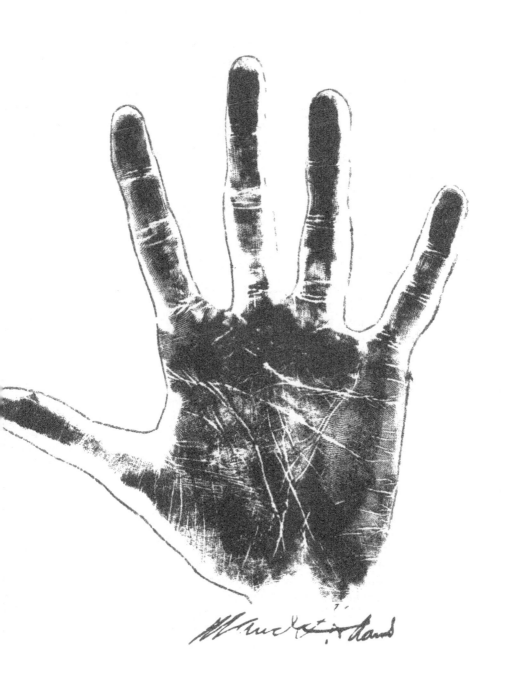

art. In Miss Adams' hand the mount of Venus is almost flat and firm. Her interpretations are based upon a subtle, imaginative, mental analysis, fired by a whimsical imagination. Maude Adams possesses great powers of intuition, but before using them she submits them to mental analysis. Helen Hayes does the same in lesser degree, but the basis of the two mental processes is different. Any theatre goer who has seen them both in "What Every Woman Knows," by James M. Barrie, will recognize this basic difference. What Barrie meant "Maggie" to be we shall never know, but that Maude Adams' "Maggie" and Helen Hayes' "Maggie" would be different is as it should be.

If you will look closely at the prints of Maude Adams' hands you will see that there is a line rising on the percussion of the hand between the heart and head lines, a sign of recognition from beyond seas. James M. Barrie, visiting New York, saw Maude Adams as Dorothy Cruikshank in "Rosemary." "There," he said, as the final curtain descended, "is the woman to play my Lady Babbie." At that time he had written the book, but not the play. When Maude Adams opened in the play she became a star over night.

It is half a life time since I first met Otis Skinner and first read his hands. He smiled as I finished.

"You certainly know me better than I know myself," he said. He would not say that today. In Mr. Skinner's left hand the space between the life and head lines shows an impulsive nature. He would speak before he thinks, leap before he looks. This, together with the stiffiness of his thumbs, shows his inclination to follow his own ideas and emotional impulses, and to discount the advice given by others. But in his *right* hand the life and head lines are joined. He has disciplined those inclinations; he still has the impulses but he has trained himself to consider his leaps and where they will take him. Otis Skinner's hands lack the sixth sense mark upon the mount of the Moon. But under the finger of Apollo the talent lines are in the form of a trident: fame, fortune and honor are his. There is another line, flaring up from the heart line at the meeting of the talent line, which tells of aid and encouragement through those allied with him through affection or kinship. Mercury is long, with a pointed tip; he has the gifts of expression and diplomacy. On the mount of Mercury is a mark which is called the "Merry Thought." It tells of its owner's gift of repartee and badinage.

Otis Skinner's hands show plainly a well-balanced mixture of the practical and artistic. The breadth of the palm under the fingers marks his practical nature; the slope of the palm towards the wrist, the artistic side. His stiff thumbs tell of a stubborn perseverance that has stood him in good stead through the years. The second finger, that of Saturn, shows a certain distinction. The shape and length of the nail phalange tell of a man who has dignity of bearing and savoir-faire and an understanding of the deeper meanings of life. His first finger, Jupiter, shows ambition with a quickness of perception and a sense of justice which have marked his dealings with his associates.

When I first met Miss Barrymore she was on her initial professional tour. She was fresh from a convent school and was playing a small part with Maude Adams and John Drew in "Rosemary." Seven years later when she was playing in "Alice-Sit-By-The-Fire," I made these impressions. The outstanding characteristic of her hand is its diverse qualities. The great spread of the fingers, almost like a starfish, shows extreme independence of thought and action which can easily become recklessness. Her palms are exceedingly resilient; she has no liking for taking thought for the morrow. Her thumbs show a strong will in the long first phalange —so long that it dwarfs reason and logic, the second phalange, and becomes obstinacy where "an ounce of opposition would create a whole pound of incentive." With the long first finger of Jupiter, it also shows a love of power and the desire to rule, regardless of consequences. The pointed tip of her thumb shows impatience over results. Here is a restless, imperative, reckless temperament. But her gifts! Her fingers, beautifully placed upon her palms, are nicely shaped and extremely flexible. They show her versatility and a mental elasticity and brilliancy that masters a portrayal of kaleidoscopic range of emotions. Her smooth fingers, rather short, indicate a dislike of detail. And then, common sense in the length and position of the head line, prudence as shown in the second phalange of the finger of Saturn—these two carry her through situations in which others less strong, less determined. and less gifted would come to grief.

In the lines under her third finger is additional evidence of her great ability. In the left hand, the "natural" hand, there are many lines of almost equal clearness and depth. Miss Barrymore could undoubtedly have succeeded as a musician, perhaps as a writer. The fork of brilliancy shown in the right hand is clear; she wisely bent all of her varied gifts into the one channel of dramatic expression, using her beauty of voice and ability as an instrumentalist as an added charm in the portrayal of her roles. Her quickness of eye for lines, shown in the nail phalange of the third finger, together with the love of color shown in the development of the second phalange, are assets in the planning of her gowns and of the sets which are her background.

Actors are not usually credited with shyness, but Walter Hampden has a persistent shyness or aloofness which is evidenced in the stiffness of

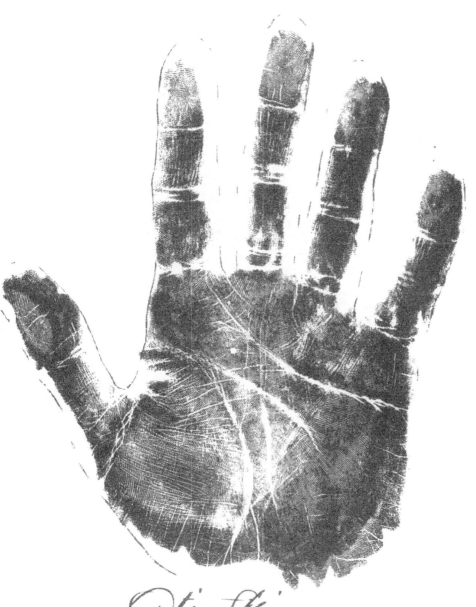

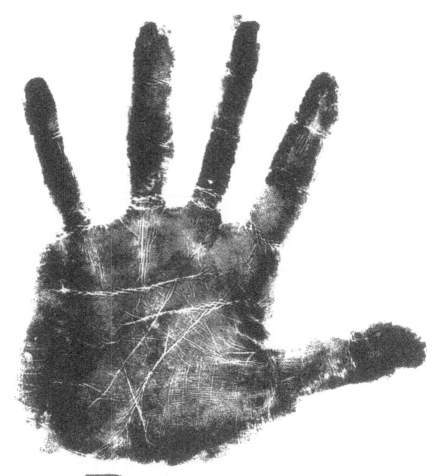

Ethel Barrymore

Ethel Barrymore

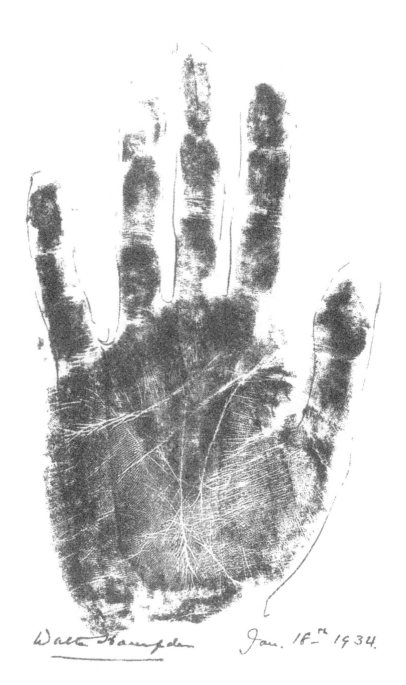

Walter Hampden   Jan. 18ᵗʰ 1934.

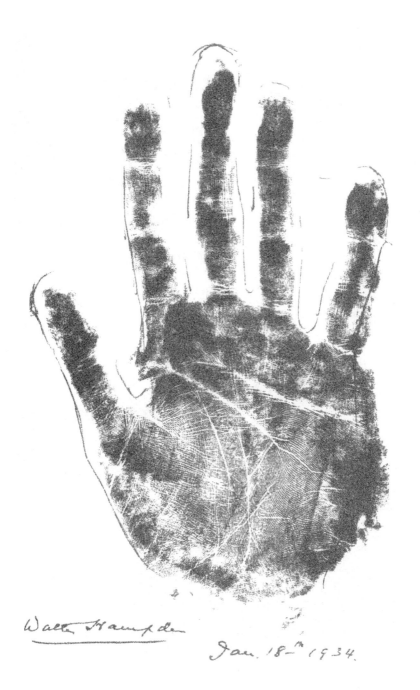

Walter Hampden

Jan. 18—th 1934.

is left thumb, together with the development of the cushions of his fingers. He is supersensitive to mental atmosphere. He never wanted to appear before an audience unless he was certain that it would welcome and applaud him. In his long years of service to his art his right hand shows how he worked to correct this condition. His right thumb is much more flexible than the left; and has a much greater flare from the fingers. Hampden has disciplined himself so that he is willing to take a risk of failure in order to reach his goal. His long first finger, Jupiter, shows ambition and executive ability. Coupled with the diplomacy shown in the long fourth finger, Mercury, he has assets in the management of others. His fingers are smooth only to the second joint. Inspiration is checked by conscious processes; often he defeats his flashing intuition by trying to reason it out. He has the sixth sense which could be his infallible guide if he would permit it. He is proud of his mentality and has reason to back his judgment. The length and depth of his head line in both hands show his ability to grasp a subject and to make it his own through the clarity and power of his intellect. He trusts his mental powers, but he has trusted too little to the gift of the gods, intuition.

Look at the hands of the man of one role, Anton Lang, who for years at the Passion Play at Oberammergau, portrayed the role of the Christus. These impressions, made in 1905, are unusual in that they are made in the clay used by Lang in his trade as a potter. Although Anton Lang is very reticent and shrank from publicity, the idea of reading his hands interested him, and he readily gave his consent. Again I found the sixth sense, the spark of genius indicated by the whorl on the mount of the Moon. Inspiration and intuition lead Lang in the playing of a single character. Another curious fact is that the right hand shows a developed imaginative quality, indicated by the drooping head line, and an acquired supersensitiveness to spiritual influences is shown in the finger tips of the right hand. The actors who present the "Passion Play" try earnestly to live as much as possible the lives of those whom they impersonate. Anton Lang has made a sincere and tremendous effort to be worthy of his role.

Chapter 5: *Camera! Shoot!*

After I had visited Harold Lloyd, I knew that I should always think of him in a dual role, Lloyd the screen actor, producer of mirth-provoking comedies, and Lloyd the lover of beauty, who spends much of his spare time in a wonderful garden of his own planning. For sheer beauty and originality I have seen nothing to equal that garden, even among the many lovely gardens of the screen stars. When we had spent some time reveling in the glory of bloom and the marvels of the landscaping, I looked with interest at Lloyd's hands. Somewhere they must show this intense love of growing beauty. Look at the impressions. You can see that the second and third phalanges of the second finger are of equal length, which is an indication of a great love of the land and all that grows upon it, especially in connection with home. Harold Lloyd's love of beauty is more comprehensive than this however; he is capable of understanding it in many forms. The breadth of his palms under the fingers shows a love of the out-of-doors, together with a great deal of physical energy.

His thumbs are stiff. Despite his kindly nature Harold Lloyd is indifferent to people who are not congenial. He picks his friends from those whose standards and interests are similar to his own.

His smooth fingers indicate inspirational qualities that are reinforced by the imagination shown in the high development of the mount of the Moon. The whorl distinctly etched on the upper part of this mount is a sign of the gift that enables him to envision that which he desires to achieve, his pictures or his gardens or the road by which he may attain success in both.

The clear head line drooping to the mount of the Moon reveals an intelligent use of his powers of prescience. With all his ability to see in visions, Harold Lloyd has a practical nature. The breadth and firmness of his palm signifies a comprehension of the need of the work and of the self-discipline necessary to make his dreams come true. His forefinger is long and denotes decided executive ability, a gift that makes it easy for him to plan his time and the work of those who assist him. The tip of the third finger indicates the outstanding quality that has made Harold Lloyd's work in the motion picture field unique. It shows originality, and coupled with the length of the first phalange of the fourth finger, originality in expression. Added to these gifts, the high mount of Venus evinces an abundant vitality and sympathetic understanding, both qualities that come through to us in his pictures. Under his little finger the high mount of Mercury is developed towards the mount under the third

39

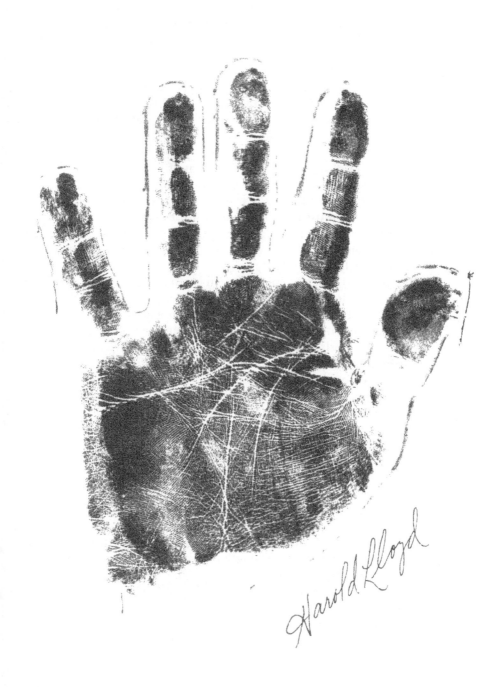

Harold Lloyd

finger, Apollo, a sign of a strong sense of humor, another gift that comes to us through his work. He is ambitious, as is shown in the full and long third phalange of the first finger, and this ambition is guided by the wisdom revealed in the long second phalange of the second finger, a combination of qualities that makes for commercial success.

Since my reading of her hands Mary Pickford has added to her laurels. The little book, "Why Not Try God?" has been published, and was a best seller. Actress, producer, and now author, Mary Pickford is a highly gifted woman. The prints of her hands show clearly her two dominant characteristics. The first is found in the shape and tip of the second finger, the finger of Saturn. This is the sign of the inborn optimist. Mary Pickford is, and always will be, dauntless. No matter what disappointment and griefs she suffers, she can emerge. She carries with her conviction that clouds must pass and the sun shine again—for her. The second characteristic, hardly less dominant, is shown in the curve of the second phalange of her thumb, the curve of logic and reasoning. Such a curve indicates a brilliant mentality.

Her personal charm is enormous. In her home at Pickfair she received me in her boudoir, a large room of many windows, a cheery fire of burning logs in a French fireplace and many photographs on the walls, including a rarely beautiful painting of her mother. She came to me with outstretched hands, and the clasp at once told me that she is both sincere and friendly. Her palms are firm and resilient, a revelation of a power of concentration with the open mind of intelligent understanding. Her fourth finger, Mercury, flares from the hand, a sign of an independence in thought and action that has helped to make her an outstanding personality. The pointed tip of this finger shows her gift of expression, and its length indicates the diplomacy that has stood her in good stead. The first phalange of her thumb is very long; Mary Pickford has great will power, and directed by the logic and reason shown in the second phalange she has the ability to be impersonal in self-appraisal and to use mental discipline when it is needed. Her palm, sloping to the wrist, denotes her love of the artistic, and the breadth of the palm under the fingers shows that she prefers mental to physical activity. She has decided executive ability as is shown in the length of her first finger, and decided ambition indicated in the length of the third phalange.

The development of the mount of Venus denotes that her affections have great power in determining her course of action. The middle phalange of her first finger discloses a strong sense of justice, and, again, with her gifts of logic and reason, makes it possible for her to be impersonal n reaching her decisions. Her long fingers show her consideration of very important detail in all things, and their smoothness reveals an in-pirational quality that prevents her from being fussy.

Under the third finger in her left hand is a marking called the star of elebrity, in addition to the fork of brilliancy illumined by that mystic marking like a finger tip. Ahead of this remarkable woman is additional ecognition through some method of expression as yet but partially re-ealed.

While I was in Hollywood the office of Metro-Goldwyn-Mayer called ne to ask if I would make a reading of the hands of Walter Huston. Vhen I arrived he was in a great hurry, saying he must leave within an ıour. Since he had planned to leave town early the following morning I ould make no appointment to read his hands. He offered to drive me ıack to my hotel, and watching his hands on the wheel I told him what raits they revealed—not all complimentary. By the time we reached the ıotel he decided to postpone his departure, and arranged for a nine-hirty appointment. He was there on the second, as the owner of such ıands would be!

His palm is square and very firm showing a positive nature and indi-ating that he investigates carefully, and gives due deliberation to any ıew project before making his decision. His fingers, smooth to the second oint, show inspirational qualities which he has restrained by his desire o apply the tests of material law and order to all problems, a desire :learly shown by the development of the second joints.

The comparatively small flare of the thumb from the palm and the lares between the fingers, likewise rather small, indicate a conservatism n expressing his opinions and a tenacity in holding to his point of view. The wide space between his life line and his head line shows initiative ınd independence, but these have been decidedly curbed as the closer ıoining of these lines in his right hand reveals. He has learned from ex-perience to "make haste slowly" in reaching his decisions.

The rounded mount of Venus signifies great vitality and great powers of physical and mental endurance. If obstacles are placed in his way by nature, or by conditions of living or by opposition to his plans, he can fight, and usually is victorious. But when those he loves are involved he has a quiet depth of tenderness, a great loyalty and understanding in dealing with his real friends and intimates. His is the love and friend-ship based on respect with a patient tolerance except when, in his opinion, a fundamental principle of right is violated.

His innate dramatic ability is revealed in his double jointed thumbs.

41

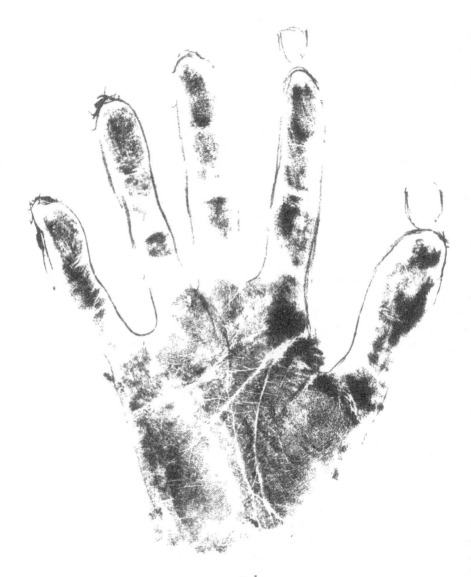

Mary Pickford
april 11th 1938.

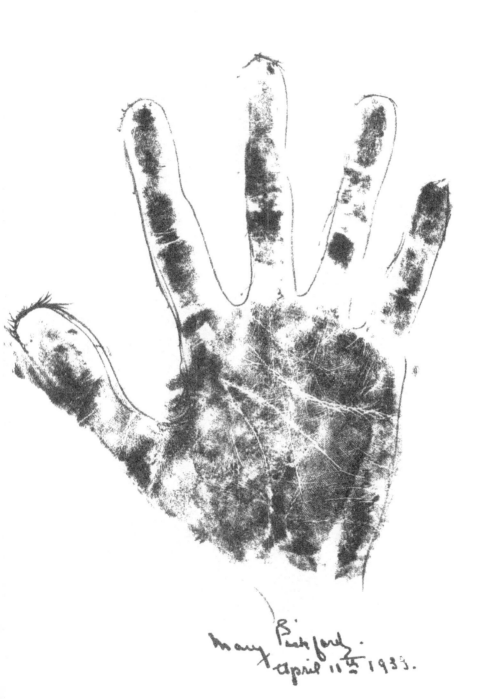

Mary Pickford.
April 11th 1935.

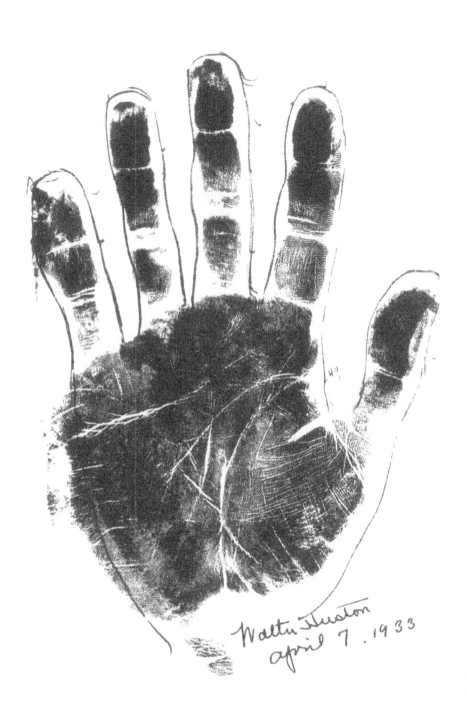

Walter Huston
april 7 . 1933

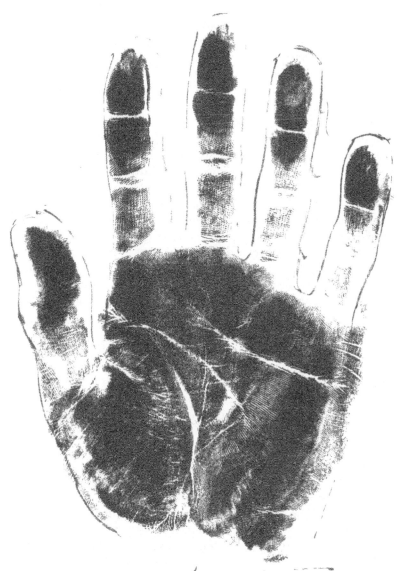

Walter Huston
april 7 1933

Together with his inspirational qualities, his great vitality, his ability to fight, and his care in making decisions, it has brought Walter Houston to the heights of his profession.

The radiant, friendly personality of Marie Dressler was a natural gift. Anyone's troubles were her troubles, anyone's sorrows her own. Literally she obeyed the Scriptural injunction,

"Rejoice with them that do rejoice, and weep with them that weep."

It was Easter Sunday, 1933, that she came to me, full of apologies that, as it was a holiday and she had given her chauffeur, her cook, and her secretary the day off, she was a full five minutes late. It was her fault, every bit of it. That was an outstanding characteristic of Marie Dressler's. If she could blame herself she would, and even when I tried to tell her that since she was there with me, the five minutes could be forgotten, she continued to blame herself for being late.

Look closely at the impressions of her hands. You can see a finger-print marking on the palm of her hand where the head line droops towards the outside of the palm. This is a sign of a nature that absorbs an understanding of life and life's problems as affecting others. The development of the mount of Venus shows the sympathy and the tenderness that accompanied that understanding. Marie Dressler's emotional nature was something like a highly sensitized photographer's plate: it caught the fleeting impressions of the passing moment. The flexibility of her palm offered repeated evidence that here was a woman who understood people and could adapt herself to their conditions of life and their responsibilities. The exceedingly flexible first joints of her thumbs told the same tale; she was tolerant, kindly, and wanted to make everyone feel her true friendliness. The flexible second joints of her thumbs indicated unusual dramatic gifts, which she evidenced not only in her work but in her service, in friendship and in life at large. The flare between thumbs and fingers and between the fingers themselves, coupled with the development of the mount of Venus, indicated spontaneous response to the appeal of others, especially if her affections were involved. The only check upon this tendency was to be found in the long nail phalanges of her fingers. These are the phalanges of conscience, and Marie Dressler found in her conscience a limitation of her otherwise unbounded response to others. She was conscientious too in fulfilling obligations of professional transactions, especially when they involved others.

On the mount of the Moon was a clearly marked swirl, a gift of intuition that carried her through many emotional and mental depressions. It was this gift that enabled her to *be* the character she sought to portray,

42

ther than to act it, and to send through the impersonal medium of the screen, the warmth of human traits.

The rounded mount of upper Mars showed the bravery of the woman. She resisted care and worry until she was able to face any personal crisis not only with courage but with an understanding smile at the frailties of mankind, including Marie Dressler.

The work of Grant Mitchell has always interested me because he brings such an impeccable finish to the character he portrays. Because of this quality, his work is outstanding. His palms have the delicate tracery of a steel engraving which makes the major lines stand out with a staring clarity. This texture of the palm indicates a temperament which reflects the varying phases of his environment upon the surface only. He has the power to retain what he likes and to efface the remainder. His deep, rather short head line shows he absorbs as much knowledge through personal experience, travel, association and environment as he would through a college training. The long first phalange of his thumb reveals his strong will by which he can hold under restraint his emotions and desires.

On the mount of the Moon there is a pronounced whorl, which in this case shows an uncanny ability to read the thoughts and motives of associates as well as to sense impending changes or conditions which affect him personally. There is another whorl under the third finger which discloses that his portrayal of a character is through intuitive understanding of human traits—not a studied mental picture.

My first impression of Elizabeth Patterson was when I saw her in the role of Virginia, the devout, down-trodden, neglected maid-of-all work in "The Miracle of St. Anthony." In the years since that time she has made a great success on both stage and screen as one of the finest character actresses.

Her palms are conic, and together with her long smooth fingers indicate the inspirational faculty that seeks absolute perfection. The flares of the thumbs from the hands and the flares between the fingers show that she will go to any extreme to gain this end of perfection in its finest details. It is a standing joke among her stage associates that "Patty" must have her shoes fit her role, if not her feet.

The satiny smoothness of the skin of her palms shows her native ability to absorb any phase of a role, and to *be* herself the character she portrays.

The space between the life line and the head line reveals a woman given to act upon impulse and, with the wide flare of the thumbs men-

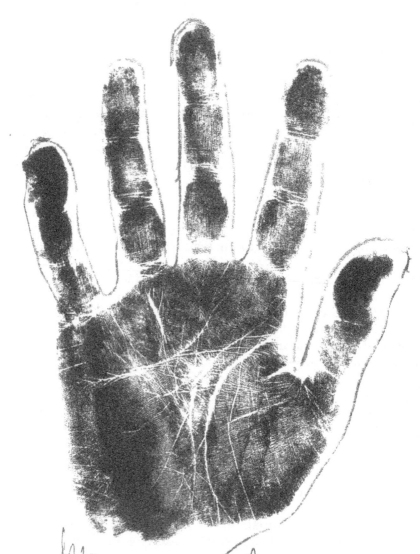

Marie Dressler
april 16th '33 —

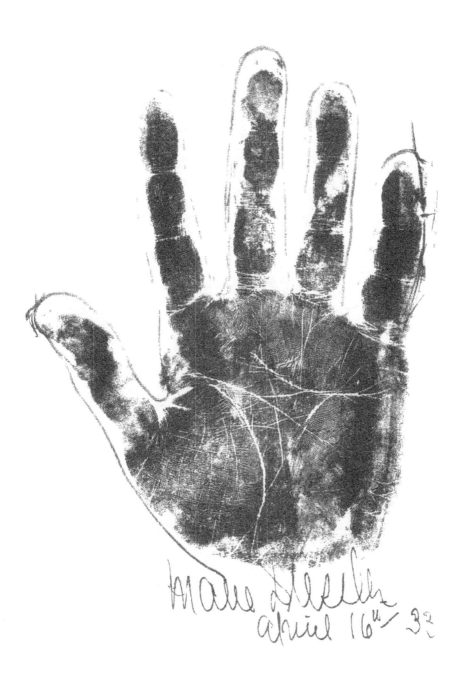

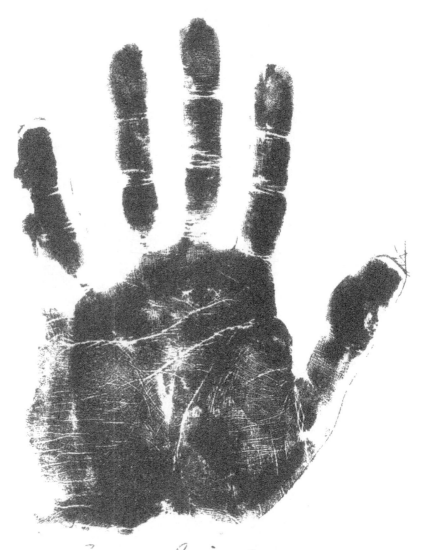

Grant Mitchell
April 6th, 1933.

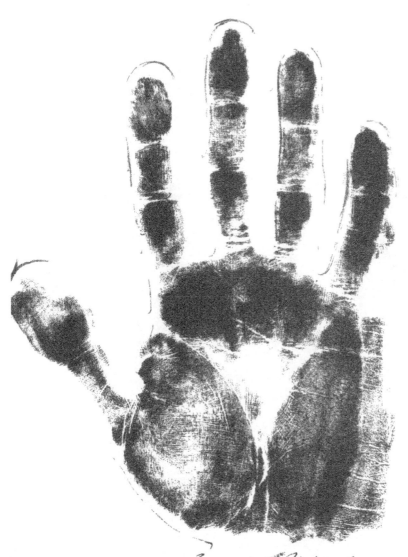

Frank Mitchell
April 6th 1939

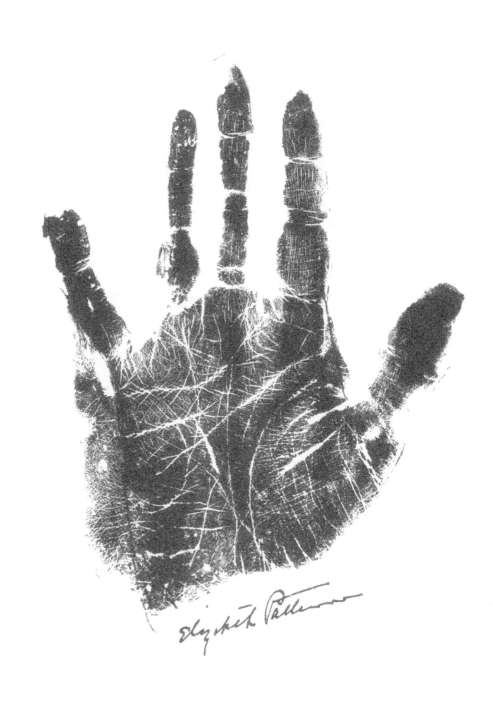

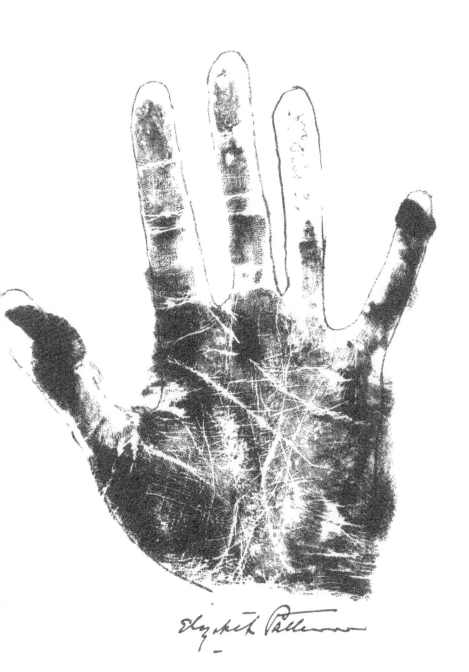

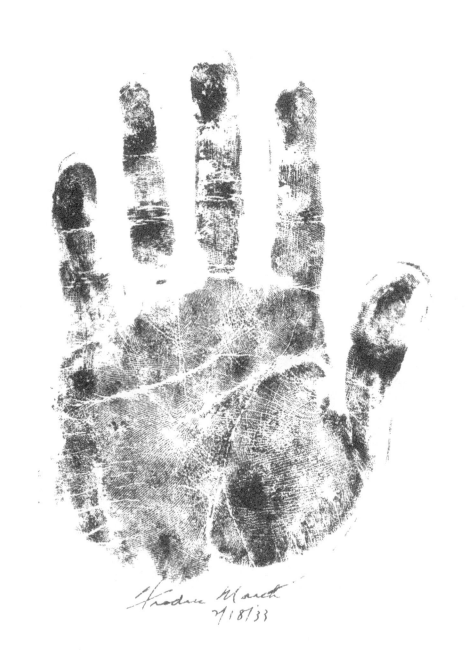

Fredric March
7/18/33

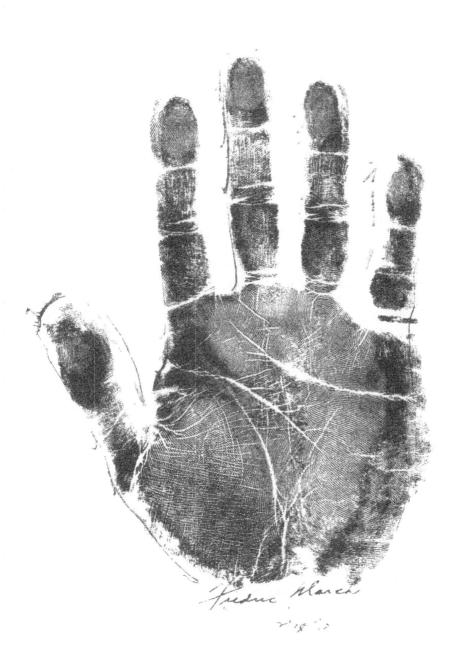

Fredric March

tioned, repeats again that she is an extremist giving largely of her time, strength and money to others, particularly to those who have any claim upon her affections. The decided will power shown in the long first phalange of her thumb, together with the sign of prudence in the long second phalange of her second finger, are the necessary "drag-logs" to her tendency to act first and realize her mistake afterwards.

The flexibility of her long smooth fingers reveals that, notwithstanding her desire for perfection and her infinite care in detail in her work, she is careless about practical matters.

The conic tip and the length of the first phalange of her third finger denote the restraining influence the technique of her art exerts over the influence of her emotional nature, in the love of color, mental and material, indicated in the length of the second phalange, and the influence of her imagination shown by the development of the lower part of the mount of the Moon. These qualities, tempered by tenderness and warmth, evidenced by the development of the mount of Venus, enable her to portray her characters through the fine shades of subtle suggestion rather than in the primitive colors of obvious action.

Fredric March of the screen was known to me first as Fredric March Bickel of the stage—he was playing in "Duberau" under the direction of David Belasco. I met him again when he appeared with Harry Beresford in "Shavings" and saw him advance to stardom in "Tarnish." When, as Fredric March, he shook hands with me in Hollywood in 1933 that clasp conveyed the poise and quiet force of the man who had become "the master of his fate."

Fredric March's hands are an interesting study, the right differs so vitally from the left. In the left hand the thumb and fingers are decidedly flexible, and there is a wide flare between thumb and hand, and again between the fingers. These tell of a man who is exceedingly adaptable to all sorts and conditions of people and to varied circumstances and surroundings. The double joint of the left thumb shows him a mixer in every sense of the word, the second joint with its definite suppleness is the sign of the love of the dramatic. The first phalanges of his fingers are also unusually flexible. He is a born gleaner of dramatic episodes and all is grist that comes to his mental mill in this way. With the wide flares mentioned, he stood in grave danger of becoming an extremist in his desire to experience dramatic reactions and allow himself to be carried away by extravagant giving of his time and strength. But fortunately Fredric March has introspective tendencies, as the shape of his nails shows. The length of the nail phalanges of all of his fingers reveal his

44

bility for self-analysis. Assaying himself, he knew that to be successful he would have to crystallize his effort in one definite direction.

His right hand shows that he has succeeded. The thumb is not nearly so flexible as that of the left hand; he has developed will power and perseverance.

He has the smooth fingers that are the signs of inspirational qualities; his first fingers are long, showing executive ability and the qualities of leadership, aids to his ambitions. The close joining of his life line and head line denotes his reticent nature. He dislikes plumbing his emotions even in the interest of dramatic necessity. Innately reserved and aloof, it has been a long and difficult struggle for Fredric March to use convincingly the fire and ardor revealed in the fulness of the mount of Venus, and so color his impersonations with passion and desire.

Chapter 6: *In the Spotlight*

My collection of hand prints must number among the thousands. I have never counted them, but they fill a great chest which I call my treasure chest, for surely no treasure of gold and silver can be compared to these hands, each pair revealing to me the character of the owner. From among them I call to the spotlight of this chapter, certain personalities who have literally stood in the spotlight of the material stage, and who have held that spotlight focussed upon them. Of them all perhaps none is dearer to me than these prints of the hands of Mrs. Thomas Whiffen, affectionately known as "the grand old lady of the stage." To the very end of her ninety odd years of living she was as keen about the stage as when she was in her first season.

Her small beautifully shaped hands were, as you will agree, youthful in vigor and contour. In the lower part of the mount of the Moon in each hand is the clearly marked whorl showing the spark of genius that illuminated all efforts she used in developing her gifts. Her inclination towards the stage is revealed by the flare of her long straight finger of Mercury from the hand, a sign of quickness of action, together with the gift of words disclosed in the long first phalange, and a keen sense of humor shown by the high mount directly beneath the finger.

Her fingers were relatively short, indicating a dislike of detail, a dislike accentuated by the smoothness of the fingers, which is a sign of inspiration. The wide flare of her thumbs from her hands added a tendency to be an extremist, but the long first phalange of all her fingers had the saving grace of a strong sense of duty that enabled her to control impulses towards extravagance in action.

In her left hand the wide space between head line and life line revealed an independence in thought and action that might have become aggressive if it had not been curbed by the diplomacy shown in her long fourth finger; her independence was thus modified by a natural graciousness towards others. The long first phalange of her thumb, with a tip that might be called paddle-shaped, showed a will power and determination that sustained her throughout her long life. She had ambition as shown in the length of her forefinger and in the mount beneath, but all through her life she used her strong will and her sense of duty to those bound to her by ties of affection to curb the desire for personal achievement. Under the third finger in her left hand was the star indicating a recognition which she perhaps did not fully realize in her chosen profession. In the right hand this developed only the fork of brilliancy—she

46

deliberately sacrificed personal achievement again and again in order that she might fully respond to the call of affection.

In the words of Proverbs, "Length of days" was "in her right hand"—the long clear life line showed them—"and in her left hand" were the "riches and honor" of a life well spent, divided, it may be, between responsibilities and ambition, but who can say to the detriment of either? Mrs. Whiffen lived to see herself regarded, not as the greatest genius the stage has produced, but as a most honored and revered ornament.

Peggy Wood needs no call to the spotlight; she is in the spotlight. In musical comedy, in comedy and drama on stage and screen she has been a great success. I first met her when she was guest artist with the Stuart Walker Players, and during the years that have followed it has been a great pleasure to watch more and more of the spotlight fall upon her.

Peggy has hands in which contradictions abound. In the rounded tip of her second fingers with their long nail phalanges are indications of an innate gaiety, a fount of perpetual youth. Hope springs eternal within her, and her outlook is naturally buoyant. Yet the pointed tips of the first phalanges of her thumbs disclose impatience. Hers is an enthusiastic and spontaneous nature, and she wants quick response. The shape of her nails, which are broader than they are long, tells of her tendency to be analytical, introspective, and mentally irritable. If you look at her head line you notice at once its great droop towards the mount of the Moon, a sign that the owner goes into periods of mental depression and despondency. The space between her life line and her head line shows impulsiveness in speech and action with an independence that is almost aggressive. She is the kind of person who is likely to make unfortunate decisions on the spur of the moment and to find it difficult to extricate herself from the consequences. Between the third and fourth fingers is a fingerprint whorl, an indication of talent amounting to the spark of genius.

How reconcile all these diverse qualities? Peggy has distinct helps. Her palms are firm and rather square, common sense palms, and with the stiffness of her thumbs, they indicate a practical outlook accompanied by a great deal of perseverance. The length of the second phalanges of her thumbs shows strong reasoning power, while the length of all her fingers is a sign of her ability to handle the most minute details connected with her artistic work.

The middle phalanges of her second fingers show in their length the wisdom and prudence that are hers. Peggy Wood has enough of the "temperament of an actor" to enable her to portray the gamut of emo-

47

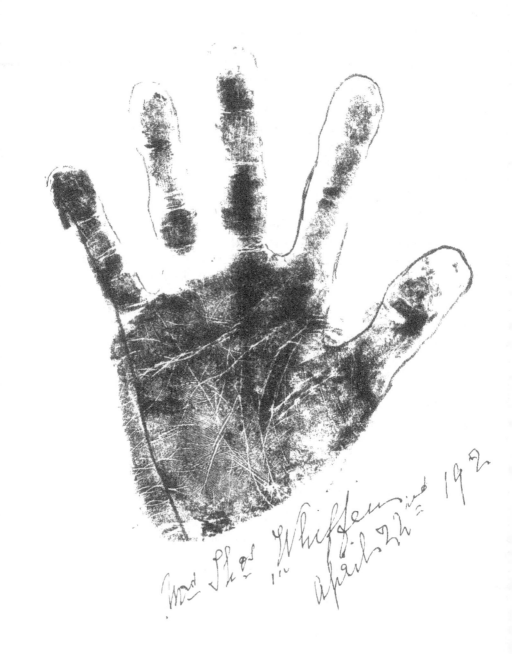

Mrs Thos Whiffen "" April 22nd 192

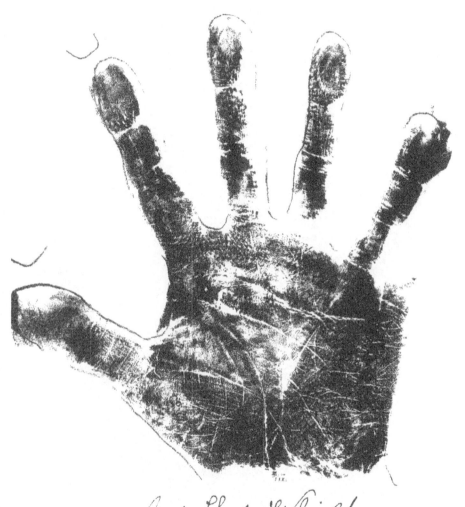

Mrs Thos Whiffen

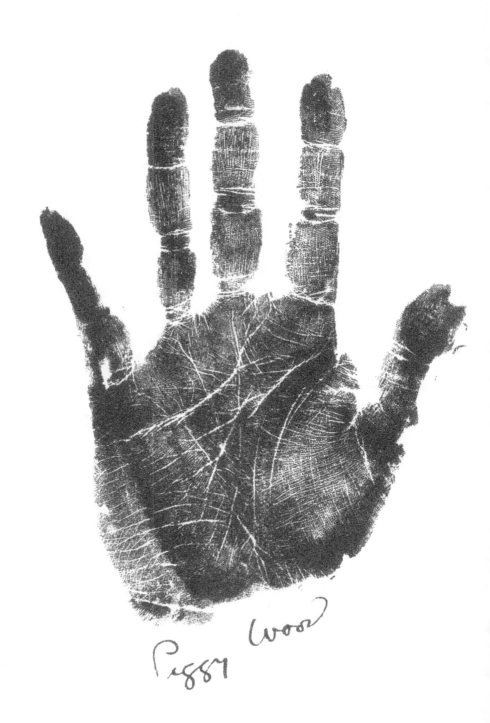

Peggy Wood

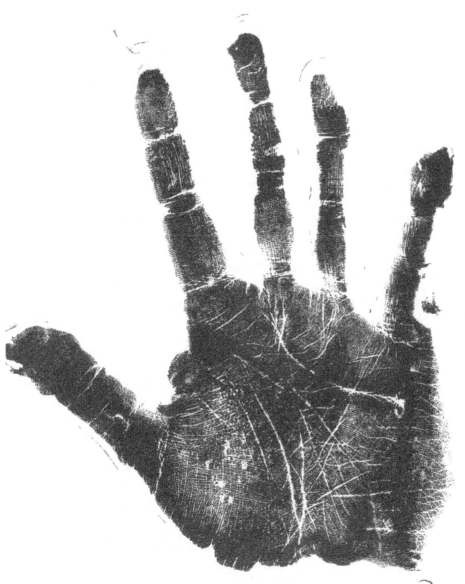

Peggy Wood

tions. In addition she has the disciplinary qualities that raise her art to a high mental level.

The third phalanges of her second fingers show in their length and breadth a "love of the land" which will not be denied. Although she can spend comparatively little time there, she has found her farm, "Buddy Brook," essential to her happiness.

The lines of talent under the third finger in her right hand show that Peggy Wood has not yet arrived at the zenith of her career. In her left hand is the trident of fame, fortune and honor, yet to be realized in the right.

Calling the name of Fanny Davenport into the spotlight is sheer presumption on my part. The name of Davenport will always be in the spotlight in the archives of the stage.

The English laurels won by her famous father, Edward L. Davenport, were sustained when he came to America and took his place as one of the groups with Jefferson, Booth and Barrett, that constellation of stars whose light never dims. Fanny Davenport is remembered for her work with Joseph Jefferson, with Mrs. Drew as a member of the famous Augustin Daly Company, and finally for her presentation of the Sardou dramas.

My first reading of her hands was in 1896. At once I was impressed by her thumbs, with their long first phalanges so well balanced with the long second phalanges. Only a character of great force could possess such thumbs. I said as much and she replied,

"Miss Simmons, I have yet to know what it is to fail in what I undertake to do."

Her career to that time sustained her assertion, but its very nature led me to turn at once to her head line. Its length, depth and clearness showed such remarkable ability that it would be called a "business head line." Keenness of judgment and an amazing and prodigious memory were indicated as among her great assets.

She was an extremely ambitious woman. Her long first finger showed her desire for power, while the high mount at its base denoted a love of the approbation she earned by her efforts. Her smooth fingers are those of the inspirational artist. The highly developed mount of Venus revealing a high abundant emotional nature, disclosed the inexhaustible source she could draw upon in her portrayal of dramatic roles. Her line of destiny showed unremitting success until her forty-fifth year when losses were shown. I spoke of this and two years later she again sent for me.

"I would love to have you read my hand again," she wrote. "I am so anxious to know if my luck will change."

Fanny Davenport could have won fame as a writer, an artist, a lawyer, or a painter. Her mentality plus her gift for words, her painter's grasp of technique and love of color and form as shown in the first and second phalanges of the third fingers, and a highly developed imagination shown in the mount of the Moon would be of value either in writing or in painting. That she chose the stage was inevitable, it was family history. In the lines under the third finger of her left hand were signs of many talents; in her right hand was a single deep, clear line; she had fused them into one.

Julia Marlowe's hand is an intuitive hand, and the intuitive qualities are fired by ambition. The highly developed mount under her forefinger, Jupiter, shows a strong love of approbation, and again, where her head line begins can be seen a little line running up towards Jupiter, reinforcing and strengthening that desire to succeed above all things. Her intuitive qualities are marked by the whorl on the lower part of the mount of the Moon, in this case almost at the wrist, a sign of a personality which can project itself without much effort, towards others. Almost in the center of the mount of Apollo under her third finger is another whorl, a second sign of intuition. She could understand without conscious thought. At the same time her intellectual assets are of no mean kind. The smooth skin of her palms is that of those fortunate persons who almost unconsciously absorb from environment anything that is likely to be of interest or of use. Her head line is deep in both hands, fairly level and well-defined. She can think clearly and with balance. Her lacks are shown in the character of the flexibility of her thumbs and their pointed tips, which, while they indicate suavity, charm and adaptability, also show a spasmodic will power. Often she had to drive herself to work. The space between the life line and the head line shows in its width a tendency to independence in thought and action and an impulsive disposition that would lead her into many difficulties. Her long fourth finger with the very decided flare from her hand discloses all the Mercurial qualities essential to an actress, gift of expression in the long first phalange, and the gift of mimicry and humor in the high mount of Mercury and sloping head line leading to imagination in the mount of the Moon.

Her finger of Jupiter is curiously short. She dislikes responsibility. Motivated in part by this dislike of responsibility, in part by impulse and by that intuitive quality that told her that her laurels were not

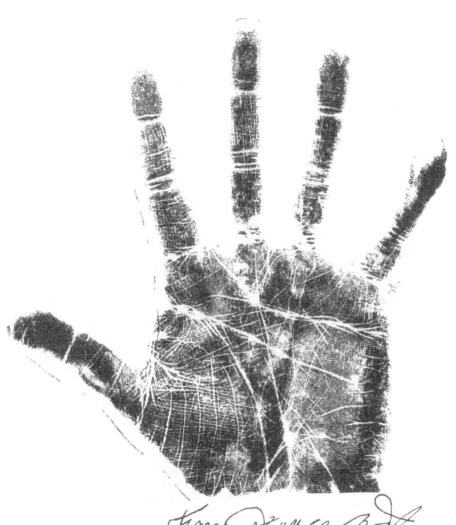

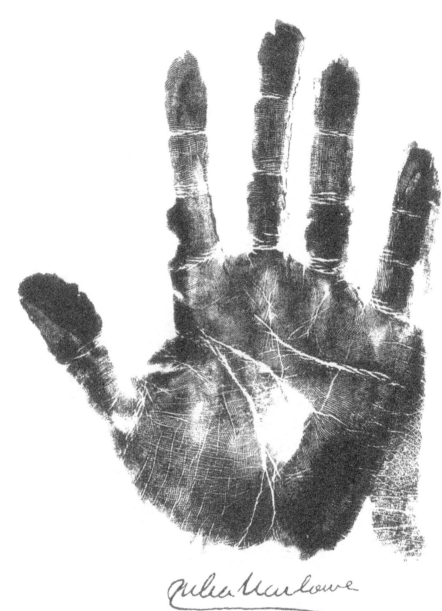

Julia Marlowe

ely to be greater, her retirement from the stage left a beautiful memy to her public.

From among our younger actors I call Morgan Farley into the spotght. This young Lion was presented to me, as a person of great distinction, by Stuart Walker. Farley was at that time "the youngest assistant age manager in the world." As I shook hands with the lad I realized his persensitive nature, eager for truth in art, eager to contribute all that could.

A young idealist then, and as I made the impressions of his hands I w that the handshake had been truly informative. Farley has large horls upon the mount of the Moon, whorls towards which his head ne droops. Other large whorls are marked between the first and second ngers. All of these prints are so clearly etched that they stand out in allenging fashion. He is gifted; he has rare intuitive quality, and the ip of the head line shows that his mentality is led afar into fields of imgination.

With these alone, Farley might run amuck. But his hands also show ecided balances. The first is the decided firmness of his palms. He has ne ability to restrain himself. The long first phalanges of his thumbs peak of decided will power, which is all the more noticeable because of ne decided flexibility of the first joint. Morgan Farley dislikes social onventions, but adapts himself to people with ease. The second phalnges of his thumbs show well developed reasoning powers, another heck upon imaginative and intuitive gifts. The curve of the thumb into nis particular waistlike formation indicates that he possesses both tact nd patience in dealing with himself and with others—a third check. he wide flare of his fingers and thumbs shows extreme independence. Ie might be an extremist, but he is more likely to put his balances to use. he wide flare of his fourth finger, indicating quickness in thought and ction is dominated and directed by the love of the dramatic shown in is double jointed thumbs. Add to this the emotional nature shown in he developed mount of Venus, and with the imagination, intelligently irected, you have the stepping stones leading to the realization of his iramatic goal. Will he go far? He must if he uses his gifts and the tools or their development.

From my treasure chest I lift the hands of Lynn Fontanne, exquisite ands that remind me of a Fragonard painting. These impressions were nade fifteen years ago when Lynn, a gifted young girl, was touring with aurette Taylor's company. The spotlight had not touched her then.

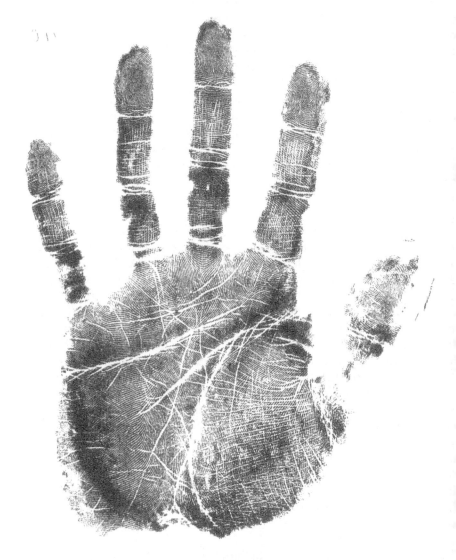

Morgan Farley
New York May 25 1924.

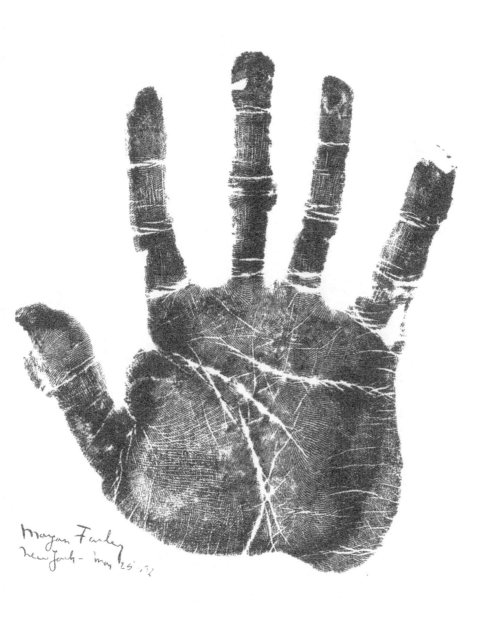

Morgan Farley
New York — May 25 '72

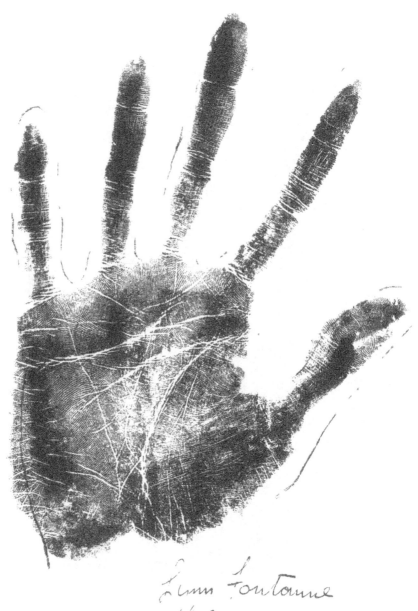

Lynn Fontanne
February 12 1919

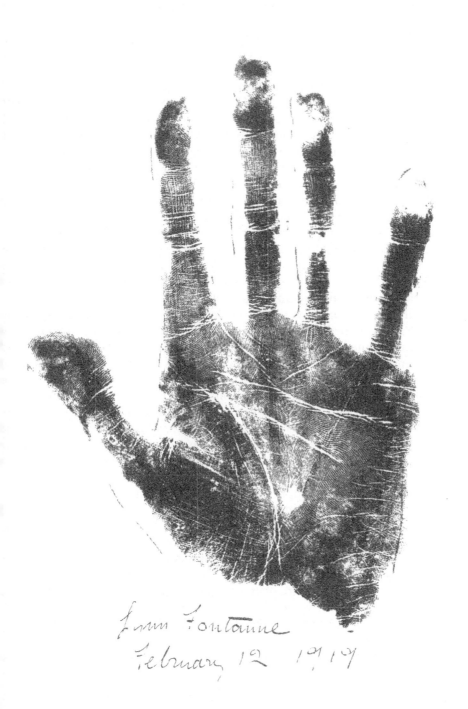

Lynn Fontanne
February 12 1919

Today, as an outstanding player of The Theatre Guild, she is known from Coast to Coast—and across the seas to England.

Rarely have I looked at hands that show so clearly the truth which every palmist who heeds the creed of her science must preach, namely that the making of life is in your hands.

Lynn Fontanne's thumbs are flexible and so are her fingers; she is eager to gain from life's experiences that which will further her career. She lacks perseverance, but the logic shown in the long second phalanges of her thumbs strengthens her will power. Her head line has both depth and length, and its closer joining with the life line in the right hand indicates a developed caution. Impatience is again shown in the pointed tips of her thumbs, but the second phalanges of her second fingers are unusually long and indicate a wisdom and prudence that seems utterly at variance with impatience.

Her long smooth fingers reveal an exquisite sense of detail and decided inspirational quality. The pointed tip of her first finger discloses quickness of perception, while the roundned tip of the second indicates a nature not easily cast down. She is not likely to hold post mortems over disagreeable or disappointing past affairs.

Her rather small flat mount of Venus shows a lack of all the qualities one might expect in an actress of her power. But she has the girdle of Venus, a line broken in the middle, starting from between the first and second fingers and ending between the third and fourth—a sign of warmth, tenderness and sympathy that finds an outlet in expression. In her left hand running in almost continuous fashion from the line of alliance or marriage line under Mercury to the line of the heart is a definite line which indicates her dependence upon someone else in her advance in her career—someone to whom she is bound by ties of affection. As Lynn Fontanne's success has been most marked when she appears with her husband, Alfred Lunt, this line seems justified.

Under the third finger of her left hand is seen in shadowy outline what seems to be a trident, marking the growth of fame, fortune, and honor. If I were examining Lynn Fontanne's hands today, I should expect to find this trident much more clearly defined.

Lynn Fontanne has not occupied the spotlight alone. In her greatest successes, "Reunion in Vienna," "The Guardsman," "Queen Elizabeth," she has shared honors with her husband, Alfred Lunt. These two in reciprocal acting, that has rarely if ever been surpassed, have chosen to remain in the spotlight together, although each is in his own right a center of attraction.

The hands of Alfred Lunt are among the latest in my collection. Look

51

at the prints. Lunt's hands appear one mass of clear, well-defined lines. Such hands belong to those whose lives are very full of all kinds of activities, both physical and mental. In the early part of Alfred Lunt's life his physical activity was decidedly limited, as is shown by lines crossing the life line. At the time he must have found his schooling and his planned physical recreation much interferred with. Even his active brain was forced "to make haste slowly." The years have established his health, as the life line indicates in the depth and length. In the close joining of his life and his head line, with the islanded condition, is shown his tendency to permit his mental outlook to be biased by his physical condition and vice versa—if he is mentally troubled, it is prone to affect him physically.

The length of his first finger, with the dominance of the third phalange, marks the man of ambition and love of approbation, with decided executive ability. In the wide flare of the thumbs is shown Alfred Lunt's dislike of limitations that might be imposed upon him by social conventions or because of environment. The stiffness of his thumbs indicates considerable will power. His executive ability, plus his will power and the reason powers shown in the second phalange of his thumbs, enables him to straighten out stituations arising from temperamental maladjustments. He has a keen sense of justice, shown in the length of the middle phalange of his first finger, and by applying this he can bring harmony and understanding to his relations with others. His will power, however, often dominates his judgment. When his heart is set upon a thing he can bring the diplomacy shown in the length of the fourth finger, persuasion and argument shown in the breadth of his finger nails —a little broader than they are long—and so make a platform on which he may triumphantly stand to vindicate his avoidance of common sense and reason. This attitude applies especially to health conditions. His zeal to complete some cherished plan may place heavy demands upon him which he thus manages to justify.

Alfred Lunt's fingers show inspiration, but he is not content with inspiration. He must know how, technically, to express the fire and passion, sympathy and tenderness shown in the development of his mount of Venus, the ambition indicated in the developed mount of Jupiter, the somber tragedy indicated in the development of the mount of Saturn under the second finger, and the buoyancy shown in the rounded tip of the straight finger of Apollo, and the wit and humor disclosed in the developed mount under the fourth finger of Mercury. Quickness of thought and of action are revealed in the flare of the fingers of Mercury, and the length and roundness of the tips indicate the gift of expression and of tactful consideration for others. As this first phalange of Mercury domi-

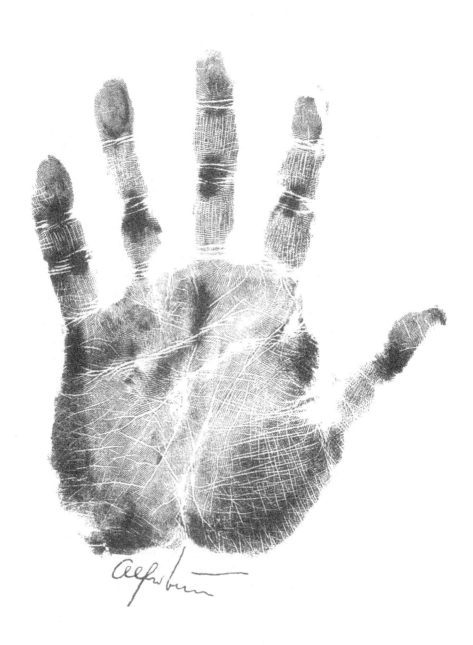

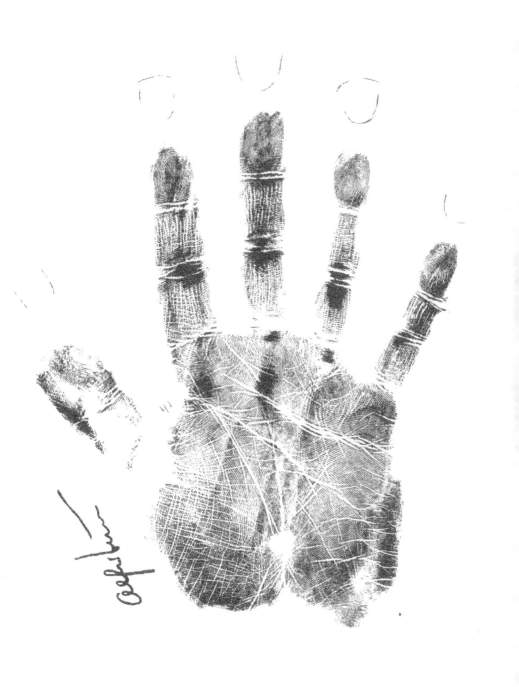

nates the other two, Alfred Lunt is one whose "word is as good as his bond." Between the head and heart line is a wide quadrangle—tolerance. Combine this with the quality of mercy shown in the length of the first phalange of the forefinger, and you have a man who may be unsparing when it comes to his own shortcomings, but who has a vast forgiveness towards his fellow beings.

Like his gifted wife, Alfred Lunt possesses the girdle of Venus, broken in both hands, an indication of dramatic gifts of emotional quality. Under the third finger of the left hand is the trident of fame, fortune and honor. In the right hand this is as yet the fork of brilliancy. At the end of the life line on the mount of Jupiter is a star. Lunt has still greater possibilities of realization in his career. He has not yet reached his greatest height. There await him more distinguished honors.

Chapter 7: *"The Play's the Thing"*

The spotlight would never shine or the camera shoot, and the kings of make believe would have nothing to make believe with, if two figures who never stand in the spotlight or face the camera, i.e., the playwright and producer, ceased their labors. "The play's the thing," asserted the Master Playwright, who was his own producer, and the play is still as much the "thing" as it was in the time of Shakespeare.

I wonder what Shakespeare would have thought, could he have joined me upon my journey to the twenty-sixth floor of the Hotel Lincoln in the city of New York in the summer of 1933, a journey to secure the impressions of the hands of a modern Lion, playwright and producer both, one John Golden. We—I was accompanied by my New York representative, Marian Gillespie—, entered the office suite bearing our passport, a letter from Golden's private secretary, which served as a ticket to the first office. In this ante, ante, ante, ante-room sat people of many kinds, actors, aspiring playwrights, perhaps, whose eyes followed us with a twinge of envy as we passed into the ante, ante, ante-room, occupied by three or four persons at desks, who surreptitiously gave us the once-over to decide whether we did, or did not, belong. Past them in triumph into the ante, ante-room which was evidently a place for the heavy thinking of the solitary young man absorbed in his cigarette and the beautiful view from the window. Into the ante-room, where the Personal Secretary of our Lion greeted us affably and ushered us into the Den, in which the Lion was roaring mightily. Since there was no other exit save the window, we had our quarry cornered.

I began to make the impressions to the tune of the Lion's roars as to the value of the prints, comments upon the method I used in making them, much ado of the valuable time being consumed, the enumeration of engagements, work, reading of plays, re-writing of scenes—at this point I finished.

"I have the prints," I said, beaming upon my Lion. "Do you want me to read your hands now, or is your time too much occupied with more important things?"

His eyes twinkled as he stretched forth his hands. When John Golden comes across, he comes all the way. If I said something about him that seemed to him particularly true, he called in the Personal Secretary to hear it repeated, and to assure me how right I was. I stopped thinking about Shakespeare and the four ante-rooms; after all, this is the twentieth

54

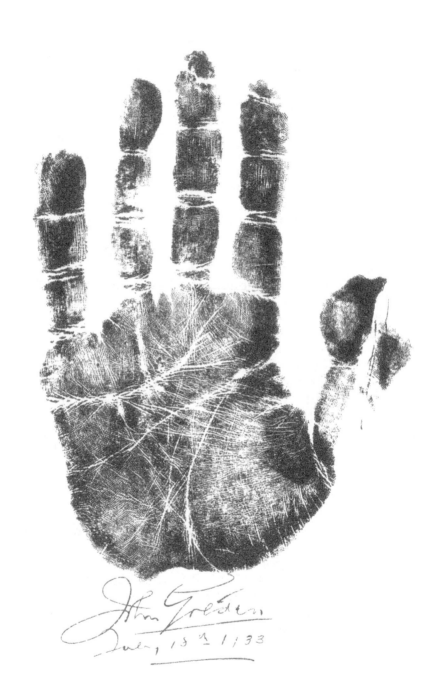

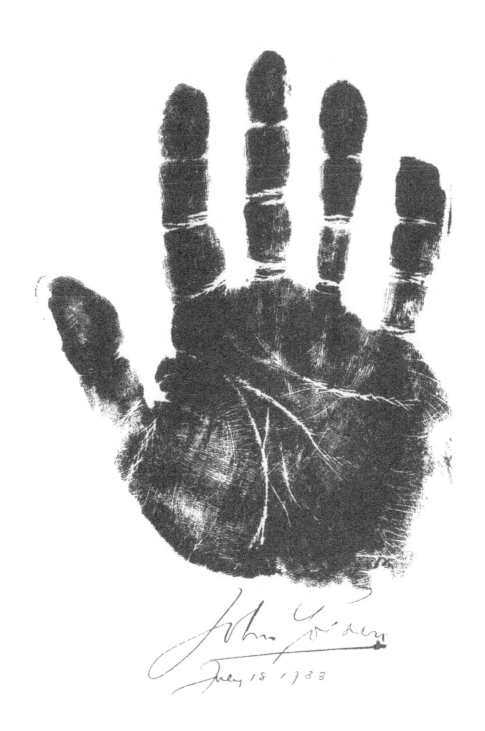

John Gordon

July 18 1933

century. When I left I carried with me a photograph, a reproduction of a sketch by James Montgomery Flagg, on which Golden had written,

"Dear Mrs. Meier, How in God's name did you know?"

His thick, powerful fleshy hands are those of a person of abundance of vitality and of energy. The flexibility of his thumbs, especially of the right thumb, coupled with the wide flare from the hands, indicates his dislike of convention, as well as an easy adaptability to his surroundings, and to the foibles, limitations and work of others. His fingers are short, and show how he dislikes detail. But his life line and head line are closely joined, a sign of caution in matters of enterprise affecting himself. The long straight head line in his left hand also indicates an underlying adherence to method.

Despite his dislike of detail this man is both cautious and methodical. His long, first finger is that of the true executive; he can when he wills, dispense with all detail, giving it over to others. His long fourth finger shows a power of diplomacy, and its pointed tip tact in management, while the long first phalange reveals a gift of expression in words and action. His double joined thumbs also declare John Golden to be an actor. In actual life he was that for four years, playing in stock and in Shakespeare. Since then he has played the part he likes best.

The wide stretch between his first and second fingers shows independence of thought, a trait that leads him to defy criticism. But his love of power and his caution enable him to make good use of his diplomatic gifts to attain his ends.

In his right hand his head line droops to the mount of Imagination. This man sees visions of what he wants to do. In the rounded tip of his second finger there is an optimism hard to beat, and again, prudence and wisdom in the second phalange, as a balancing power. His line of fate or destiny is crossed again and again, his is a life of many ups and downs. But his enthusiasm remains intact. His nails are long, and sufficiently broad to cover the ends of the fingers, thus protecting those delicate nerve centers which are such perfect barometers of human temperament. When a man has nails of this shape with a cordial handshake and an upward tilt to his mouth, he is of the unquenchable kind that meets defeat with a smile and turns it into experience to be used at the next opportunity. Add to this John Golden's amazing vitality, strength and endurance, and you can understand his outstanding record, as comic journalist and rhymster, writer of one thousand songs, composer of music for a score of musical comedies, playwright and producer of thirty odd comedies and dramas, one of which, "Lightnin'," ran for over twelve hundred consecutive performances, almost as lusty a product as its producer.

55

Contrast these vital hands of John Golden with the prints of the hands of Eva Le Gallienne, prints that show the dominance of the intellectual. Eva Le Gallienne can truthfully be called a fine actress. But she has chosen to be both actress and producer, and in both, her intellectual qualities are supreme. Her clear, straight head line, the development of logic and reason in the second phalanges of her thumbs, the wisdom shown in the length and shape of the middle phalange of her second finger—all bear testimony to her mental gifts. Driven by ambition, shown in the development of the mount of Jupiter beneath her first finger, she has managed to discipline both physical weakness and temperamental deficiencies to her desired ends.

Eva Le Gallienne is a supersensitive, reticent human being. The close joining of the life line and the head line in her left hand, together with the development of those sensitive nerves shown in the whorls of her finger tips are signs of a nature that is unusually shrinking and retiring. She avoids criticism, constructive or destructive. Combine these characteristics with the noticeably short first finger, a sign of dislike of responsibility, and you realize how many obstacles were placed in the path of her ambition. In the right hand the head line and life line are rather far apart, clear testimony to the success of her self-discipline. The thumb in her right hand is more supple than that in her left, another indication of her success in adaptation. Her thumbs also show in the length and development of the first phalanges the tremendous will power that has made such changes possible. This force of will is in itself both an asset and a liability. It is a will that can easily degenerate into stubborn obstinacy and an almost sullen quiet resentment, and be swayed by desire rather than by intelligence. In Eva Le Gallienne's early life such fits of sullen resentment must have come often. The network of cross lines in the left hand shows impaired health and overstrained nerves. But in the right hand the health conditions have much improved. Her firm elastic palm indicates an abundance of nervous energy and above all the deepening of her head line shows how well she has overcome her chief barriers to success. Her line of destiny shows success beginning in her early thirties, gathering momentum into her forties and finally culminating in the three short lines leading to the whorl between her third and second fingers. The first indicates a definite recognition; the second, financial recognition; and the third, the honor conferred in recognition of her outstanding attainments.

Daniel Frohman has been connected with the stage so long that he is almost a legendary figure. To have reached four score years and some, to

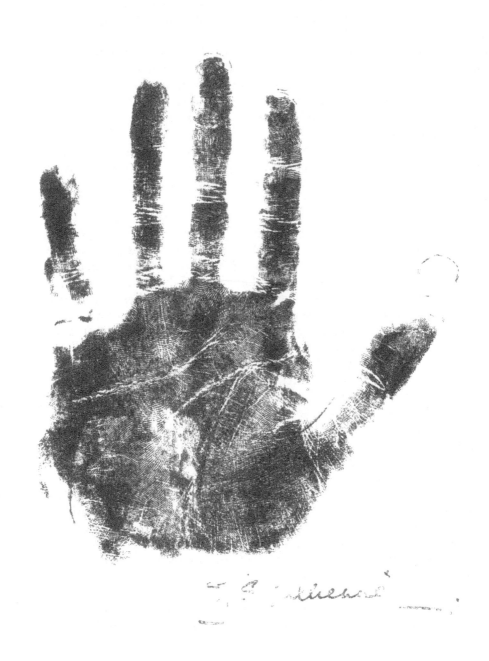

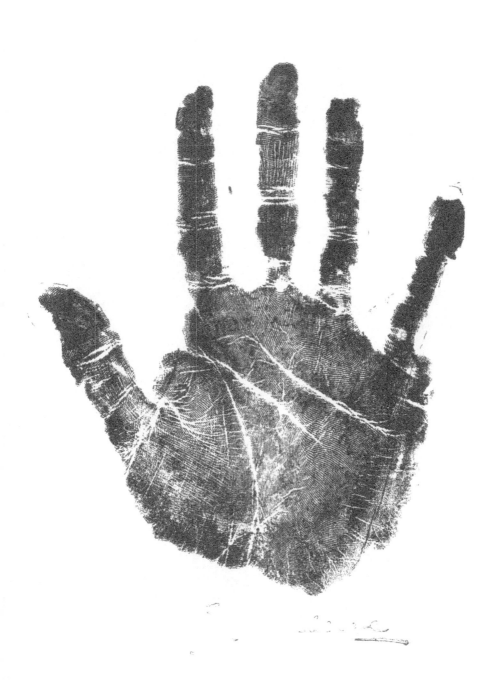

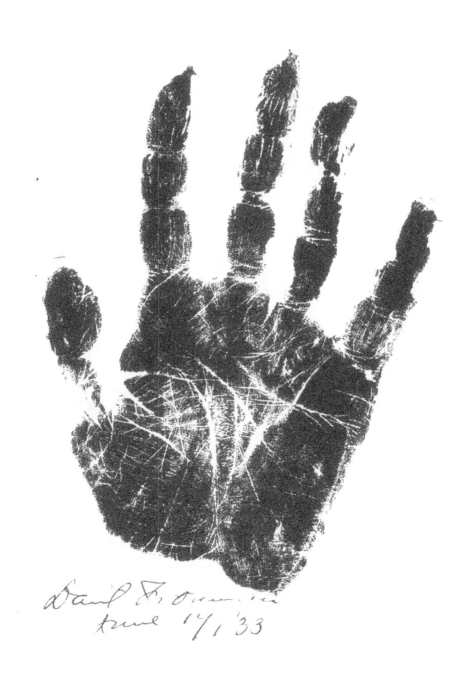

David F. Orwin
true 17/1 '33

maintain an erect figure, an alert mentality, and a vital and eager interest in the world is in itself an achievement of no mean order. I met Daniel Frohman in 1933, and the prints here shown indicate the vitality of the man.

He loves life. His thumbs are double joined and flexible. a sign of the actor who participates in everything as a part of a master show. His fingers and palms are likewise supple and flexible, indices of a mentality that develops through keenness of observation, association with people in every walk of life, and an ability to jump at a conclusion remarkably near the truth. He has a tendency to be influenced by intuition as the first phalange of his second finger, together with the droop of his head line, indicates. The tip of the second finger, however, is square, a sign of common sense. From the combination, Daniel Frohman has evolved a philosophy of compensation, "no loss without gain."

The slightly spatulate tip of the third finger shows an originality in constructive work, which would mean stage settings or direction. The broad space between the life line and the head line is a sign of impulsiveness in speech and action, and it has taken much hammering of adversity to make him realize the necessity for curbing both. This is indicated by the heavy cross lines on the line of destiny—fate—success, etc. His clear long life line has all the signs of the years he has enjoyed.

Kenyon Nicholson, whose latest success, "Sailor Beware," left New York after a two-year run, lived near me in the neighboring town of Crawfordsville, Indiana. When I met him first, in 1921, he was a likeable, shy lad, and I was at once interested in the possibilities of success so plainly indicated in his hands. Kenyon Nicholson's unusual thumbs, finely shaped, perfectly placed, with the long will-phalange motivated not by desire but by reason, as shown in the relation of the two joints, together with the degree of stiffness, a sign of steadfast perseverance without wilful obstinacy, are those of a man competent to work towards the goal he selects. That goal is revealed by the long first phalange of his fourth finger, indicating the gift of expression, while the straight head line and the stiff thumb point to writing rather than speaking, as his outlet. Like most producers and playwrights, he has double jointed thumbs, the sign of the love of the dramatic. The mount of Venus is particularly well developed and indicates warmth, fire and ardor, while the fine texture of his palms is that of the man who can reflect the surroundings and characteristics of others as does a mirror, and having made them serve their purpose, turn the mirror to a new reflection. Meanwhile the inner life goes on quite undisturbed, his natural traits and

57

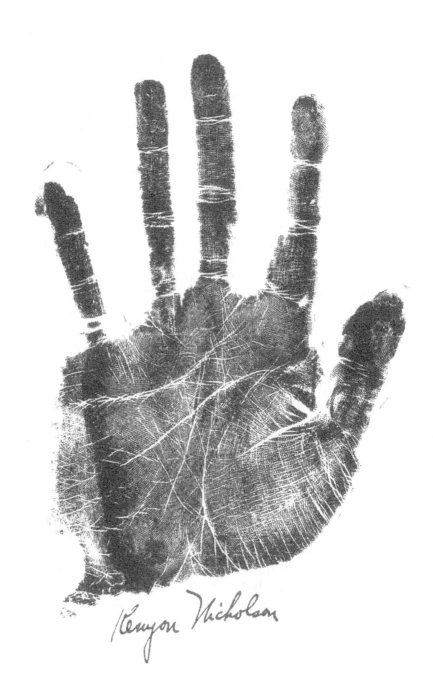

Kenyon Nicholson

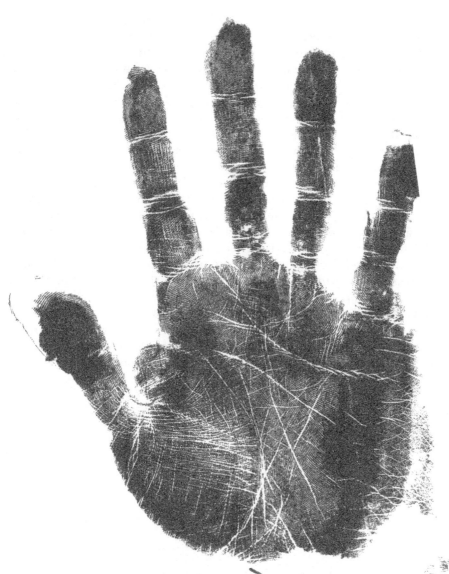

Kenyon Nicholson

personal interests are barely touched, if touched at all, by the mirror and its reflection.

Kenyon Nicholson began as a self-effacing person. The rather short first finger in the left hand, and the close joining of the life and head lines in that hand, are contradicted in the right, where the first finger is much longer and the life and head lines are separated. The thumb in the right hand has a much greater flare from the hand and marks a distinct growth of self-assurance and independence. This growth is not a result of ambition but of the conscientious qualities shown in the very long first phalanges of all of his fingers. To write with convincing truth and accuracy he had to become more independent and more self assertive; it was essential to his honesty of purpose.

Kenyon Nicholson is a man of many assets, but the most striking is the repetition of the quality of what might be called "double mindedness." Not only the texture of the skin of his hands, but also the character of his fingers, smooth to the second joints and then developed in a way that shows how he erects a wall between the varied expressions of life envisioned through his inspirational qualities and his own personal views, emphasize this particular quality. The long sloping head line with its deep channel reveals a tenacious memory as well as an ability to concentrate doggedly and persistently towards a desired end. A well-defined line of talent which runs from the head line in the right hand straight between the second and third fingers shows that he has gained name and fame by concentrating on the development of this one definite aim.

Chapter 8: *They Know Their Jungle*

James Whitcomb Riley was our close friend. To this fact I owe the only impressions of his hands that were ever made, and I suppose that mine was the only hand reading to which he ever listened. His hands were, first of all, always super-immaculate in their appearance. Mr. Riley was ultra fastidious with regard to his hands, and the texture of the skin was remarkably fine. The most striking quality of the pair lay in the difference between the left or "natural" hand and the right, the hand which shows what a man has made of himself. In the impressions, the left hand shows a diffident, a shrinking, secretive, rather timid nature. The right hand reveals self-reliance and initiative. The head line in the impression of his left hand shows a long droop, an indication of great imagination, which found expression in gloomy forebodings or in humor and gaiety. In the right hand the droop is much modified; the periods of depression came less frequently and were less intense as the years passed. James Whitcomb Riley was a self-made man in the highest sense.

The qualities that made him a poet were easily found. His smooth fingers showed inspirational qualities, and the pads or cushions on the inside of the nail phalanges revealed him to be supersensitive to everything that went on around him. The mount of Venus was well developed and smooth, indicating a deeply emotional nature responsive to mental contacts and material conditions.

The mount of Mercury, largely developed, indicated his great sense of humor and the mercurial characterstics—humor, gravity, versatility, high spiritual understanding, and plain homespun living. The length of the first phalange of the finger of Mercury with the pointed tip showed his gift of expression in speaking or writing. Riley had dramatic gifts which, if he had overcome his sensitiveness to appearing before the public, would have placed him with the great actors of his day. His heart line was the saddest kind of a heart line, for when he lost faith and belief, which he gave in extremes, the awakening disappointment brought poignant suffering, which found its outlet in his work and enriched his poems.

On the mount of the Moon was a whorl, a mark that looked like a thumb print which, with a similar print under and connecting the fingers of Saturn and Apollo, told of extraordinary intuitive powers.

All of these gifts would help a writer, but why did Riley become a poet? A poet is a writer who must express his thought in melody and

59

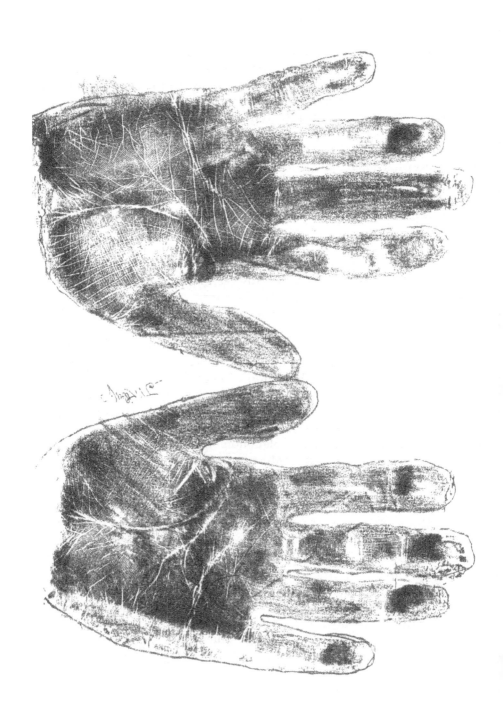

rhythm. The modernistic poets dispense with melody and use rhythm alone. He used both. His gifts of rhythm and melody are shown in the development of the lower mounts of Venus and of the Moon. He, like many poets, had a beautiful singing voice, and had he chosen to develop that gift, would undoubtedly have been successful.

The whimsical side to his nature was even more pronounced in the man than in his work, as shown in the development of the mount of Mercury. In the left hand there was a faint trace of what is known as "the sign of Mercury," a mark under the fourth finger. When this sign appears it means that the Mercurial powers are raised to the highest possible degree.

A touch of fantasy was shown in the development of the mount of the Moon with the large whorl—"Whose sword is sharp enough to cut the line twixt fact and fancy?"

As I recall my personal contacts with James Whitcomb Riley, I remember one afternoon when he was talking of the spiritual world, predestination and fatalism.

"I always think it wonderful," he said, "when I go to the circus, to see a man riding around the ring on a bare-backed horse, keeping a number of colored balls passing from his hands into the air and back again and again, without dropping one. But the Great Power has been keeping the rainbow balls of many universes moving through space as He rides in His circuit."

Perhaps it was this power of whimsy and fantasy that made him appreciate my reading of his hands. A few days later I received his photograph. On the back was written,

> "The Poet to the Palmist
>
> If she as happily had read
>   His poems as his palm—
> 'Now by God's rood,' he would have said,
>   'How satisfied I am.' "

If this left me in some doubt as to my ability as a reader of poetry, at least I was satisfied—as a palmist.

The hands of Edwin Markham are those of a thinker and of a seeker after truth. The length of the second fingers shows his mental power to grasp life and its serious problems, and the length of the nail phalanges of these fingers shows his demand for truth as far as he can find it. The rounded tips of the fingers show the poet. Mr. Markham wants to find the silver lining, no matter how heavy the cloud. As a thinker he demands

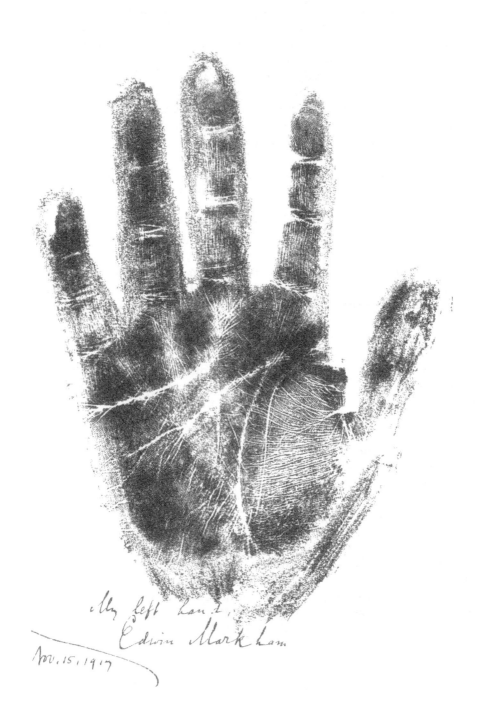

My left hand,
Edwin Markham

Nov. 15, 1917

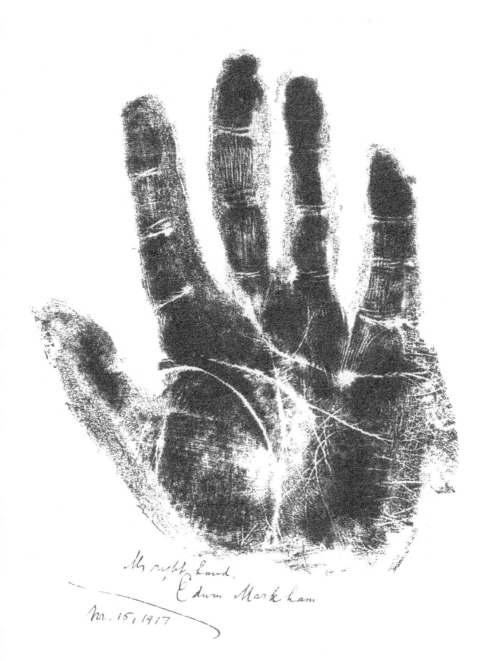

My right hand.
Edwin Markham
Mr. 15, 1917

truth, as a poet he wants to sing, and to sing he must find joy. Melody and rhythm, showed in the rounded mounts of Venus and the Moon are highly developed.

Edwin Markham is an old friend to most of us. Every school child knows his name. Thousands of them have recited his "Man with the Hoe." His hands show him to be an unusually fine type of human being as well as a poet. His handshake is that of a man who is level-headed, resourceful in emergency, and who has taken to heart Alexander Pope's admonition,

> "Know first thyself, presume not God to scan;
> The proper study of mankind is man."

Markham's long first finger marks him as ambitious, and the pointed tip of this finger discloses a quickness of perception that is almost prescience, and enables him to recognize and take advantage of opportunity. The middle phalanges of the second fingers have a development that signifies prudence. His search for truth and his natural sympathies are checked before he reaches extremes. His prudence prevents him from becoming a fanatic. The length of the first phalange of his third finger shows the quickness with which he discovers any flaw or makeshift in the technique required in the development of any phase of creative art or in intellectual or commercial activity.

Edwin Markham has many gifts. The unusual length of his fourth finger, Mercury, extending even above the first joint of the third finger, marks a natural diplomat. The length of the nail phalanges of this finger and the pointed tips show that he can express himself equally well in speaking or in writing. He can make himself clear in reading his poems; no one is at a loss to know what he means. The length of his fourth fingers coupled with the length of his first fingers show that Markham is a born leader. He has the ability to plan for others, to execute, and, with his extreme diplomacy, he could have been a great executive.

The fundamental traits in the development of the nail phalanges of all the fingers are integrity and sincerity. The will power shown in the long nail phalanges of the thumbs has been converted into a driving force which he has used to bring forth concrete results. Markham would have been happy to have lived in his castles in the air in his search for truth. His silver lining would have made them castles of loveliness. But the demands of practical needs developed the good common sense shown in the length of the head line. Desire yielded to the logic and reason shown in the second phalanges of the thumbs. With kindliness and good will he directed his poetic qualities to practical ends.

Why have I put poets and humorists together? Because while they must express that which they feel in words, as do all writers, these two must express it also through a second medium. The poets see their themes through imagination in terms of rhythm and melody; the humorists through that rare angle of vision that brings him who reads the gift of laughter.

The hallmark of a humorist, as seen in his hands, is to be found in the mounts of Mercury, below the fourth fingers towards the outside of the hands. The length of the first phalange of the fourth finger shows the power to use words to express that humor.

Look at the hands of Irvin Cobb. He has the signs of humor in the developed mount of Mercury, the gift of repartee in the pointed tip of his fourth finger.

In the extreme flexibility of the thumbs, coupled with the wide flare between the thumbs and fingers and the fingers themselves, is denoted an outwardly gay unconcern as to daily happenings in his life.

The second finger, Saturn, which is square tipped and heavy, denotes prudence, wisdom and thrift. These qualities act as a needed stabilizing force and enable him to get into harness and plod along carrying the responsibilities which life holds.

He is genial, as is shown in the suppleness of the thumbs, and the flare of the thumbs and fingers shows also that he is unconventional and likes Bohemian type of living. He has a great deal of the milk of human kindness in his temperament, indicated in the fulness but not the thickness of the mount of Venus, which also tells of a quick sympathy. Such sympathy, together with the flexibility of his thumbs, makes him adaptable to people whose lives differ widely from his own. The man and his work are much alike. His humor is genial as Cobb is genial, it is sympathetic as the man is sympathetic, and it is painted in with a broad brush—almost as broad as Cobb himself. He does not criticize; he interprets the foibles of his fellowmen in the light of his large geniality.

His fingers are the smooth ones that indicate inspirational qualities. His second finger, Saturn, shows in the length of the nail phalange a deep appreciation of that phase of life that we call spiritual force. He believes in it, and shows the belief plainly in his writings. He has an open mind towards the varied beliefs of all mankind. His third finger, Apollo, has an unusually long nail phalange that tells of his desire for reason and truth in all art, and of his fidelity to truth as he sees it.

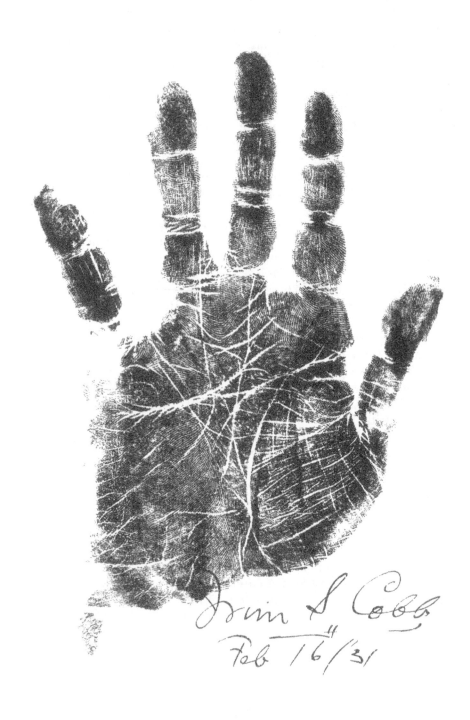

Irvin S Cobb
Feb 16 / 31

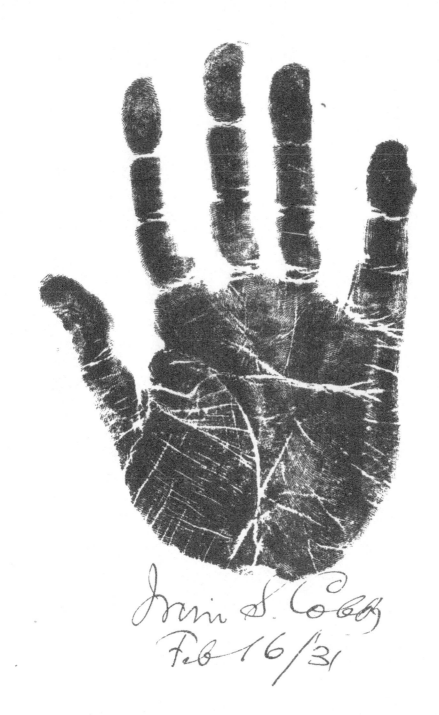

Irvin S. Cobb
Feb 16/31

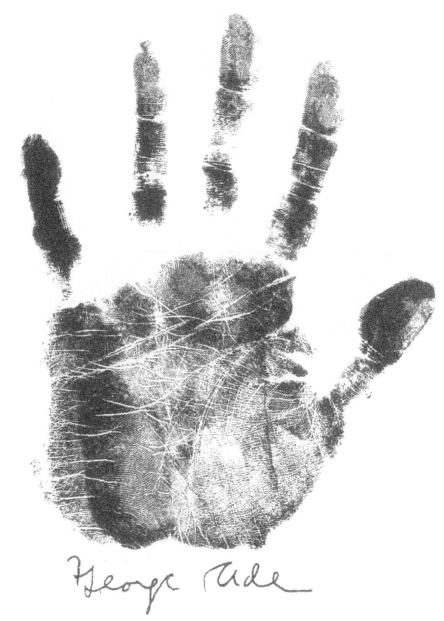

George Ade

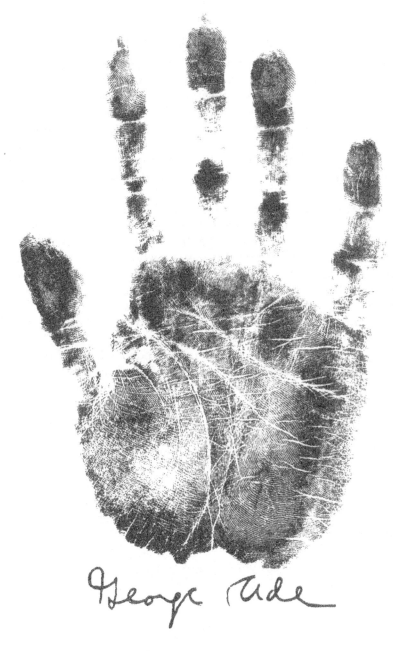

George Ade

George Ade chose for his sphere of humor our pseudo-social world. His "Fables in Slang" were read by many social aspirants who never realized that they were being portrayed. After I had read his hands, George Ade gave me a copy of the "Fables" which he inscribed to me in the terse but flattering words,

"To get a fair trial of speed, use a pacemaker."

He did not need my pacemaking. Ade is an extremist. The wide flare between the thumbs and fingers shows independence of thought to an unusual degree. It is this quality together with his sense of humor, shown in the development of the mount under Mercury, that is the basis of his work. He writes of extremes in extreme fashion. His fingers, smooth and comparatively long, show that he has inspirational qualities that can be applied to the detail he had the patience to acquire, and to use. His gift of expression is shown in the length of the nail phalange of the finger of Mercury.

George Ade has an unusually good head line. It tells of the ability to grasp a wide range of subjects and without the drudgery of deep study to assimilate enough of each one to enable him to use all with a degree of accuracy that defies challenge. He has the whorl on the mount of the Moon that is indicative of the sixth sense, intuition. With the exceptional head line and this sixth sense, the fortunate possessor need not labor through a heavy grind to accomplish results.

Ade's thumbs are well balanced. Reason and logic, shown in the second phalange, are equal to will, shown in the first phalange. The same tendency to extremes that characterizes his independence of thought is likely to make him a hard worker at times, bringing his powers of endurance to their limit and then going to the other extreme when he decides to rest, ignoring any claim upon his time or talent. Longevity is indicated in both hands. His life line has the recuperative qualities that enable him to recover after a prodigal use of his vitality.

Looking back over our poets and humorists, what makes them what they are? How do they differ from ordinary men? All the poets have in large degree the gift of expression plus a high development of melody and rhythm. The humorists have the full development of the mount of Mercury, which is the sign of a keen sense of humor, plus the gift of expression as shown in the length of the nail phalange of the little finger. These are the abilities or traits common to them. Beyond that, their particular brand of humor is a personal possession.

Chapter 9: *Story Tellers*

In the chapter entitled KINGS OF MAKE BELIEVE, I stated that of all the questions asked by the owners of the thousands of hands I have read, two concerning careers were general. The one universal question, of course, is

"How long will I live?" Then come,

"Can I succeed upon the stage?" and

"Can I write?"

The last question is put to me by people of all ages from eighteen to eighty—the desire for expression seems to live as long as the individual. The great majority of these questioners want to write fiction. They have felt and seen, and they want to express what they have felt and seen, not in exactitude, as biographers or journalists or fact writers, but through a medium that will veil their direct connection with events. Lions among story tellers are logically, therefore, of great interest to all would-be writers. What enables them to get across to others what they see and feel, through the medium of a story of imaginary persons, when so many seeing and feeling people fail utterly in the attempt?

I do not know that I can answer the question. But looking at the hands of the Lions of story-tellers who appear in this chapter may help. Meredith Nicholson naturally heads the list for two reasons: he is a fine Lion, and he is a friend of many years and the writer of the foreword to this book. He is not only a teller of tales, he is a poet and essayist and at the present time our U. S. Minister to Venezuela. So gifted a man is difficult to catalogue. But with twenty-one novels to his credit as against two books of poems and five of essays, I have placed him primarily as a story teller, and those who have read his "House of a Thousand Candles," will agree, I know, that here he belongs. I first met Meredith Nicholson at the home of James Whitcomb Riley. In 1917 and again in 1935 I took the impressions of his hands. It is the latter impressions at which you are now looking.

Meredith Nicholson's hand shows him to have the triple mental personality which he has manifested as the scholarly essayist, the poet of vision, and the novelist of imagination.

His long fingers with their long second phalanges point to the meticulous care which he would bring to intellectual expression. The close joining of his life line and head line are signs of an innate caution and, combined with the intense sensitiveness to criticism shown by the development of the little cushions of his finger tips and the great gift of

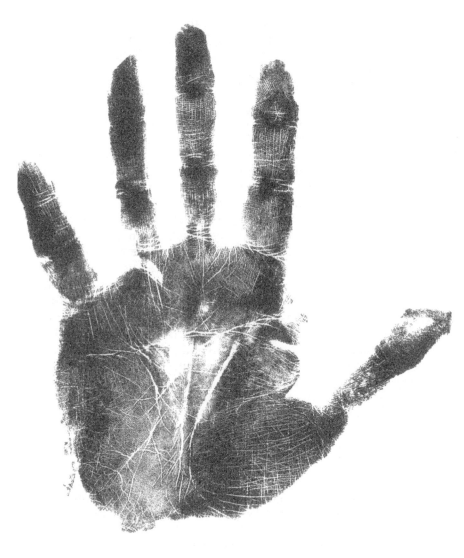

Meredith Nicholson
March 22 1935

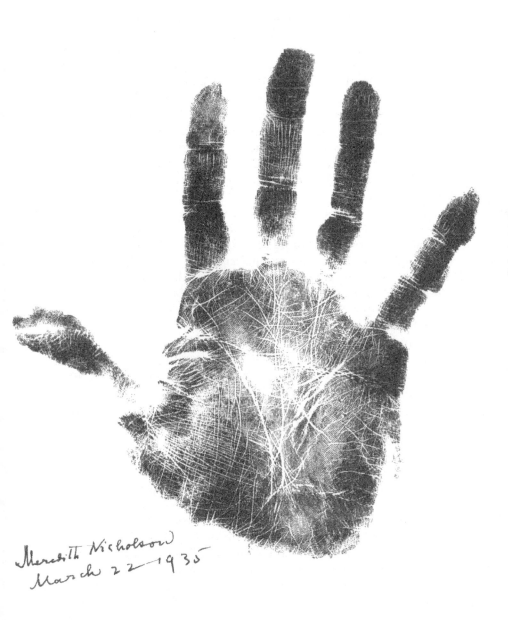

Meredith Nicholson
March 22—1935

words indicated by the nail phalanges of his fourth finger, Mercury, establish the essayist, the fact writer who carefully garners his material, sifts it and assays it and as carefully presents it.

To these charactertistics add the inspiration shown by the smoothness of his fingers with the drooping of the head line on the mount of the Moon, an indication of an apparently inexhaustible imagination. Here are the requisites for poetic expression, which in the work of Meredith Nicholson is decidedly influenced by his great love of the beautiful, as revealed by the slope of the palm to the wrist.

The circle of intuition clearly marked in the left hand, running from the mount under the fourth finger towards the base of the mount of the Moon, coupled with the long nail phalange of his second finger, discloses a certain phase of mysticism which is a recognized characteristic of Meredith Nicholson's fiction. Added to his gifts as essayist and poet, it enabled him to write the famous fantastic mystery, "The House of a Thousand Candles."

Meredith Nicholson's thumbs are well placed, but the nail phalanges of will overbalance the second phalanges of logic. He can shut his eyes to reason and carry out his impulses, which is often an asset to a writer. The "waisted" shape of the second phalanges of the thumbs shows a brilliant mentality and a power of analysis, a quality that enables him not only to see an act, but to understand the motivation back of it, another powerful asset to a writer. While his smooth fingers show inspiration, the limited stretch between the thumb and fingers and between the fingers themselves indicates a conservatism which often hampers inspiration.

He has done much for himself in overcoming his dislike of responsibility and lack of initiative, as revealed in the rather short first finger, through his driving ambition, disclosed by the full third phalange of the first finger, and his love of approbation also shown in the high mount under this first finger. His long nail phalanges of conscience and the stiff thumb of determination in the left hand are the disciplinary factors needed to enable him to stick to the drudgery and toil necessary for literary expression.

The greater flexibility of the thumb in the right hand shows that he has acquired a savoir-faire that enables him to be something of a mixer, a quality much needed by an ambassador to a foreign country. as well as by a man who wishes to write what he knows of people.

⸱ That he has achieved his ambition to an unusual degree is indicated in the definite star of unexpected honor and elevation on the mount of Jupiter under the first finger. That he has gained the recognition of fame, fortune and nonor to which his career as a writer, a poet and a novelist and a diplomat justly entitles him, is shown in the trident under the third finger in the right hand. The triangle clearly marked on the mount of Mercury in the right hand is supposed to indicate success in connection with diplomatic mission. Meredith Nicholson is fortunate in having attained outstanding success and recognition commensurate with his definitely varied and brilliant gifts.

Like Meredith Nicholson, Stark Young has written books of poems, many essays and short stories. He has also published four novels since 1926. His latest, "So Red the Rose," definitely places him in the ranks of Lions of story tellers. He called upon me in New York City at the request of a mutual friend. I liked his handshake; it is cordial and sincere. His hands show, even in these impressions, the mental versatility that has made his articles as well as his novels, of high order. Under the third finger, Apollo, leaning toward the fourth finger, Mercury, is a whorl, a finger print marking. This is a sign of an accentuation of his artistic qualities, and also of a considerable commercial ability which will make it possible for him to gain financial as well as artistic reward.

Stark Young has a wide stretch between his thumb and fingers which indicates a tendency to fly off at a tangent. The distances between the fingers strengthen this sign, and add indications of independence in thought, and what may be rashness in action is shown in the wide flare of the fourth finger. In the right hand all these flares are modified. He becomes more conservative as he works on. Such qualities are those of the writer who uses facts. The novelist is shown in the head line. In both hands it droops to the mount of the Moon, and reveals that imagination must play a large part in his work. Added to this, the development of the mount of Venus discloses potential emotional ardor. He has a distinct liking for life seen through glamour. His novels will always be logical romances, i.e., based upon unquestioned facts, seen under a veil of glamour. His gift of expression is two-fold. His fourth finger, Mercury, shows in the length of the nail phalange that Stark Young is both a ready speaker and a ready writer.

Stark Young has greater recognition awaiting him, provided that his personal ambition is strong enough to drive him to the necessary effort. He is inclined to be mentally and physically indolent, and needs the stuffed club of necessity to live up to his abilities. He would much prefer to dream away his time. The drooping head line in both hands shows his tendency to allow his imagination to over-rule his clarity of vision. As a result, his heights of elation are balanced by depths of depression. And Stark Young is something of a philosopher, which does not accelerate

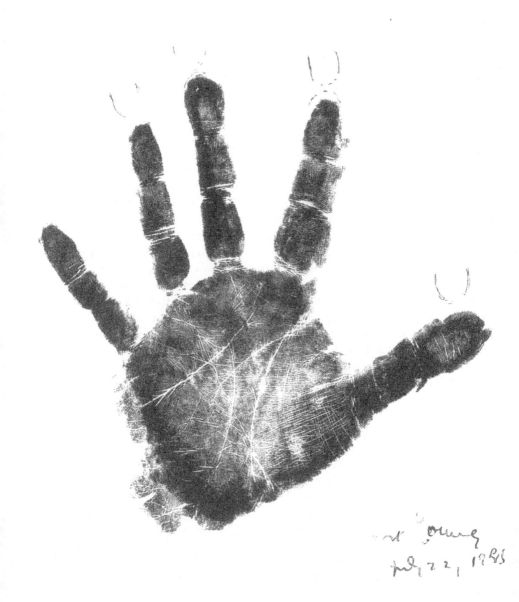

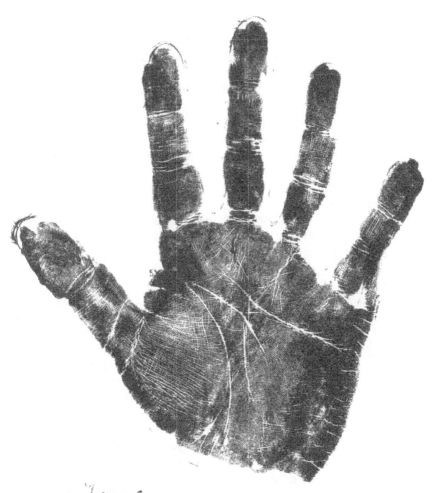

Harold Young
July 22. 1933

action. The long middle phalange of his middle finger suggests a philosophic wisdom. This is increased by the square tip of his finger, an indication of a demand for reason. The length of the nail phalange of the third finger reveals that, while Stark Young is a lover of beauty expressed in art, nature and life, he has also the discriminating eye of the critic, since lines and technique constitute the standard he unconsciously uses to form his judgment.

Under the third finger in his left hand are a variety of upward lines revealing a variety of decided gifts in the expression of which he has received definite recognition. In his right hand there is one deep line from the center of the mount under the third finger to the base of that finger. Stark Young is conserving his gifts and directing his forces into one definite line of expression.

In the past forty years, thirty-seven books, almost all of them novels, the latest her autobiography, have appeared over the signature of Gertrude Atherton. I met Mrs. Atherton in Hollywood through the well-know columnist, Mollie Merrick, and found her very dubious about "fortune telling."

"But I am not telling your fortune," I replied. "I am reading your characteristics as shown by your hand and comparing them with those shown in the hands of other writers."

At once she was eagerly interested. I looked at her hands and saw—what I cannot show here—how pink her palms are, those of a person in excellent condition. Her mount of upper Mars called my attention because of its unusual development; here is a woman of great courage, both physical and mental. The square tip of her third finger—indicative of creative ability—denotes a characteristic that is evidenced as well in the straight, clear head line in her right hand. Mrs. Atherton must have definite facts from which to build her novels. Unexpected and original as their denouements have been, she has found a basis for them. Not only is she courageous, she is also combative. The mount of aggression shown in the development of the mount of lower Mars, which is the upper part of the mount of Venus, shows a born fighter. Add to this, that Gertrude Atherton's hand shows her to be a conservative, and you have a nice little problem for a palmist. Her thumbs and fingers are stiff, and her life and head lines are joined, and those are all characteristic of conservatives.

Also, consider that the whorl on the upper part of the mount of Luna shows a deep sense of the poetic, which is both an inspirational fount and a haven of refuge. And finally, note the smoothness of her long finger, an indication of the gifts of inspiration, intensifying the qualities marked by each finger and mount, and carrying their varied traits to the depths of the clear, straight head line. Here is a woman who dreams, but who comes out of her dreams to fight. Heeding the practical urge to find facts to back up her dreams, she has entered the fields of history and science—her keen interest in science is indicated in the shape of her finger of Saturn—and using what she finds, she spins her yarns. Her courage and combativeness have been used in the selection of her subjects. Not knowing fear, and loving a fight, she has logically chosen those which would give her a chance at arousing dramatic climax. Do you recall "Black Oxen"?

The star of celebrity in her left hand under her finger of Apollo is only faintly shown in her right hand. She has not yet realized to the full her potentialities.

James Whitcomb Riley gave me a letter to General Lew Wallace, and also gave me permission to read it. It was so complimentary that I did not want to part with it, and when I had given it to General Wallace I asked for its return. General Wallace frowned, and with much dignity and formality, intended I am certain to inspire diffidence in me, asked,

"Which would you prefer, the impressions of my hands or this letter from Mr. Riley?"

"The letter from Mr. Riley," I replied truthfully, and waited in some trepidation for the reply. The General made a deep bow, handed me the letter and said,

"You may have both."

I sold that letter afterwards for funds for the Red Cross for War Relief, but by that time I had it by heart. The last sentence read,

"When I meet you again you will express your gratefulness for my thoughtful thoughtfulness in opening the door of opportunity for this interesting experience." No wonder I wanted that letter! even at the expense of losing the hands of the author of "Ben Hur" and "The Prince of India."

The palms of General Lew Wallace were so smooth that it was a difficult matter to obtain prints that show the markings. Hands like these simply could not do the great amount of research involved in both of these books. The firmness of his palms, together with this unusual texture of his skin, reminded me of the hard, smooth surface of the lithographer's stone—a quality of reflection without fixation. General Wallace was one of those persons who can give forth the present and its reactions with no deep impression upon their inner selves. He registered facts, impressions, episodes as something aside from his own personality,

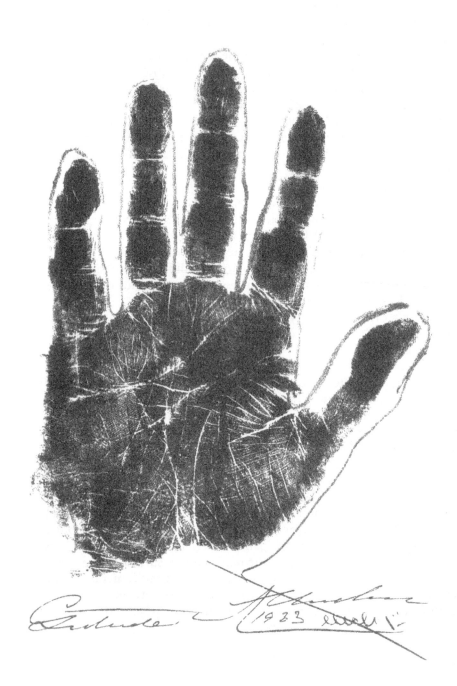

Gertrude   A Einstein
1933

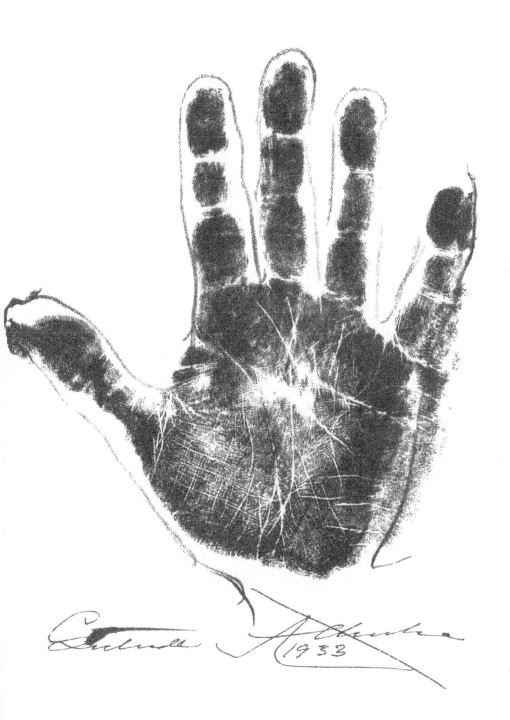

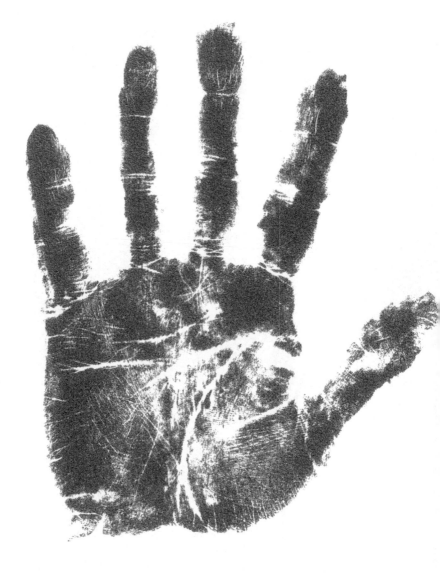

Geo Waldron
Feb 915, 1901

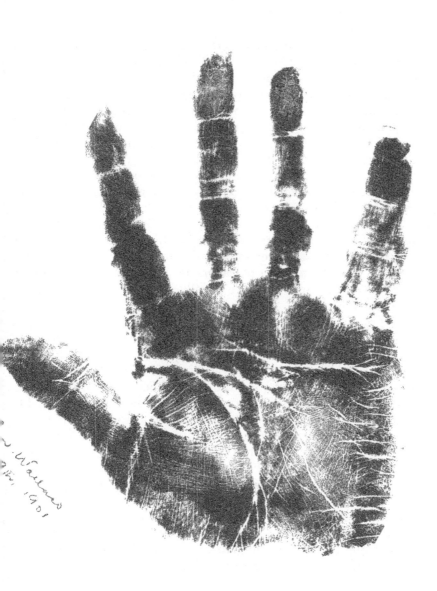

and yet he registered them in intensity sufficient to have a carrying power in his work.

I had heard of the invaluable assistance of his wife, in gathering the enormous amount of data necessary for his writings, hence it did not surprise me when General Wallace said, "My wife, Susan Elston, did that work."

This gallant soldier and able general who rendered our country such signal service during the Civil War, and who afterwards served us again as our Minister to Turkey, was primarily a restless personality. The high mount under the fourth finger, Mercury, showed that this quality dominated his life, his soldiering was one outlet, his writing another outlet. The high mount of the Moon, the mount of imagination, and the mount of Venus indicated a depth of fancy and of romance that colored his never fading word pictures. The first branch of the tripod under the second finger in his left hand revealed the strong influence of mysticism—shown in the shape of the nail phalange of this finger and the tiny finger print whorl between this and the first finger, which I call the sixth sense—which is so outstanding in his books. The middle branch was the continuance of the line of success, the financial line, and the third branch running toward the first finger showed the manner in which he dominated others through his power of leadership, and opened the road to his desires by sheer force of will or the equally strong gift of diplomacy as occasion demanded.

Whether John Erskine belongs in this chapter is a question. Noted as an educator before he began to write, perhaps his greatest contribution to our times will be finally written as a "Lion Trainer." As Chairman of the Administrative Committee of the Juillard School of Music he has given direct service of unusual character. His writings cover a large field; he had published poetry, essays, text books, and assisted in editing the Cambridge History of American Literature, all this before and while writing his novels, "The Private Life of Helen of Troy," "Galahad," "Adam and Eve" and so on. I have placed John Erskine in this chapter because he is an example of a satirical novelist who has been highly successful.

I met him in New York, and he agreed to give me the impressions of his hands, provided I got through in thirty minutes. I managed this.

"If you would like me to read your hands it would take another half hour," I offered. "I know you are rushed so ———"

I read his hands. Their most valuable asset is the large whorl upon the mount of the Moon, a psychic whorl that enables John Erskine to sense the direction of his work rather than to think it. The size of the whorl indicates a man who has great flashes of understanding that are sure guides to conduct and to work. Yet the man is a conservative. His handshake is what might be termed, limited; the stretch between the thumb and fingers and between the fingers is also limited. He possesses the ability to suppress himself, as he wills.

His stiff jointed thumb shows a strong will and more conservatism to the point of stubborn determination. He can use this quality to advantage in an impersonal, critical analysis of his work, and he has great ability in separating himself from anything he does and for getting an impersonal viewpoint. In the right hand the gain in the flexibility of his thumb shows that in one direction he has succeeded—he can adapt himself to people, at least on the surface. The depth of his intellect often shoots him over their heads, even when he does not intend to go. His head line is very deep; his intellectual possibilities are rare.

His novels, notwithstanding their satirical quality, are revelations of a rich, emotional nature. In his hands this is shown in the development of the mount of Venus, and here is the sign of melody, while directly across the palm is the high development of the mount of the Moon indicating a sense of rhythm. In his novels as well as in music, John Erskine uses these gifts to the full.

The long nail phalanges of his fingers are signs of a conscience that will admit of no half way methods to get results. Not only must John Erskine do, but he must do by methods which in themselves are admirable. The shape of the nail on the little finger, short and broad, indicates a quiet sense of humor, colored with an amused attitude towards the shortcomings and foibles of others—unconscious in their self-revelations. He might smile with or at you, and at the same time with or at himself.

Mary Hastings Bradley, writer of romances, books of travel and adventure, as well as two books for children, likewise is hard to classify. I met her first at a "Breakfast for Celebrities" when I was guest of Ruth Hanna McCormick Sims. In 1928 I made my reading of her hands. The width and charter of the stretch between thumb and fingers and between the fingers shows an outstanding love of excitement. On the mount of upper Mars under the heart line towards the outside of the hand there is a definite sign of high courage. In seeming contradiction the head line and the life line in her left hand are closely joined, an indication of extreme caution. The idealism shown by her heart line beginning between the first and second fingers, and the fact that her heart rules her head as revealed by the narrow space between them under Saturn, account not

70

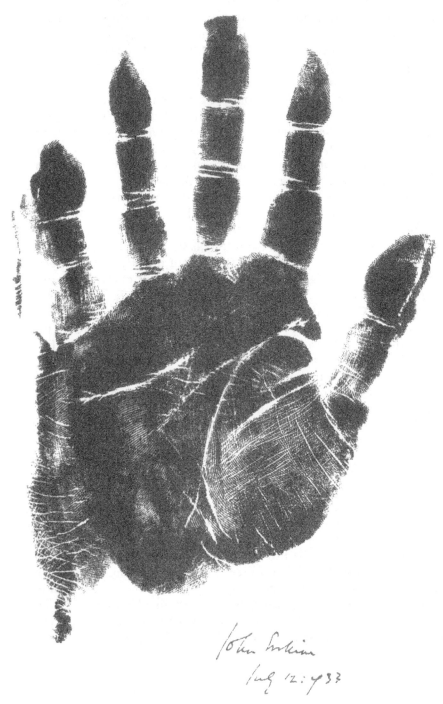

John Ruskin
July 12: 1833

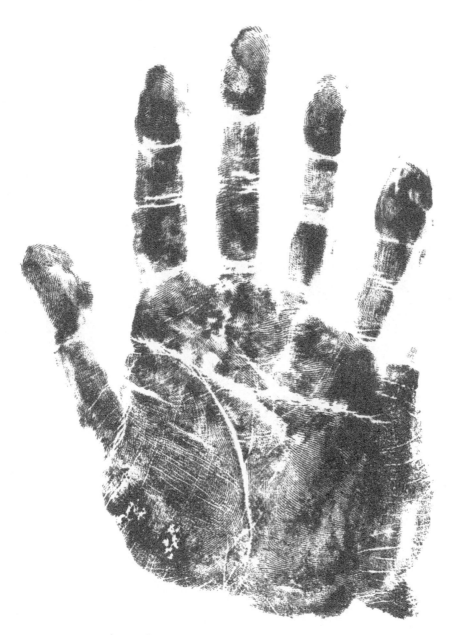

John Ruskin
July 12: 1933

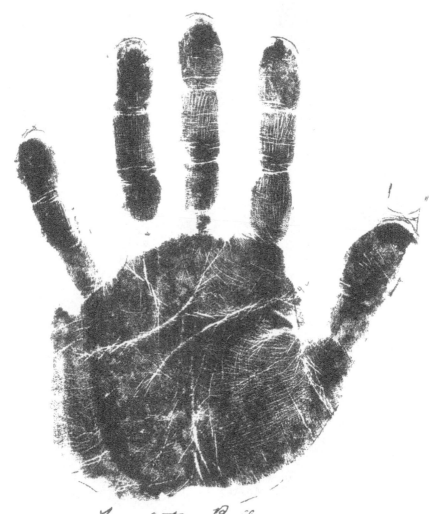

Mary Hastings Bradley

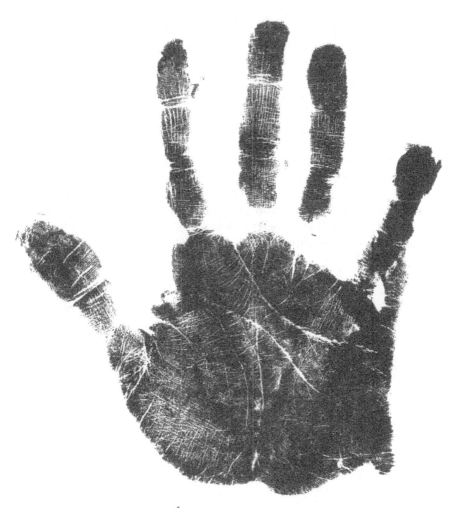

Mary Hastings Bradley.

only for her joining her husband on the Carl Akeley Expedition into the Belgian Congo on a search for gorillas, but for her taking her little girl, then five years old, with her. Despite widespread public protest she went, taking every precaution, but confident that all would be well. Their safe return was in the nature of a personal triumph.

Love of excitement accounts for her adventures and for the character of her writings. Her social gifts are indicated in her flexible thumbs, the long fourth finger, showing diplomacy, the gift of expression, and the keen sense of humor shown in the development of the mount of Mercury. Her gift as a raconteuse, which is an outstanding charm in her social contacts as well as in her tales, is shown in the long nail phalange of the fourth finger, the power of words, and of wit. Imagination is seen in the highly developed mount of the Moon, and the head line shows power of concentration in its depth with imaginative quality in the droop to this mount. The whorl on the mount shows the deep intuitional feeling, one of her "reasons" for assurance as to safety—she "feels" that she will or will not be safe, will or will not be successful—as well as an asset to her writing. The star under Jupiter in her left hand, indicative of unexpected honor and recognition, is still to be anticipated in her right hand.

Have I answered the question asked at the beginning? "Why do these people succeed in telling their tales so that men want to hear them?" I think that I have.

Looking at the Paws of these Lions of Story Tellers, you will see that they reveal many varied gifts. That means that their owners not only see and feel, but that they see and feel in many ways. It is this that gives their writings a point of view that is not commonplace; they are touched by wit, whimsy, satire, fantasy, insight and foresight, melody and rhythm in poetry and song. It is hardly ever the tale that is told, but the manner in which it is told, that makes it a tale to be read.

Chapter 10: *Their Tales Are True*

When men were little children they had to be told a story. Nothing in the facts of their lives seemed worth the hearing. But as life grew better and men grew to be what they are today, a little more than children, the day in itself became a kind of story, a tale worth repeating, if a teller who could see more than the bald fact of the moment, could be found. Today our interpreters of events, past and current, are as well-beloved as our story tellers. They take from the very air about us, the commonplace, and through their alchemy it is returned to us in a less personal setting so that, related to the past and the future as well as to the present, it takes on a new significance.

Dean of this school of writers is Ida M. Tarbell. I met her two years ago in her office in New York City. It was an odd office, with lovely old Oriental rugs and some pieces of old mahogany that rather crowded the well-filled book cases and tables piled with magazines. Framed photographs of friends filled the walls. When Miss Tarbell entered I told her that I was having an awfully good time examining them.

She smiled and said. "I am anticipating a good time, myself." When the reading was complete, she wrote for me two lines. The one on her photograph reads,

"Dear Mrs. Meier, I didn't know there were any like you." The other says, "An extraordinary reading of my character and my past, Ida M. Tarbell."

Ida Tarbell's hands are those of a well-disciplined character. Her left thumb is much more flexible than her right thumb. She has checked her natural disposition to be quickly responsive to friendly advances. The flare between the thumb and fingers of the left hand is greater than that in the right. She has guarded her natural tendency to yield to impulse, to allow others to make too great demands upon her, to overdo physically and to give extravagantly where her sympathies are engaged. The flare between the third and fourth fingers is much reduced in her right hand. She is naturally swift in thought and action, but she has deliberately curbed that swiftness to allow time for reflection. Her short, smooth fingers, indicative of a natural dislike of detail and a tendency to jump at conclusions, are tempered by the executive power in the relatively long forefinger, smooth and with a pointed tip, revealing an inspirational quickness of perception that enables her to put her detail in order ere she arrives at a conclusion. The first and second phalanges of her forefingers are equal in length—a sign of her ability to balance justice with

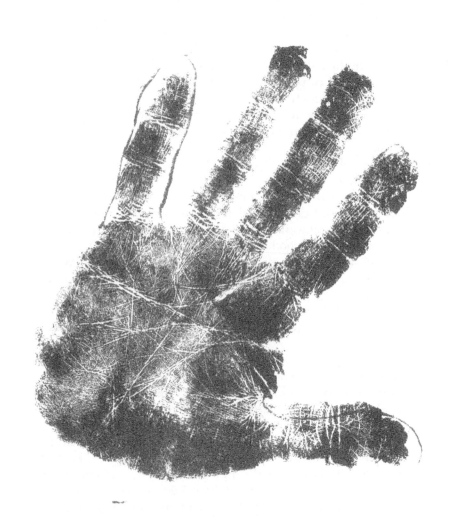

Edn M. Parhill
December 7 - 1933

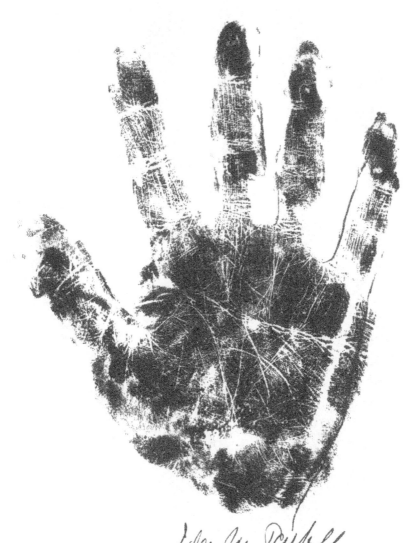

Lee M. Parkell
December 4 - 1983

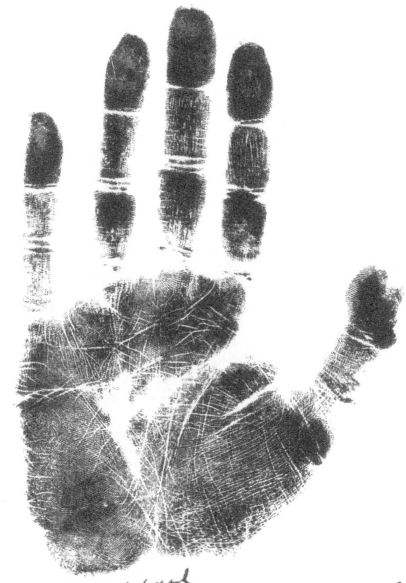

Elbert Hubbard   Left hand 2
Elbert Hubbard
Oct 6th 1903

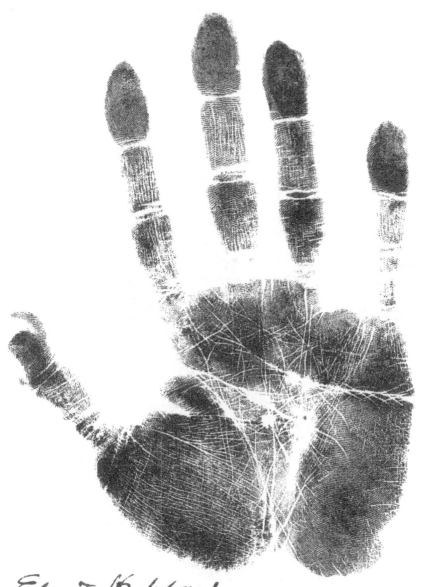

Elbert Hubbard
Right hand of
Elbert Hubbard

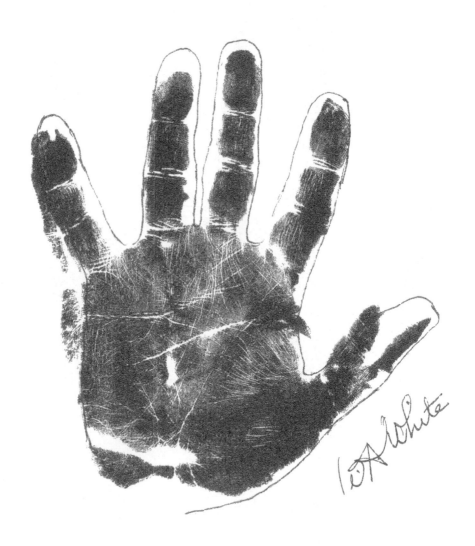

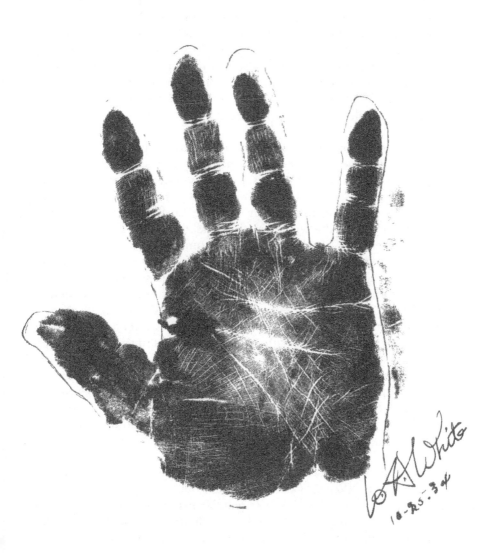

mercy. The shape of her nails, wider than they are long, shows an argumentative nature, while the shape of the second phalange of her thumb indicates that she will pursue an argument with logic and reason as her guides.

The tip of her second finger, definitely rounded, reveals the optimist, while the second phalange shows wisdom. She is far from a sedate character however. Her left thumb is double jointed; she always sees drama in life and has a great enjoyment of the unexpected. Her fourth finger shows not only the gift of words, but in its length, diplomacy, and in the pointed tip, tact. In the centre of the mount of Jupiter under the forefinger is a very definite star, a sign of honor, and the lines under the third finger of her right hand have formed the trident of fame, fortune and honor to which she is justly entitled.

If Elbert Hubbard had never written anything but "A Message to Garcia," his name would still be remembered. His work at East Aurora will always stand as one of the first examples of the William Morris movement to combine beauty of expression with forms of labor. And perhaps Hubbard's death—he went down with the Lusitania, trying to save his wife, who chose to die with him—but added another imperishable dramatic moment to a life that was always dramatic.

At the time these impressions were made he was at the height of his fame. There was an excessive flare between the first and second fingers and between the third and fourth which disclosed extreme independence in thought and in expression. A flare of this size and shape usually characterizes the man with the gift of showmanship. Together with his double jointed left thumb, and the gift of words as shown in the first and second phalanges of his fourth finger, is revealed the master showman with drama at his command. He was impatient of results, as is shown in the rounded tip of his thumb, and he had both an analytical and argumentative nature shown by his short broad nails. Under his third finger in the right hand is the star of celebrity, a star justified both in life and in death.

Since 1895 William Allen White has been owner and editor of the Emporia Daily and Weekly Gazette. He has done many other things besides getting out his newspaper, but it remains his outstanding achievement. He has been a delegate from the United States to France, Russia, Haiti, on various commissions, has written extensively for magazines, and is the author of a number of books. "A Certain Rich Man," and "The Marital Adventures of Henry and Me," are perhaps the best known. The tribute

73

to his daughter, written after her sudden death, has always seemed to me his highest distinction in the field of literature.

His square, firm hands indicate the firm, square qualities of the man. Apparently often irresponsible, as is shown by the suppleness of his thumbs with the wide flare between thumb and fingers indicating a disregard of conventionality, he will be found following standards of obedience to recognized authority. His long straight head line is that of the fortunate possessor of a big stock of common sense. This has prevented William Allen White from being the extremist the wide flare of his fingers shows that he might be. His first finger, moreover, has a very long second phalange, the phalange of justice.

His fingers are smooth, the fingers of the man of inspirational qualities, and on the mount of the Moon under his head line is the whorl of the sixth sense, of intuitive qualities that have aided him throughout life. The shape of the tip and the length of the first phalange of the forefinger added to the innate understanding of human nature the sixth sense provides, show his comprehension of the problems of the less fortunate of the world, and a broad tolerance. His fourth finger with its long nail phalange shows his gift of expression. His nails are interesting. Naturally he dislikes an atmosphere of contention, but roused, he can meet fire with fire. With all his mercy he has a critical attitude; he will be easy going if he can, but when his sense of justice is disturbed he will fight with all his powers.

If you will go over these writers who have come so much to the front in public favor, you will see that all of them possess the gift, either in love of the dramatic, development of the sixth sense, or some particular power of imagination, that enables them to glorify what once was the commonplace, and to their vision we owe from day to day a new valuation of our present world.

Chapter 11: *The Fearless*

The aviators whose paws are read in this chapter will shake a disapproving head at its title. For fear, in the sense of shrinking from hurt, is something they all have known. That fear will always be a part of every human being, it is the fear which induces the quick reaction that serves as protection. Fear in the acute sense, that is shrinking from hurt to the point of avoidance of action, they do not know; their hands show it. All of them have in their hands significant characteristics that mark their owners as brave, courageous, audacious, aggressive. Any one of these words implies fear reduced to a protective minimum, reduced to the point where it cannot interfere with action. Not without fear, but with *less fear* than the average human being, these Lions of the air have taken their wings.

A second possession which their hands declare common to most of them is that of a mind which has worked for some time in a single track. This is shown in the depth and clearness of the right head line. No matter what diverse gifts they originally owned, their mentalities have been concentrated voluntarily upon one line of activity.

Amelia Earhart might stand as a model of courage and caution. The head line in her right hand shows no trace of a period of traveling on one track. It does show mental ability, and the stiff thumb and long nail phalange of the thumb in the right hand, together with the straightness of the head line, indicate great power of concentration directed by will. Her courage is clearly told in the development of the upper mount of Mars, but it is a courage directed by the mental powers; in fact Amelia Earhart possesses what is called a mental type of hand. The length and breadth of her palm indicate her love of physical activity, and her long fingers show her carefulness in detail ensuring perfection as far as possible. In many signs her hands repeat her cautious qualities. The close joining of the life and head lines, the length of her fingers, reason and logic in the developed second phalanges of her thumbs, the long nail phalange of conscience on the fourth finger, all show her tendency to stop and consider—to weigh probabilities before making her decision. The extremely waisted shape of the second phalange of her right thumb again shows mental activity. She can and does make quick decisions when they are imperative.

One charming quality is shown in the check upon the very long finger of Jupiter. Miss Earhart has ambition, and she likes commendation, but her long straight head line is a sign of clear thinking. She listens to words of admiration, but before she believes them she examines them in her pellucid thought. She does not allow anything to remain in a pleasant fog of uncertainty. She must get everything straight and clear. So she is rarely misled or influenced by flattery. Her desire for power is balanced by her desire for clarity.

In January, 1934, newspaper and radio reported the non-stop flight of Commander Knefler McGinnis, U.S.A. at the head of his squadron from San Francisco to Honolulu. I looked at the head lines in rather bewildered fashion. For when you have known a man since his babyhood you are not likely to recognize him when he is described in superlative terms. Commander Knefler McGinnis, U.S.N. Air Service, was to me simply "Knef." His waiving of honors in the simple statement,

> "It was merely in the routine of the Navy's
> air activities and carrying out the orders
> of my superior officers,"

seemed quite in character with what I knew of him. But I wanted to secure and go over the impressions of his hands.

The close joining of the life and head lines in both hands shows caution in action. The breadth of his palms under his fingers denotes a natural mental and physical restlessness. The wide flare of his thumbs from his hands shows an extravagant nature, in the use of time and strength in line of duty or personal aid to others. Prudence, indicated in the development of the middle phalange of the second finger, has acted as a check upon this extravagance. Courage and coolness in danger are shown in the high mount of upper Mars. His short fingers show a definite dislike of detail, but the developed second joints, indicative of law and order, together with the long nail phalanges on all his fingers, showing strong traits of conscience and responsibility to others, have enabled him to overcome his natural tendency to take things in their entirety. His is the hand of an extremist, and in applying his will power towards the improvement of care in detail, he has become a mental martinet. He spells Duty with a large "D" and is zealous in seeking its most infinitesimal associations. He goes round and round looking for that which he may have left undone. The fullness of the Mount of Venus shows great vitality, and the flexibility of his thumbs shows that he is adaptable to circumstances or to people. His clear deep head line in both hands shows that he has realized his potential ability for concentration on a particular line of work.

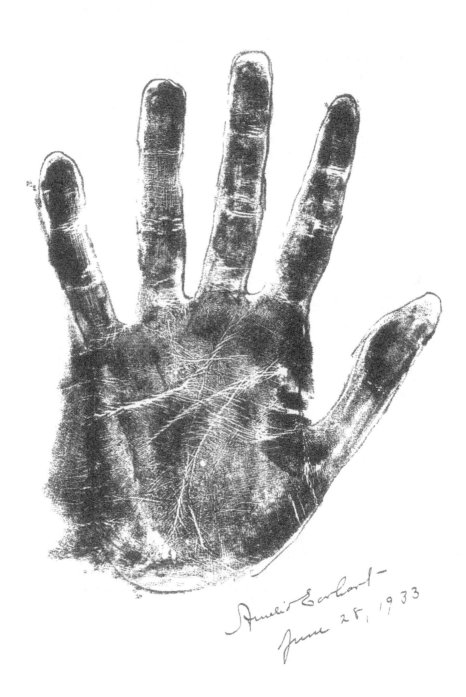

Amelia Earhart —
June 28, 1933

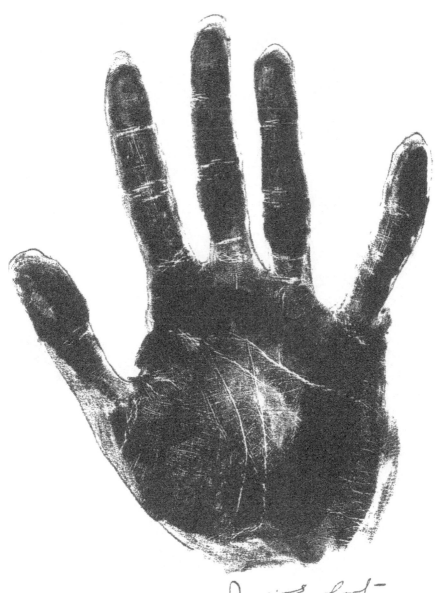

Amelia Earhart

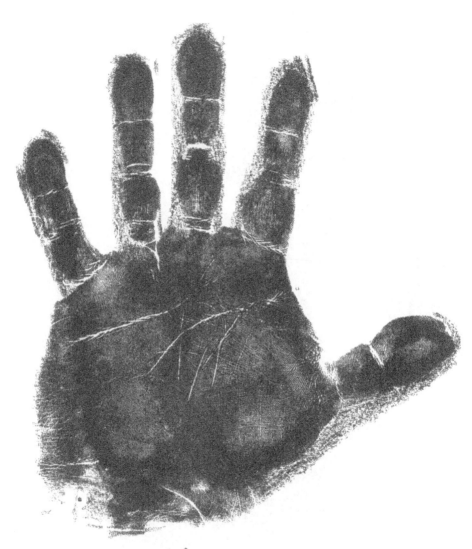

K. M�°Ginnis
4/25/34

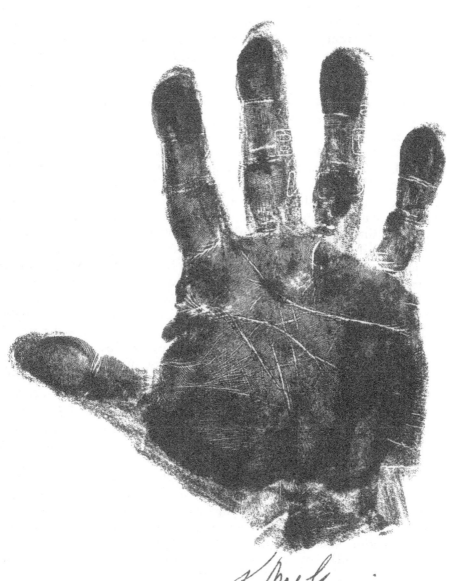

K. McGinnis
4/25/34

Chapter 12: *In Many Fields*

To this point I have been making a rather hard and fast classification of my Lions, according to their achievements. But now I find among my prized collection, many hands that do not readily lend themselves to such arbitrary usage, but which belong, without shadow of doubt, in this book.

There is Louise Ward Watkins whose achievements have been in the less recorded world of living—not money making or record breaking. To my mind. however, she is a record breaker. In the club, civic and social life of Pasadena, Hollywood and Los Angeles she is outstanding, and perhaps her chief value is that she gets others to work with her for ends that benefit the community at large. In addition, or first, she is the mother of seven charming, well-cared for children.

The impression shown here was made in April. 1933. and my notes tell me that her palms can be very hard and at the same time are resilient and yielding to the touch. Louise Ward Watkins sees all detail but selects what she intends to use. The breadth of her palms under her fingers adds a mental eagerness to attain as much breadth of outlook as possible and to absorb as much of the detail as she can. The pronounced tapering of the palm towards her wrist informs me of her interest in all phases of art expression, and helps to explain why, in addition to her listing as official in civic, municipal and political organizations, she is also prominent in associations devoted definitely to creative arts.

One of the most interesting features of these interesting hands is the slight curvature of all the other fingers towards the second finger. The second finger, Saturn, is the finger of wisdom and of sober thought. This curvature affects all the attributes of the other fingers. Her first finger, for example, indicates in its length executive ability, in its rounded tip, quickness of understanding. Her third finger shows, in its long first phalange a capacity for judgment of technique in art expression or construction, and in the shape of the middle phalange a love of color. Her fourth finger is the long finger of diplomacy, with the long first phalange telling of gift of expression, and the rounded tip, tact. All these qualities are curved toward sober thought and wisdom, while her strong emotional nature, shown in the roundness of the mount of Venus, tells of sympathy, tenderness and devotion extending beyond those she loves to those who need her efforts. The width of this mount of Venus shows that Louise Ward Watkins is also endowed with a great vitality that stands her in good stead in her varied activities.

77

In her left hand is one straight channel of talent in the deeply marked line under the third finger, in the right hand this has forked into several lines, indicating success in her objectives and recognition from her fellows.

It was in the studio of Serge Yourievitch, the famous sculptor, that I made the impressions of the hands of H.R.H. Alexander, Grand Duke of Russia. Alexander was a very tall man, something over six foot three, and he looked even taller, for despite his sixty-five years he stood erect, the result of years of military training. So this large hand was in keeping with the size of the man, and the rather square palm showed what we might expect to find in a man of this rank: belief in custom and authority, tenacity of inherited rights, punctuality and precision, and a certain methodicality of mind.

The large first phalange of his thumb showed a great will power, which he would use in forcing the activities of others and justify his methods by the results he gained. The second phalange denoted logic and reason, and his head line in his left hand a clarity of judgment, with broad tolerance towards the opinions of others as revealed in the wide space between the end of the head line and the heart line. In his right hand the decided droop of the head line towards the mount of Luna showed great imagination, and, coupled with the long first phalange of his second finger indicating a strong influence of mysticism, showed how heavily the sudden change from recognized position, wealth and prestige in Russia to the poverty, uncertainty, and anomalous existence of an exile weighed upon him.

Alexander was a great lover of music; the mount of Venus and the mount of the Moon both denoted this. But the gifts he had were blocked. The star of brilliancy shown on the talent line under the third finger of his left hand revealed great natural endowments. But in the right hand the line cutting across the mount under the third finger from the life line, right through the head line and the heart line marked a definite barrier. His position, his heritage of power, and perhaps the threat of the future forced him to turn his talent into intelligent appreciation of the gifts of others.

The long first phalanges of all his fingers indicated: in the first finger with the rounded tip, quickness of perception with a desire for reason; in the second finger a strong religious attitude tending towards mysticism; in the third, originality in lines related to the technicalities of invention; in the fourth, the ability to express himself and with the rounded tip, tact.

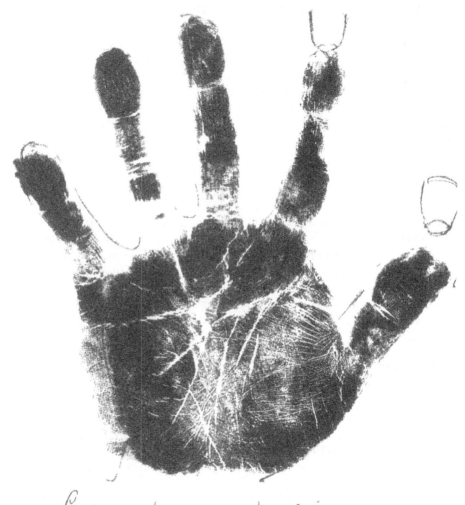

Louise Ward Watkins
April 8 1933

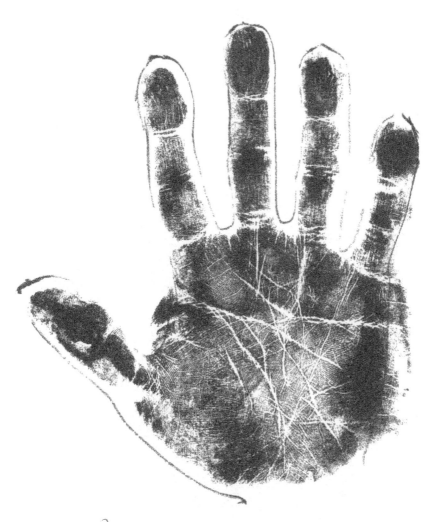

Louise Ward Watkins
April 8, 1933

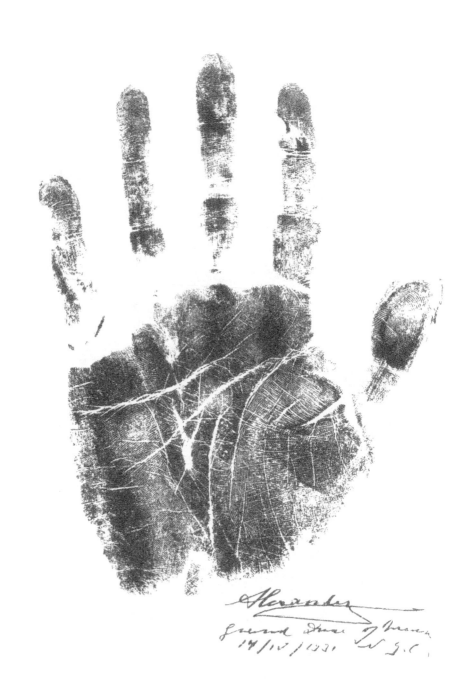

Alexander
Grand Duke of Russia
14/IV/1931 N.Y.C.

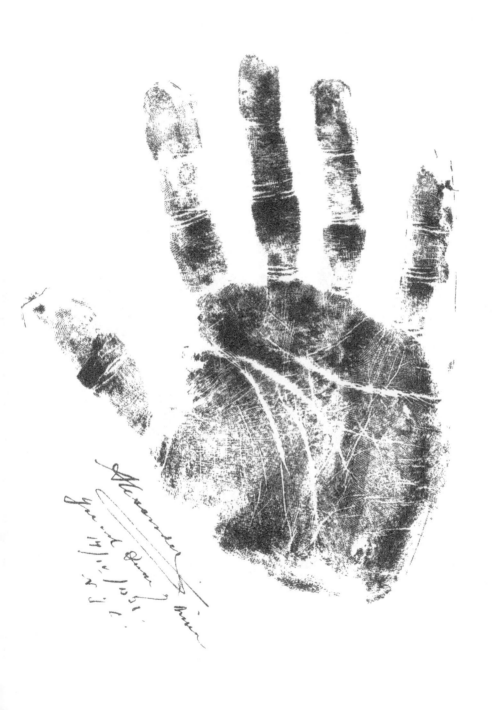

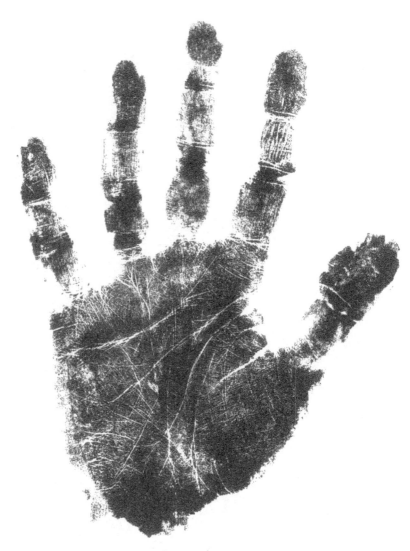

Mary Louise Curtis Bok

12/16/33

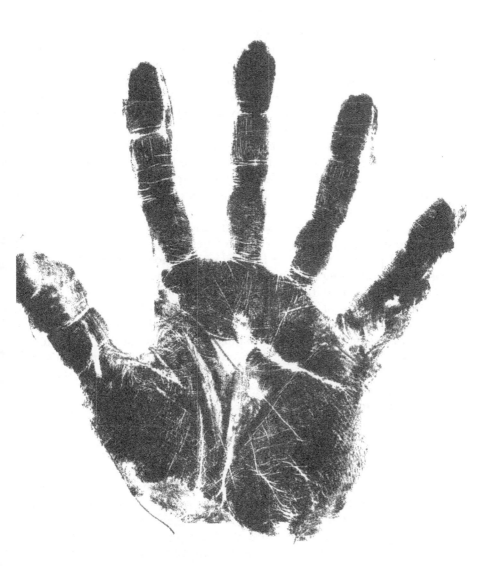

Mary Louise Curtis Bok

This man was not only an aristocrat, he was a highly gifted individual. Had he been given another five years, the characteristics shown in his hands lead me to believe he would have been a factor in the development of a united Russia.

Mary Louise Curtis Bok, in less spectacular fashion, has lived up to the inheritance bequeathed by her father, Cyrus W. Curtis, publisher of the *Saturday Evening Post*. Mrs. Bok's work in the field of music is well known. It has helped Philadelphia to establish an enviable reputation as a city of music, and the Curtis Institute which Mrs. Bok founded and endowed has not only helped many aspiring, talented young musicians, but has been a decided asset in the raising of musical standards.

Mrs. Bok's palms, with their decided curve towards the wrist, show at once her love of beauty both in nature and in art, they are "artistic" palms. Her long head line, clear and deep, tells of a naturally keen mentality. It is, together with the palms, an indication of the happy possessor of good, plain common sense.

The wide space between heart line and the end of the head line denotes tolerance without a yielding of her personal point of view. The long nail phalanges of all of her fingers are those of the person who is susceptible to strong religious beliefs and who uses such beliefs in molding her life and activities.

She is a person of many and varied abilities. Leadership is shown in the length of her forefinger, with quick perception in its rounded tip. The equal length of the first and middle phalanges of this finger, mercy and justice, reveals she is not an emotional giver nor a sentimentalist, but is guided by her judgment and understanding. Though the space between her head line and life line, at its beginning, is a sign of an impulsive temperament, the developed second joints of all of her fingers reveal that impulse is made to accord with law and order, or it is discarded.

The rather square tip of her second finger is again a sign of the practical; she turns her religious and spiritual ideals into active use. The long third phalange of the second finger shows a love of the land. The rounded tip of the third finger, Apollo, with the long first phalange shows recognition of the need for technique in expressions of creative art, and the fulness of the mounts of Venus and of the Moon indicates that the art which will interest her most is that of music. Under this finger is shown the fork of brilliancy, but the line going from the heart line to and crossing this fork of brilliance shows that the desires of others interfered with her own desire for personal recognition of her gifts.

79

Her fourth finger shows diplomacy in its length, tact in its rounded tip, and the gift of expression in its long first phalange.

The hands of Mary Louise Curtis Bok are an interesting study: sincerity and truthfulness, shown in those long nail phalanges; keen mentality revealed in the dominance of the middle phalanges and in her long head line; tolerance between head line and heart line; and great will power shown in the first thumb phalange, backed by logic, reason and a brilliant mentality denoted in the waisted second phalange. Words of praise mean little to Mrs. Bok. Her reward is in what comes of her work.

I cannot think of Martin and Osa Johnson without having in mind that quatrain from Hiawatha

"As unto the bow the cord is—
So unto the man is woman,
Though she bends him, she obeys him,
Though she draws him, yet she follows."

In all my years of research work in hands I can recall none like those of the Johnsons, whose lives have been so closely joined in experiences involving danger and the possibility of sudden death. Martin Johnson, over six feet, broad shouldered, hard muscled and sinewy, fulfilled your imaginary picture of the daring explorer. But little Osa, vitally and energetically feminine, challenges the imagination.

In six expeditions that circled the globe, through twelve years in the South Sea Islands, two years in Borneo and five in Africa, much of which time was spent in the jungle or among tribes reputed savage, Osa was her husband's inseparable companion. Together they made their wonderful motion pictures, together they wrote "Cannibal Land," "Camera Trails in Africa," "A Saga of the African Blue," and, singularly fitting for this book, "Lion—African Adventure with the King of Beasts." I am reading their hands together because they belong together.

My notes tell me that Martin's palms were firm and pink, as are also Osa's, indications of robust health and strong vitality. Martin Johnson's palm was practically square—he was a man of orderly and disciplined habits with respect for authority. Osa Johnson's palm is spatulate, broad under the fingers and sloping decidedly towards the wrist. Hers is a nature that is capable of great enthusiasm and purpose. She would brush away hardships or obstacles. The wide flare of her fingers shows independence of thought and action to the point of recklessness.

Martin's stiff thumbs, coupled with the comparatively short but very

80

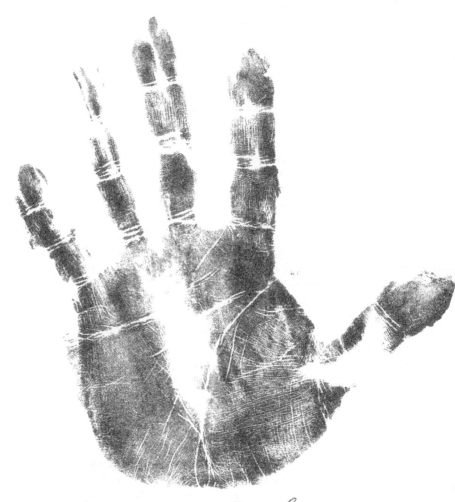

Martin Johnson

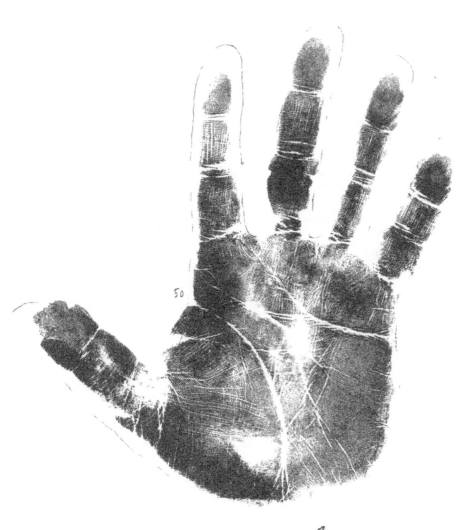

50

Martin Johnson

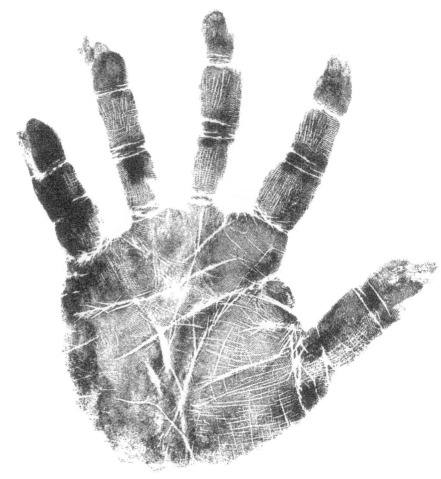

Osa Johnson

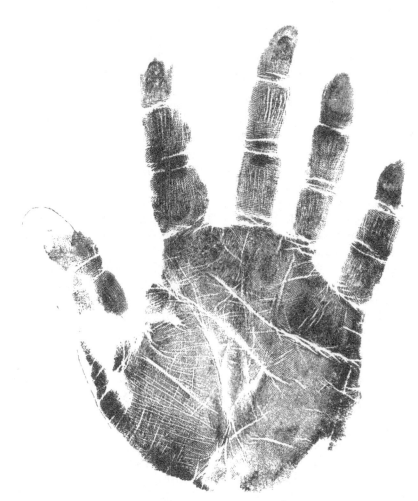

Osa Johnson

deep head line, tell of the dogged determination with which he pursued his course. Osa's thumbs are flexible; she has the graciousness that disarms antagonism and can adapt herself to uncomfortable surroundings and uncongenial people.

Martin Johnson's fingers were stiff; he was the kind of person who gets knowledge for the affair in hand, rather than assimilating it for future use. He was cautious in accepting statements and advice and took time to consider both carefully. Osa's fingers are flexible showing that she absorbs knowledge from everything about her. Her straight deep head line shows that she can sift the wheat from the chaff and retain her harvest for her purpose.

The fingers of both, being smooth to the second joint, indicate inspirational qualities, and the first phalanges show integrity and sincerity. Martin's second joints were developed, thereby acting as the "Stop, Look and Listen!" sign on the path of his advance. Osa is saved from recklessness by the close joining of her life line and head line, a sign of caution.

Martin Johnson had nails broader than long, the nails of a man who was mentally irritable and rather argumentative, but the length of his fourth finger showed diplomacy. The pointed tip of Osa's fourth finger shows great tact, and the first phalange of that finger, in its length, declares that she has the gift of expression.

They were one in independence of thought, shown by the wide flare of first and second fingers, and their "taking no thought for the morrow" is indicated in the flare between the second and third fingers.

In both pairs of hands upon the mount of Jupiter under the forefingers is a cross. This is an indication that their lives knew one great love.

Under her third finger Osa Johnson has a straight line of talent with a definite whorl on either side. She has the sixth sense; she sees beyond and before that which others may not see. Under Martin Johnson's third fingers were outstanding lines of ability running parallel to each other.

Osa Johnson possesses upon her mount of the Moon another whorl, which intensifies those near the talent line and gives her an uncanny premonitive sense which must have been helpful many times in guarding both herself and her husband against danger. These charming, talented young people who brought so much richness to us from their explorations, were ideal partners, each complementing the other.

I waited for Ely Culbertson. I have been in many offices teeming with feverish activity, but never before had I been in a home in which one could feel the live currents even if one could not see them. I met him in the large apartment at the Sherry-Netherland in New York where the Culbertsons and their two unusual children were living. In other rooms a bridge tournament was being directed by the high priest and priestess of the game. Finally Ely Culbertson came. He was willing to give me the impressions of his hands, but he did not care to hear my reading.

"I know myself" he said, "no one can tell me more than my own knowledge gives me, and I know quite a little of palmistry. Only thieves, gamblers and musicians have long fingers, especially a third finger longer than the others."

"I am no authority on thieves and gamblers" I admitted, "but Leopold Godowsky and José Iturbi have unusually short fingers, and some name and fame." Mr. Culbertson raised inquiring eyebrows.

Ely Culbertson has a controversial nature; the high mount of upper Mars under the lifeline on the upper part of the mount of Venus showed belligerence, the long first phalange of the finger of Mercury adding the power of words disclosed this as I made his impressions.

The long first finger denotes his love of power, and good executive ability helped by the will power, shown by his thumbs. On the first finger the almost pointed tip shows the spark of inspiration, but the square nail informs me that when Mr. Culbertson has an inspirational urge it is interrupted by the demand for reason. He does not follow his hunch unless reason approves it.

Again, in the second finger, the long first phalange indicates a trend toward mysticism, but the square tip again demands reason and mysticism resolves itself into the practical. The length of the third finger indicates his love of games of chance. He is a mental soldier of fortune and would risk money, liberty and safety for the zest of uncertainty. That is a reason which satisfies those square nails; he is a conscientious worker.

His thumbs in both hands are fairly flexible denoting his ability to express an outward suavity, but showing that he is a mixer only on the surface. The shape of the tip of the thumbs is indicative of impatience. He is easily bored and often has to call upon the diplomacy shown in his long fourth finger to enable him to get through. His left thumb is double jointed and this gives him additional aid. It indicates a love of the dramatic in every expression of life, and some suavity which, with the love of the dramatic makes intolerable situations bearable. The intensity of his profession, the unexpected, all the thrills of the expert at cards bring to Ely Culbertson the keenest enjoyment.

Josephine Culbertson whom I met later, is a woman of great charm and decided beauty. Her palms are lined, etched I might say, with fine lines; the texture of the skin is satiny and smooth, indicating a nature

with kindest regards

Ely Culbertson

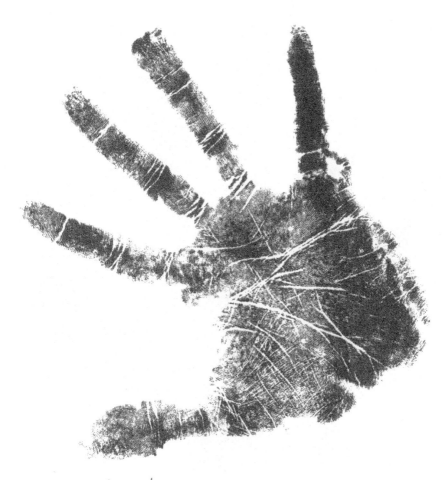

Good Luck!
Ely Culbertson
December 5th 1933

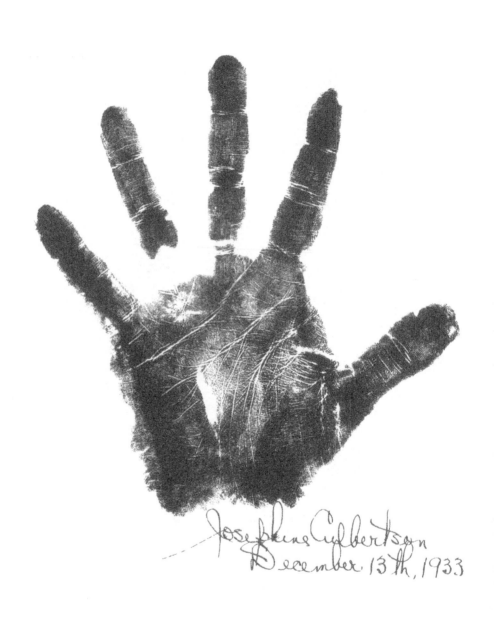

Josephine Culbertson
December 13th, 1933

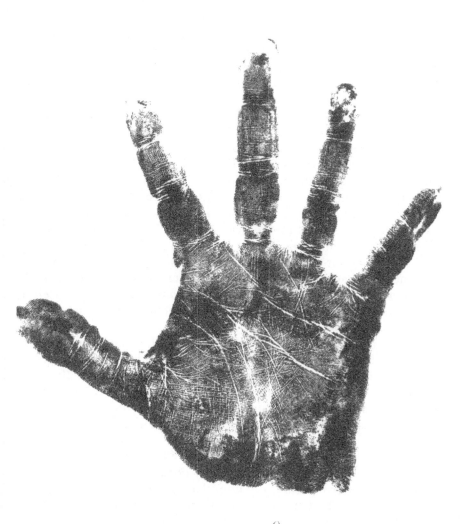

Josephine Culbertson
December 13th, 193?

which would not neglect the details of daily life but which would put them aside as of minor importance in the time of greater happenings. Her fingers bend back at the tips and this with the satin skin denotes a mental aptitude for absorbing a minutiae of detail from which she selects with discrimination only that which fits into the scene as she wishes to see it. The long smooth fingers reinforce this tendency to be careful in detail but not to clutter up her life with unnecessary infinitesimals. There is further aid in the flare between her fingers and thumbs, the flare of the person who decides immediately on what is necessary and what is not.

Her left thumb is unusually stiff. Mrs. Culbertson would persevere to the point of stubbornness in sticking to anything upon which she decided. In her right hand, the thumb is not so stiff. She has learned to employ the diplomacy indicated in the length of Mercury, her fourth finger. In her right hand too, the space between heart and head line is wider than in the left, another sign of tolerance gained. She has used considerable self-discipline to attain these gains as she is naturally impetuous, which is shown by the space between her life and head line in the left hand. She has great love of power, revealed in the high development of the mount of Jupiter under the first finger. Her straight head line and the shape of her thumbs show Josephine Culbertson to be slow in accepting new beliefs or ideas. It is only after she has carefully assayed them by the reason, shown in the second phalange of her thumbs, that she selects those she means to retain.

Her third finger with its square tip reveals her tendency to accept rules and regulations as well as to demand established and recognized technique in any phase of art expression, shown by the length of the first or nail phalange. The second phalange of this finger which denotes color is subservient to the first, while the length of the third phalange indicates an ability to turn all expressions of art into commercial channels.

Withal, she is buoyant. The rounded tip of her second finger declares that when she is downed she cannot stay down but just floats again to the surface. In her left hand the lines that radiate and cut through the lines of ability under her third finger show that her heart ties and loyalties will always come before gratifications of ambition. Her fourth finger in its long first phalange denotes a decided gift of expression and its pointed tip reveals the tact she uses both as professional organizer and in the home. Her hands show that she has earned her place beside her husband as world authority on the playing of contract bridge.

Chapter 13: *Their Voices Are Heard*

The woman who has the courage to read the hand of a prima donna should, it seems to me, merit especial attention upon the part of her readers. In this chapter I have the temerity to read not one, but five hands of five famous divas, and to add to these, three well known and loved male Lions among singers.

In the hands of all musicians we expect to find a great development of the lower part of the mounts of Venus and of the Moon where the signs of love and rhythm and melody are found. The hands of Lucrezia Bori show the high development of these mounts. Bori, who came to us from Spain twenty years ago, is one of the leading sopranos of the Metropolitan Opera Company, and is known all over the country for her concert work.

The square shape of her palms shows the foundation of her character, a love of order and the ability to maintain that order. She has a disciplined personality. She is capable of planning and maintaining a schedule of practise, coaching, study and action. The wide flare between thumbs and fingers and between the fingers, shows impulsiveness in speech and action with decided independence of thought. Yet the close joining of the life line and head line indicates again the discipline imposed upon herself in continuing the daily grind essential to technical perfection. When she has mastered the technique, the enthusiasm and spontaneity shown in the flexibility of her thumbs and fingers, the wealth of imagination shown in the development of the mount of the Moon, and the varied gradations of sympathy, fire and passion indicated in the development of that rounded mount of Venus, lift her impersonations from the mechanical to the inspired.

Bori's hands show unusual developments. Her long, slim figures with their conic tips, indicate her inspirational qualities, and the slightly marked circle of intuition running from just above the heart line curving and ending on the lower outside of the mount of imagination can be called the warning signal by which she knows when to stop, look, and listen, and, equally important,—when the tracks are clear and she can forge ahead.

She might have all of these gifts and have failed to make the remarkable record in the world of song and dramatic art if she had lacked the motive power so plainly shown in her fourth finger. The length of that beautifully shaped finger is to Bori a well-oiled piston rod in the machinery of personal action. She is diplomacy itself, and the pointed tip

84

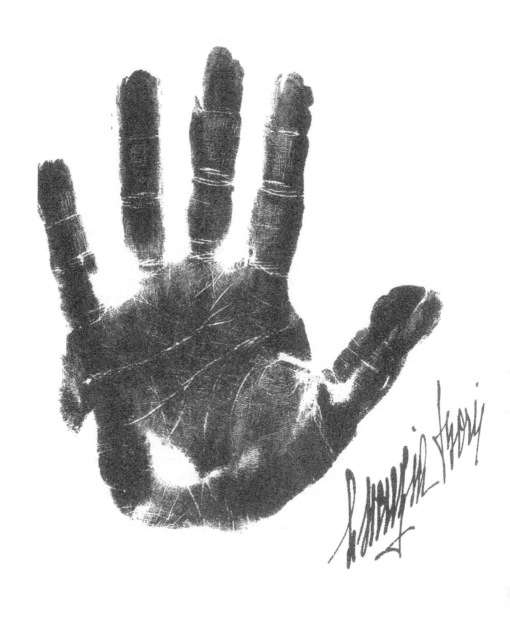

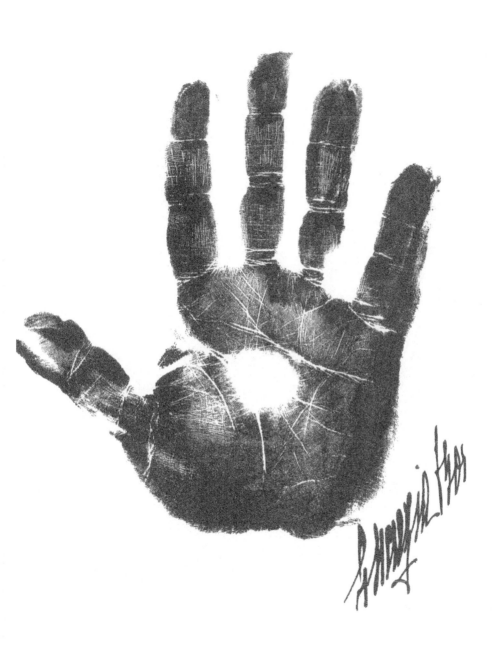

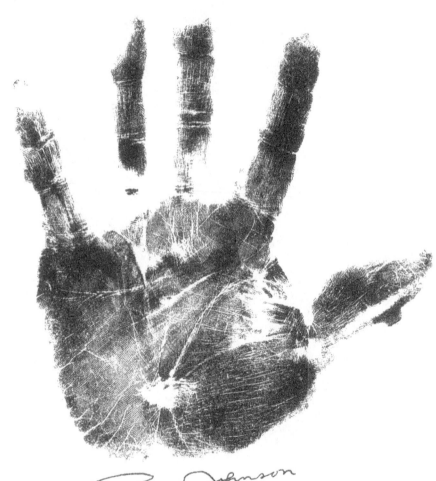

Edward Johnson

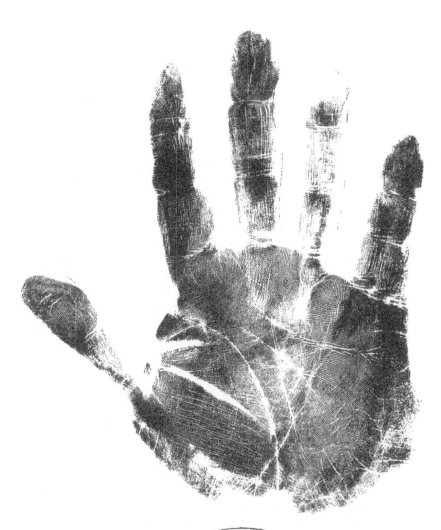

Edward Johnson

and shape of the first phalange show tact in management of organizations or people. Her first finger shows in its length decided executive ability, which, directed by her diplomacy, has enabled her to accomplish results for which she hardly dared to hope.

The expected trident of fame, fortune and honor appears in her right hand under her third finger.

Edward Johnson, much loved leading tenor of the Metropolitan Opera Company, came to us from Canada, went from us to Italy where he sang for ten years in many cities, but mainly in Florence and Milan. He returned to U. S. A. to join the Chicago Opera Company in 1920 and the Metropolitan in 1922. In 1935 he was made manager of the Metropolitan Opera Company.

Looking at Edward Johnson's hand one is impressed by the extraordinary length of the life line. Apparently this is a heritage from both his father and mother, with his father's side of the family slightly ahead. The hand is dominated by the length of the middle phalanges of all his fingers, which indicates the ascendancy of the mental faculties. He must have a reason for anything he does, particularly in his professional work. He will have nothing left to chance. The slightly spatulate tip of the nail phalange of the third finger denotes an originality which he brings to his roles, and which has aided him greatly as an artist. Edward Johnson is a serious person, as the long first phalange of his second finger shows. He has a desire for justice as the long first phalange of all his fingers show. His square palm is a sign of a practical nature, and its firmness and resiliency are signs of the ability to receive "the slings and arrows of outrageous fortune" and come through smiling.

Unflagging determination is evinced in the long first phalange of his thumb, and this mighty will power is directed mentally by the logic and reason of the second phalange.

Between the life line and the head line under his first finger is quite a space, an indication of impatience for results. This impatience is disciplined by the diplomacy shown in the length of the fourth finger, and by the mental dominance of those long second phalanges of all his fingers, and the second phalanges of his thumbs. In his right hand the space between heart line and head line grows markedly wider towards the outside of his hand. Edward Johnson has acquired a tolerance of opinion and judgment of others. This widening also suggest that he has made great gains in his ability to accept criticism, and to select from approval and censure that which will enable him to improve. The lines of talent in his left hand are nebulous, those in the right clear and well defined,

85

and under the third finger there is a distinct fork of brilliancy. On the mount of the Moon is the whorl which declares the possession of the "sixth sense," so valuable to an artist, and on either side of the mount of Apollo under the third finger are additional whorls. These are unusual whorls in that they are joined by a series of lines that radiate from the mount. They require more space for elucidation than can be used here, but one ability indicated is that of working "from the inside out" in depicting a character in opera. That is why Edward Johnson inspires his audience by his natural impersonation of his role. In fact, for the time being he has become that character.

When I examined the hands of Mary Garden for the first time I was a bit puzzled. It seemed to me that she had achieved all the fame, fortune and honor that one person could possibly attain. In Paris, London, Brussels, New York and Chicago she had been recognized and honored as a singer of the first rank, and at that time she was a star of the Chicago Grand Opera Company. Yet the mark foreshadowing the star of unexpected honor and elevation on the mount of Jupiter under the first finger was clearly shown in her left hand and not as clearly in her right, and the trident under her third finger, that sign of fame, fortune and honor, was not nearly as clear in her right hand as in her left. I was puzzled, but told her that greater honor was evidently to come to her. Her hands foretold a true story. In a short time Mary Garden was appointed general director of the Chicago Opera Association, the first woman or star of magnitude to be given such a position.

Mary Garden's is a fighting hand. The mount of lower Mars, under the life line above the mount of Venus, is highly developed and indicates belligerency. The thickness of the first joint of her thumbs shows persistency. The shape of the tip of her thumb and the shape of her finger nails reveal limited patience and mental irritability. The rounded mount of upper Mars indicates her high courage. The wide flare between her thumbs and fingers and between the fingers themselves declares independence of thought and action, defiance of conventionalities.

Such qualities inevitably involve their possessor in a series of struggles. But Mary Garden has on the whole enjoyed those struggles. The flexibility of the second joint of her thumbs shows not only dramatic talent, but love of the dramatic in life. Her well-known characteristic of superb indifference to criticism or comment is indicated in the length and shape of her second finger. Yet she is almost inordinately ambitious. Under her first finger is a distinct line of ambition running from her life line to the highly developed mount of Jupiter directly beneath that finger. Such a

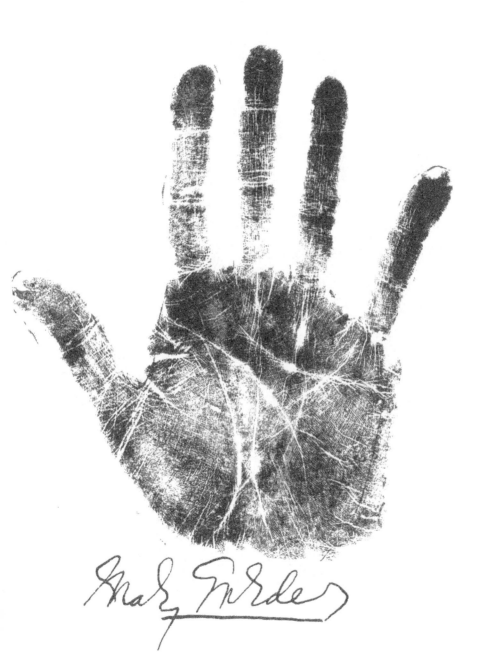

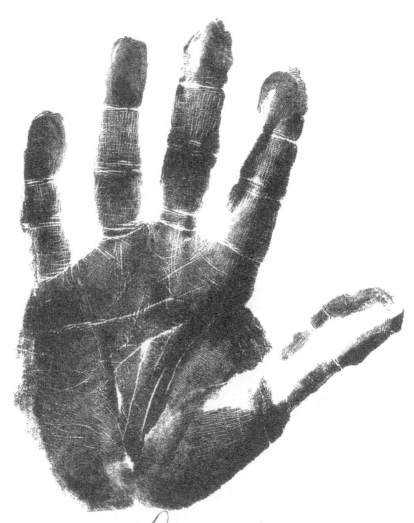

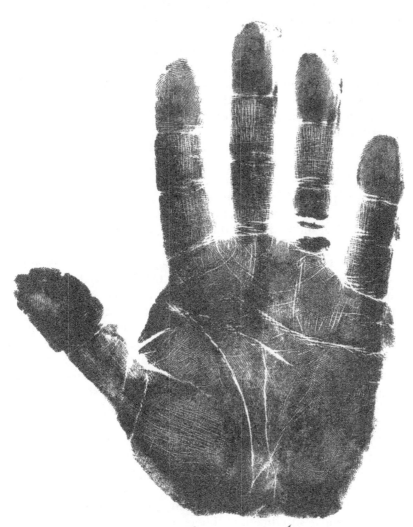

line indicates an extreme love of power. This finger has a conic tip, a sign of a lightning-like speed of perception, and the length of the finger testifies to Mary Garden's undoubted ability as an executive. Her inspirational qualities are shown in the smoothness of her fingers to the second joints, and in the stretch of the second and third fingers is disclosed originality. The development of the second joints is the first sign of her power of restraint. Her long fourth finger adds the diplomacy shown by all the Lions in this chapter so far. No matter how indifferent or how belligerent Mary Garden may be, sooner or later her power of diplomacy comes into play and helps her to smooth out the effects of her irritating qualities.

The development of the mount of the Moon and of Venus shows the usual signs of love of rhythm and melody characteristic of musicians, and her pink firm palms further testify to her enjoyment of physical activity in any form that leads to a definite result.

Mary Garden has struggled, but she has enjoyed work and life and her honors hugely, and will enjoy them while life lasts.

One who believes in reincarnation might be inclined to relate the spirit and genius of that great artist Lilli Lehmann to the new star Lotte Lehmann. Strange to say, there is no tie of kinship, other than the probability of an equal greatness as an artist. Lotte Lehmann's shoulders are formed to carry the Wagnerian tradition. Her smooth inspirational fingers hold the fire of a Brunnehilde; the long first phalanges of those fingers denote the fervor, the devotion, the spirituality of Elizabeth. The lines that apparently enclose the second and third fingers at their base reveal the love and longing of an Elsa, and the desire and warmth of Isolde is suggested by the fulness of the mount of Venus, giving a composite of Wagner's super-women.

Add to these qualities the square palm of Lotte Lehmann showing mental and physical discipline, a self-imposed regime of mental and material order, deep-seated tenacity of purpose.

Lotte Lehmann has flexible fingers and thumbs: she loves the dramatic; she has power to absorb varied experiences and also power to direct her course intelligently. There are no flashing crashing climaxes in her progress, but a rolling way of advance surprisingly free of obstacles. When she does meet an obstruction in her path she applies the clear vision indicated in her deep head line, and deals with it with wisdom.

Under the fourth finger you can see three straight lines, which indicated that Lotte Lehmann would make a fine physician or nurse. Under ner third finger are two strong talent lines, musical and dramatic gifts, that show wonderful possibilities for her career.

When one has received the warm handshake of John McCormack with his "God love you," you know it is the accolade signifying your passing through the gates of understanding. As I look at the prints of his great hands I can recall very few others with such definite markings of an un-obstructed road to success, both in recognition and in financial return. He has paved his way with notes of gold which an admiring public cashes at face value.

His palms are of the square type; John McCormack is a practical person. His long, deep, straight head line shows that he demands reason before he acts, and that if he feels it necessary, he is prepared to justify any act of his own. His powerful thumb shows force and determination in the first phalange, and that this is driven by the logic and reason of the second phalange. His driving force, his intelligently directed will power, has enabled him to hold in check the dislike of detail declared by all of his smooth fingers.

The caution shown in the close joining of his life and head line, together with the conservatism suggested by the limited flare of his thumbs from his hands and the equally limited flares of his fingers, enables him to control his use of everything that would aid in his advance. Rarely have I looked at a hand in which every quality that would be of assistance has been so assiduously and intelligently developed.

Like the other singers in this chapter, he has the long fourth finger of diplomacy. This finger governs and controls what might be mischief-making abilities. Irish wit is revealed in the high development of the mount of Mercury under this finger, a high temper in the over-developed mount of upper Mars on the outside of the palm under the head line, and further belligerence is evinced by the aggressive mount of lower Mars under the life line on the mount of Venus. All these, together with the mitigating tenderness and sympathy shown by the high development of the mount of Venus, are under the control of that finger of diplomacy.

He has a Mercurial temperament, shown in the flare between his third and fourth fingers. He knows the depths and heights, sun and shadow, but he lives in June as long as he can manage it, and he manages exceedingly well.

His line of destiny shows a practically unimpeded flow of financial gain. The lines under his third finger declare recognition of his talents, honor and fame, and his life line declares that he has lived through

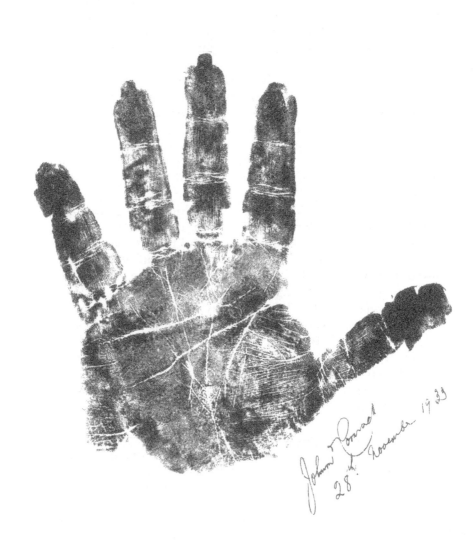

Johnn Connord
28th November 1939

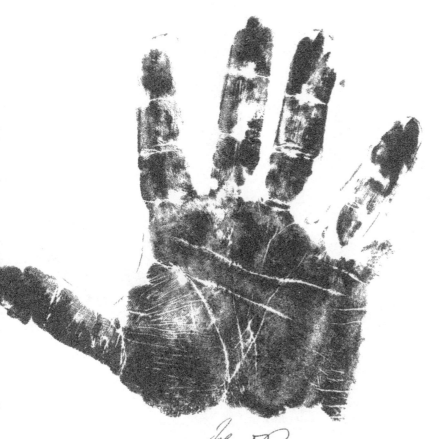

John Cormack
Nov. 28 '33

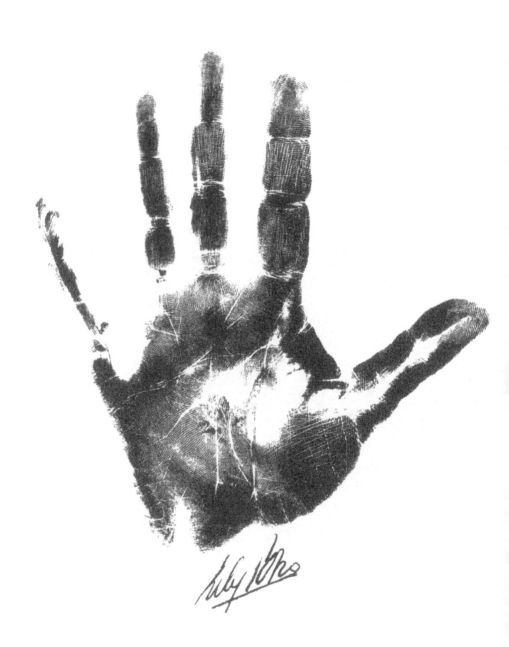

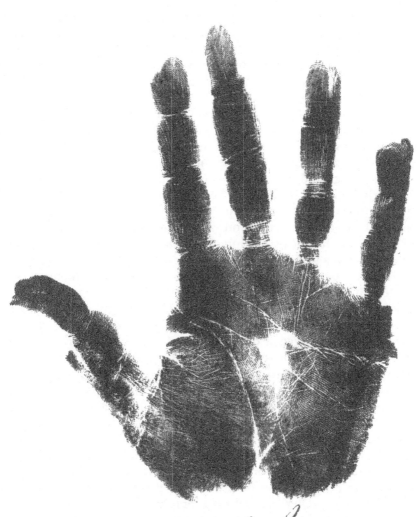

health interferences and will live through any that come to him for a long time.

John McCormack has been smiled on by the gods. His obstacles are of his own making, and his honesty and clarity of vision make him recognize this fact. He has harvested some self-sown nettles, with his eyes wide open. I know of no other singer who has a greater hold upon his public through his gifts or who holds so within himself the making or marring of his destiny. In every home in the land John McCormack makes himself felt, not only through his voice but through his personality which the radio cannot dim and which brings back to him through the ether the echo of his own, "God love you."

Not often does the lovely fleur de lis of France take such deep root in American soil as has dainty, magnetic Lily Pons. During the five years since she has been with us she has, through her work with the Metropolitan Opera Company and over the radio, won thousands of hearts.

Hers is the hand of an independent and self-reliant personality. This is clearly indicated in the space between life line and head line. Her first finger shows in its length, executive ability, and in the development of the mount beneath, great ambition. The pointed tip of her thumb is a sign of impatience for the realization of her ambitions. Her long straight head line, with but a slight droop, shows a clear-thinking mentality. With the wide stretch between thumbs and fingers and the fingers themselves, plus the length and smoothness of the fingers, there is revealed a young woman who can grasp a subject as a whole, analyze the details, curb any tendency to extremes and settle upon a sober, well-planned decision. Again we find the long fourth finger of diplomacy, and that waisted formation of the second phalange of the thumb that indicates the ability to see another's point of view and use that ability as an aid in her diplomacy. Lily Pons has her difficulties in self-discipline. The narrow space between head line and heart line shows a leaning towards intolerance; she can see another point of view, but she does not always care to consider it. It takes all of her diplomacy to persuade herself to a more tolerant attitude. Her long nail phalanges are those of the conscientious. She has a real desire to understand any cause of opposition on the part of others, even while she dislikes giving up her own way. Her pliable thumb shows a strong will that can bend her into outward compliance while she seethes within.

Under the third finger of her left hand is a perfect trident of fame, fortune and honor. This has not yet wholly developed in her right hand. But Lily Pons has the ability to discipline herself so that it will appear perfectly formed, doubtless in the not too far future.

John Charles Thomas has served his art from an apprenticeship in small stage parts, through musical comedy, concert tours, to opera with the Royal Opera Company, San Francisco, Los Angeles, Chicago Civic, and Metropolitan Opera Companies, to motion pictures and radio. An American by birth, he has done most of his work in America, and his mellow baritone, lovelier every succeeding year, is known to millions of fellow Americans. I met John Charles Thomas in New York City, through a mutual friend, Clara Bell Walsh.

His friendly looking hands interested me greatly, for they showed me a man not especially inclined to work, who had taken himself in hand. The depth and slope of the head line which droops into the mount of the Moon shows his imagination will often bias his judgment. He is a man wonderfully good at excusing himself when he does not want to do anything and knows that he should. The length of his forefinger, or rather its comparative shortness, testifies to his dislike of responsibility and a desire for others to plan his work. All of his short fingers tell of his ability to grasp things as a whole and an equal dislike of detail; he hates a plodding grind, but the smoothness of the fingers shows inspiration sufficient to act as an incentive to help him at essential study.

The breadth of his hands under the fingers shows a love of the out-of-doors, but not of strenuous physical activity. Yet this easy going charming man has both gifts and a certain self-discipline.

His gifts include the color sense in the long, middle phalanges of his third fingers—he can shade his voice as an artist shades the colors upon his palette. Ardor and emotional quality with vitality are shown in the development of the mount of Venus below the thumb, particularly the development of the lower half, and the rhythm and time sense revealed in the corresponding development of the lower half of the mount of the Moon, just opposite Venus.

This discipline is seen in the thumbs. The length of the first phalange tells of a strong and determined will. Decided assets are the whorls on the mount of the Moon, which to him are the sparks of genius, and the additional whorls on each side of the talent line running under the third finger of Apollo in the left hand symbolize the promise of fame and of success.

My first meeting with Ernestine Schumann-Heink will ever remain a red letter day in memory. On that day I met Nordica, Reuss-Belce, David Bispham, Scotti, Jean and Edouard de Reszke, a constellation of stars that have never been excelled, perhaps not equalled. In the years after that happy occasion I met Madam Schumann-Heink a number of times. I made the impressions of her hands at our first meeting, and the

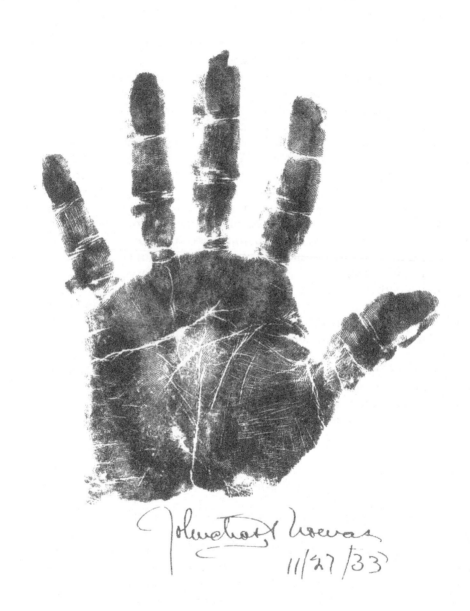

Johnathon Nuevas
11/27/33

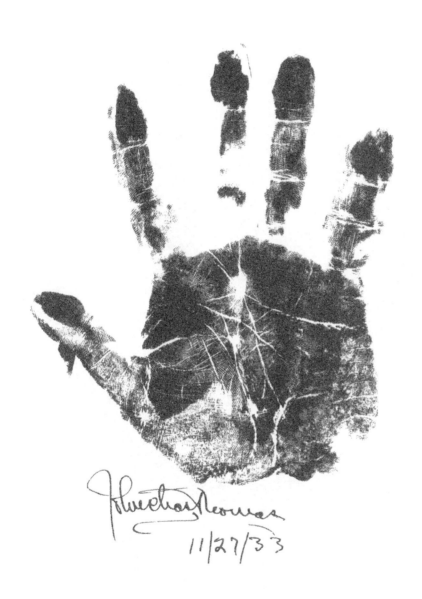

John von Neumann
11/27/33

Schumann Heink
Febr 16. 1903

woman and the prints have filled me with real reverence for all that this great human being meant, both as an artist and as a human being. Recognized in all countries of the world, she sang in many, and in her long career made a record that is unique.

What did her hands tell? Her palms, as you can see, are conic in shape, well formed and resilient. They show her to have been an artist, but also show her recognition of the practical side of life. They tell in their resiliency of the brilliancy and sparkle of a naturally emotional nature keyed by her second finger with its rounded tip of gladness and hope. This second finger is her dominant one. It reveals her wisdom and prudence, plus a deep sense of responsibility. these are shown in the development of the first and second phalanges, and again there is that sense of the practical shown in her palms.

Here then we had a happy woman, emotional but practical in tendency—what else? Impulsiveness, shown in the flare of thumbs and fingers, an impulsiveness that led her to almost unlimited generosity. She gave of herself and of whatever she had without thinking of consequences. Impulsiveness that prompted her to speak and act without considering the reaction of the person to whom she was speaking is indicated in the space between her head line and life line. A much needed curb is shown in the development of the second phalange of her thumb, the seat of logic and reason, and in the basic honesty of her motives, as is shown in the length of the nail phalanges of all of her fingers.

Her fingers are evenly placed, which gives their possessor the full benefit of the attributes indicated by each finger: in the length of the forefinger executive ability, and in its pointed tip quickness of perception. In the first phalange not only a sense of duty but a sense of mercy also. In the third phalange a liking for power, and in the mount of Jupiter beneath the forefinger, ambition. The second finger we have recognized as the dominant one. The third finger, the finger of art, shows in the nail phalange the recognition of the necessity of technique, and the third phalange again speaks of the practical, of common sense used in guarding her golden voice and her personality. See how the little finger of Mercury stands out from her hand! Schumann-Heink was the lucky owner of a Mercurial nature, one that responded to occasion, and again the long finger of diplomacy, with the pointed tip of tact. In the length of the nail phalange is seen the gift of words that was hers. She liked to please people —the flexibility of her thumbs and the development of the little cushions upon her finger tips are signs of a great desire to be liked, and the first phalange of the thumb shows strength of will.

The line of destiny running from the base of the palm outside the life line shows freedom from want to the end of her days. Her talent line, one fork starting from the line of destiny, the other from the mount of the Moon, imagination, ends under her third finger in the rare star of distinction and celebrity, in addition to the trident of fame, fortune and honor below her third finger.

Her hands show markings revealing periods of anguish and deep sorrow. Her memory was unusual. Once, after I had not seen her for some years, we had unknowingly boarded the same train, I heard a never-to-be-forgotten voice back of me say,

"You do not mind it—the luggage?"

I turned, "You do not recognize me?" I inquired. She put up a warning finger,

"Now vait! Ah I have it, your eyes they tell me and your voice helps me. You have read my hand and you make it black in Chicago, too many years ago to mention."

I had made the hand "black" for the prints you see. And as we talked on and on I wondered if there was in this world another artist who has reached such heights of stardom who remained so accessible through the rare gifts of human sympathy, affection and understanding.

Chapter 14: *With Ears Attuned*

As artists live in a world that is mainly color and line, and writers in a world interpreted through words, so musicians live in a world of sound. This is partially true of all of us who have keen ears. But the difference between a musician and the ordinary keen-eared person lies in the relation of sounds heard. Upon the musician is not only an imperative demand to express the sounds he hears, but to get them into relation to each other, so that what we might think discord, resolves itself into higher harmonies. Music appeals strongly to the type of human being students of palmistry know as the Venusian, and the mount of Venus is sometimes called the mount of Melody. If this mount is well developed and there is no like development of the mount of the Moon, the owner of the hand will prefer melodic music. But if the mount of the Moon is also well developed, harmony, fugue and counterpoint will be added.

People who have music in their souls and who have little or no facility for musical expression may have both of these mounts highly developed. Musicians and particularly Lions among musicians must add character traits of achievement to the mount development that means primarily a sensing of musical values.

Look at the hands of Fritz Kreisler, beloved violinist. You can see the great development of the mount of Venus and across from it the almost equally great development of the mount of the Moon so that the hands are exceptionally broad across the middle of the lower half. These are the hallmarks of the lover of music. The traits of character necessary to the development of Kreisler's sense of music are underwritten by the shape of the palm, which is square, the palm of the man of practical understanding of the need of discipline and of law and order in living, in work, and in society at large. His rather short fingers controvert the idea that all musicians necessarily have unusually long fingers, and tell of his natural indifference to detail. But the great thumb with its balance of the long phalange of will, together with the long phalange of logic and reason, shows a force of character that acting upon intelligence enables him to steer his course with acumen. The long deep head line adds a full quota of common sense, and an ability to concentrate. Under the third finger, Apollo, there are clearly marked lines of talent, and the smoothness of his fingers shows inspirational powers.

When I read his hands I found his thumbs flexible in the first joint, an indication of adaptability to circumstances. Kreisler can adapt himself to rough living if it is necessary, but the third phalanges of his fingers show that he is naturally fastidious. If he must accept uncomfortable or uncongenial surroundings he will accept them with an outward show of suavity. The rounded tip of the thumb and the shape of the nail, broader than it is long, reveal an impatience with results that seem to be delayed, but this impatience is likewise held in check by his adaptability.

The long first phalange of the forefinger tells of the conscientious work that Fritz Kreisler has brought to his music, which he will always bring to his work. The shape of the nail indicates a critical attitude, and with the length of the middle phalange revealing a strong sense of justice, again suggests the man of conscience who appraises his own abilities and shortcomings with his eyes fixed upon the goal of perfection.

Undoubtedly you have noticed, as you look at these impressions, the decided leaning of the second finger, Saturn, towards the third finger, Apollo, and that the third finger likewise leans towards the second. This artist is serious in his pursuit of beauty; he does not seek it through impulse but by deliberate choice, and he regards his profession with a gravity almost amounting to veneration. The development of the middle phalange of the second finger is a sign of wisdom, while the square tip on the rather long nail phalange repeats the practical point of view suggested by the square palm. Here is a sincere and serious artist, capable of appreciating the varying phases of life, capable of gaiety and possessing much of it within himself. But his attitude towards his art is that of an extremely painstaking, reverent student, who approaches it with diffidence, and yet with confidence.

The slightly rounded tip of the third finger, Apollo, is a sign of idealism, while the long nail phalange discloses gifts of construction, gifts that Kreisler uses in his work as a composer. The second phalange of this finger shows a strong sense of color, and anyone who has heard Kreisler play or has heard others play Kreisler's compositions will understand how he uses this color sense in music. The length of the fourth finger, Mercury, denotes diplomacy and the rounded tip, tact. The length of the first phalange of this finger is indicative of honor and integrity in art and in commercial transactions and a gift of expression, in this particular instance, in music and composition. In the long second phalange is revealed his ability to express himself verbally, but preferably in writing. At the end of the line of Mercury, a line running from the mount of the Moon straight to the base of the finger of Mercury, is a fork, a sign of commercial success. There is a fork at the end of the head line in each hand indicative of exceptional brilliance. The line of destiny swerves decidedly to the third finger; his commercial success comes from the use of his gifts.

94

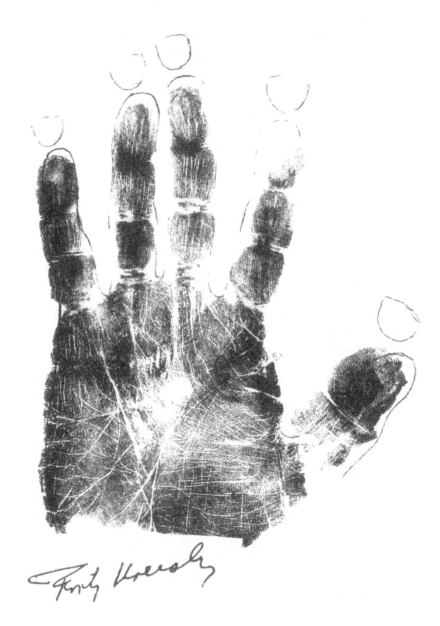

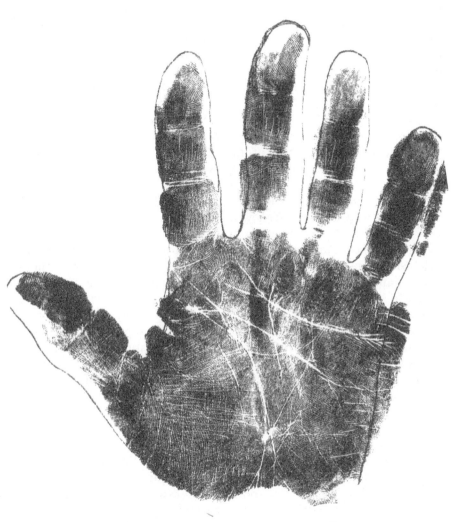

The line starting from the mount of the Moon towards the outside of the hand and running directly up under the third finger is a foretelling of recognition from across the seas. The star on the mount of Jupiter under the forefinger shows unexpected honor and ambition realized. Queer markings for a master violinist are the straight lines under the fourth finger, the medical stigmati. Although these so-named "medical" lines are present, they do not necessarily imply a liking for the medical profession. They may be used in any profession as analytical or diagnostic powers.

On either side of the gift finger, Apollo, is a definite whorl intensifying the inspirational powers revealed by the smoothness of the fingers. In his hands Fritz Kreisler has every thing he needs: common sense, clear thinking, power of concentration, idealism, conscientiousness, wisdom, abundant vitality, warmth, ardor, kindliness, imagination, sense of melody and rhythm, power of analysis—all the indices of success accomplished by the driving power of a mighty will acting through the gifts of logic and reason. A most remarkable hand, and a most remarkable man as well as a world-renowned musician.

A great contrast are the hands of Albert Spalding, likewise one of our beloved and noted violinists. He has a curious pair of hands for so famous a musician. The palm has the characteristic sloping to the wrist so often found in lovers of the beautiful. Its breadth denotes primarily a love of activity. Because of the elasticity of the palm and the length and depth of the head line, this activity will be mental rather than physical. His fingers have what is called a "perfect" placement on the palm of the hand which shows a characteristic not usually expected of a musician, a well-balanced nature. The development of the mounts of Venus and of the Moon, melody and rhythm, is quite plain.

The spatulate formation of the nail phalanges of his third fingers coupled with the length of the phalanges show originality in art. Why he selected the violin is a puzzle. I should hazard that it is probably due to the form of the instrument as that would appeal directly to his love of beauty and the mastery of the difficult technique would be a challenge to his active intelligence. His potential abilities, however, are diverse. Albert Spalding could have made a success as a critic of any phase of creative art; he has the ability to acquire technical knowledge and, as is revealed by the shape of his nails and the "mental eyes" shown on the sensitive cushions of his finger tips, signs of an unusual power of analysis.

To back these gifts he is ambitious—the second phalange of his first finger is longer than the first, and the length of the third phalange shows a love of rule and a desire for approbation. The length of his fourth finger indicates diplomacy, and the space between the life line and the head line shows great independence. The first phalanges of his thumbs, in their length, denote strong will which, if directed by the logic and reason of the second phalange, would enable him to make a success of anything he undertook. His deterrents are seen in the third phalanges of the third fingers, which show a pride which sometimes becomes an obstacle to musical expression because he is supersensitive to criticism or ridicule. He is prone to apply too great a restraint to his real gifts of expression.

The shape and length of the nail phalanges of his second fingers show reserve and innate dignity, while the third phalanges reveal a consideration of self which is dominated by the courtesy and consideration inculcated in his rearing but which nevertheless has a profound effect upon his character. Albert Spalding has a powerful personality, well-endowed. He has chosen to be a musician and to express music through the violin. His success is due to his ambition, pride, interest in personal achievement, power of will, plus his undoubted gifts.

A third of the world's most famous violinists, Jascha Heifetz, possesses like the other two, very strong hands. The even placement of the fingers on the palms is here too. This even placement is a sign of intensity, in that the qualities indicated by each finger are strengthened by the qualities of the mount directly under the finger.

In the hands of Heifetz the musical qualities of melody, harmony and rhythm, as shown in the great development of the mounts of Venus and of the Moon, are clear. The most prominent confession of this hand is that of artistic idealism. The length of the nail phalanges of all the fingers show that Jascha Heifetz is an artist who is satisfied only with the best. In the length of the second phalanges of all the fingers is found the sign of that intelligence used in his criticism of art expression, his own, or that of others. He is quick to recognize any lack of technique that must be overcome and just as quick to sense a pose or a makeshift. He is sincere and discriminating in his art.

The shape as well as the length and the development of the third phalange of his first finger and the high mount beneath it, all indicate a liking for applause, admiration, and recognition which he feels should be his because of his application and work to develop the best in his art. The length of the fourth finger, while indicating a certain amount of diplomacy, shows the influence of those long nail phalanges of conscience by which he sets an artistic standard. He shrinks from public recognition that is not merited. Jascha Heifetz does not despise the limelight, but he

Nov 26/33

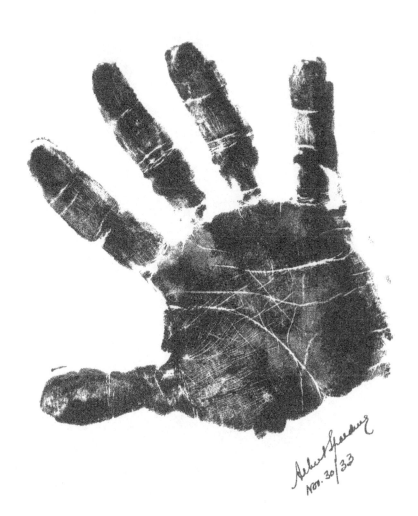

Aelbert Spaulding
Nov. 30/33

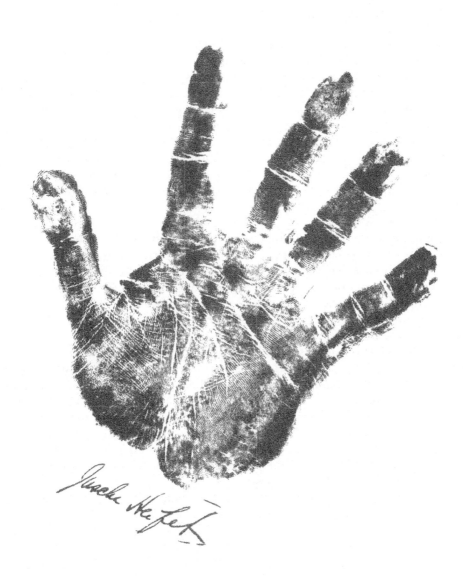

wants recognition that understands what he has to give, and appraises it accurately. He is a very clear-headed human being. His first finger, in its length, shows his ability to plan his own time and direct the activities of others, while the rounded tip reveals the quick understanding he brings to all problems affecting his life. These characteristics indicate that he has a clear understanding of the loss or gain to himself involved in attaining his desires and ambitions both in art and in pleasure. He knows what he does and what he pays or will have to pay.

Jascha Heifetz appreciates the comforts and the luxuries of life, as the length of the third phalanges of all the fingers indicate. But his love for creature comforts and luxury does not dominate him. His thumbs, in the length of the nail phalanges, show a strong will that can push aside anything that stands in the way of ambition or desire. In the past this strong will power was essential to meet apparent limitations of physical strength. The second phalanges of his thumbs show strong development of logic. Thus again in his hands Jascha Heifetz shows that clarity of vision that enables him to see results. When he acts without wisdom he knows it.

At present writing I am not certain whether by the time this book is published Jose Iturbi will be ranked as one of the world's great pianists, or one of the world's most promising conductors. Certainly his work at the Stadium in New York City, with its great radio audience as well as the great local one, proves that he has more than one string to his bow.

Iturbi again took a chance—which is his outstanding characteristic. If you will look at the impressions of his hands, you cannot fail to note the extreme length of his third finger—it is equally long in both hands. In most hands this finger is considerably shorter than the second, in Iturbi's hands it is almost as long. He loves risk where there is any possibility of gain. His third fingers also indicate in their extreme length, intensities. The nail phalanges of his third fingers with the rounded tips show love of idealism in creative art, but idealism founded on perfect technique as their length indicates. The second phalanges reveal love of color, in this instance applicable to tonal quality. The third phalanges denote a fortunate development of the practical, whereby he is able to use his talents to bring him commercial gain.

His fourth finger is likewise unusually long. When diplomacy is evidenced in this degree it can overcome many deficiencies. Iturbi's hands show impatience and irritability in the shape of the fingernails. But when he offends, this power of diplomacy enables him to reconcile those whom he has offended. The long first phalange of this fourth finger shows a great gift of words. He can play with words as with notes, and make them do his will. The rounded or pointed tip again shows tact. In its degree of development this fourth finger reveals the Mercurial temperament, a flashing kaleidoscopic temperament radiating sunshine and then retreating wrapped in depths of gloom, bursting out in spontaneous humor and wit or in an explosion of anger and withdrawing in deep melancholy, such a temperament as you might exepect in this Spanish pianist.

In his thumbs the nail phalanges, short and with pointed tips, repeat the signs of impatience for results, which are tempered a bit by the length of the second phalanges, those of logic and reason. He can delay when necessary, and he can plod when he has to. But the third phalanges of the thumbs, the mounts of Venus, are in their extreme development—as clearly shown in the prints—the source of the fire, the ardor, the passion and the abandon of his playing. With the smoothness of all of the fingers, particularly the third fingers, the development of the mount of Venus marks Iturbi as a man of such intense inspirational gifts that we may call him a genius. That he has earned the clearly defined star of celebrity on the mount under the third finger is self-evident. That he will attain the unexpected honor and ambition realized, which the star under the first finger in the left hand reveals, is only a question of time.

The hands of Ernest Schelling, pianist, conductor, composer and educator, are the ideal hands pictured by artists as the hands of a musician. Their outstanding quality is that of sympathetic understanding. His hand is that of a greatly gifted person, also that of an extremely conscientious one. The fingers equal the palm in length, denoting that intellectual qualities are always in the ascendancy. The long fingers are smooth showing great inspirational qualities. The nail phalanges of all his fingers are very long, showing a dislike of discordant conditions in mental atmosphere or personal surroundings. The long second phalanges of all the fingers show the intelligence that he is able to use to restrain an overconscientiousness which might become fanaticism. The square tip of the second finger again shows the restraining influence of his mental qualities over his intense sympathies. The second phalange of this finger shows prudence, which is an added help.

It is in Ernest Schelling's third finger that we see signs of his great and varied gifts. The shape of the tip is the clue to diversity and to originality in expression. The length of the nail phalange again shows conscience, this time a desire for truth in art expression based on perfect technique in form and construction. The middle phalange denotes the love of color which is shown in the kaleidoscopic mental qualities which

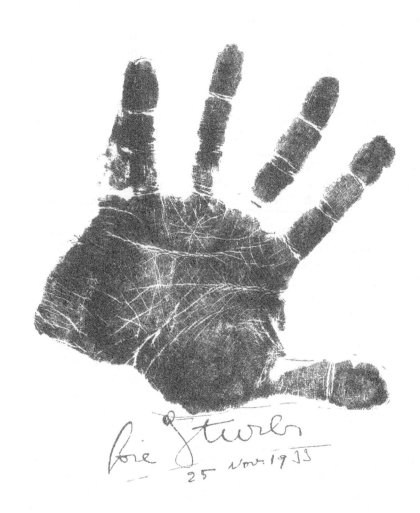

25 Nov. 19 33

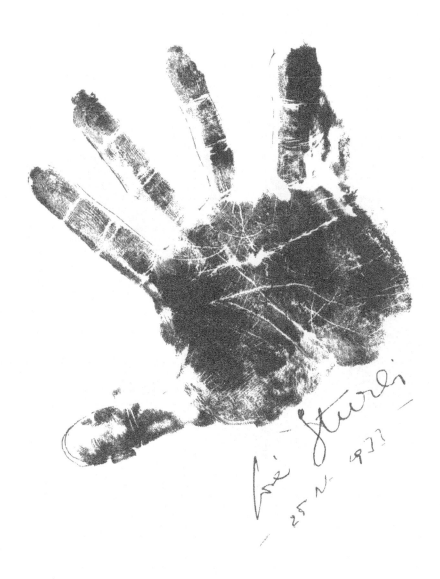

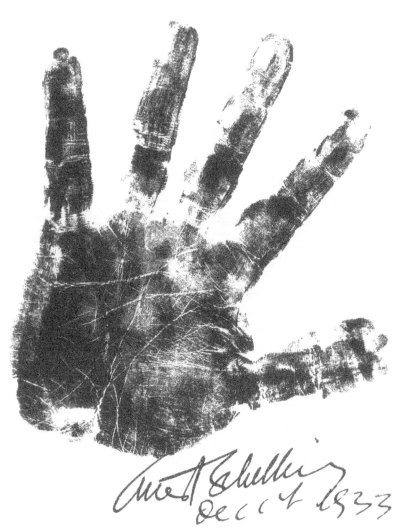

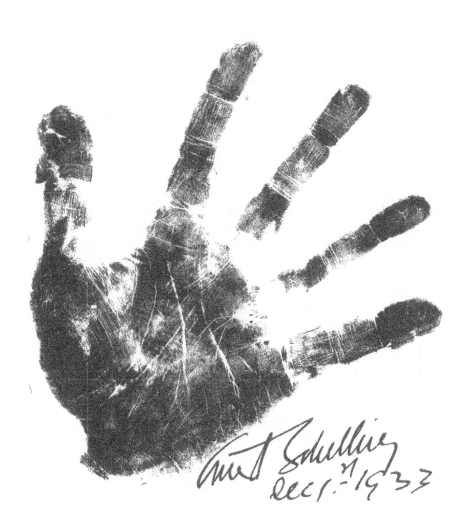

Ernst Schelling
Dec 1.ᵗ 1933

he brings to his work as a composer, as a conductor in drawing from his orchestra the tonal beauty, and as an educator—in the unique colored slides—showing the composer, his home, etc., as a part of the artistry shown in the methods of teaching the understanding love of music.

Ernest Schelling's concerts for young people conducted under the New York Philharmonic Symphony Orchestra are the effort of this sympathetic and conscientious man to extend his joy in music to all people within his reach. In the final reckoning of his achievement his work as an educator will occupy no mean place.

Under the third finger of his right hand is the formation known as the trident of fame, fortune and honor; he has earned it. Here is a man richly endowed, who has realized much of his personal ambition only to turn it to a richer form as ambition for the general joy in an art which seems to him precious. A highly idealistic character is Ernest Schelling.

Frederick Stock, conductor of the Chicago Symphony Orchestra since 1905, and general musical director for the Century of Progress, has a vital hand. His palms are firm to the touch and nearly square; he can be an almost tireless worker. His unusually stiff thumbs show an indomitable perseverance; the second phalanges indicate that he can reason if he will, but when desire rules, he may be illogically stubborn in refusing to see reason or yield to guidance. His fingers are long, showing his attention to necessary detail, but, being smooth to the second joint, reveal the inspirational quality with which he inspires his orchestra and his audience.

The wide flare of the fourth finger, Mercury, shown in both hands, indicates extreme independence in thought and action, a dominance of the mercurial traits that enables Frederick Stock to shake off the inhibitions of over-caution, seen in the close joining of life and head lines, in bringing out the emotional climaxes in his reading of a score, and giving the artist and not the technician the right of way.

Those who know Stock also know that this independence has been manifested in protests against any infringement upon his activities as conductor, in the arrangement of his programs, in his interpretations of compositions and the engaging of solo artists.

Henry Hadley is an old acquaintance; I was his guest at his first concert of his own compositions given in Berlin, December 30, 1907. Nearly all conductors do some work as composers; he has done much. He has to his credit one hundred and fifty songs, four symphonies, one of which won the Paderewski prize, three concert overtures, two operas, one of which also won a prize. "Cleopatra's Night," his best opera, was sung by the Metropolitan Opera Company. In addition he has conducted orchestras in North America, Europe and South America.

It is not surprising that the outstanding characteristic of his hands is restlessness. This is shown in the breadth of the palms under the fingers and in the resiliency of the palms to the touch. His fingers, with the even placement noted in many artists, show distinct differences in the formation of the tips, and this is indicative of versatility in thought and action. His first finger, Jupiter, shows not only executive ability, but considerable initiative and ambition, and the second finger, Saturn, in the shape and length, indicates a somberness of thought and of feeling, almost amounting to tragedy, which has revealed itself in many of his compositions. In the shape of the tip of the second finger and the tip of the third finger, Apollo, are indications of the same qualities that motivate an explorer or inventor. Henry Hadley wants to seek that which is unknown, which accounts for the great variation in his effort and in his composition. The balanced length of the nail and second phalanges of his third fingers, show recognition of rules and warmth of color animating his compositions, the former a seeming contradiction to the exploring instinct. Henry Hadley will seek the unknown, but he will reduce it to the known according to accepted formula. His warmth of color has given his compositions wide recognition for originality and beauty.

The stretch of Mercury, the fourth finger, from the third, shows quickness of thought and action, and, since he is governed largely by an inspirational temperament shown in the flare of the thumb from the hand, he is apt to disregard time and health limitations and to be provoked easily into stubbornness by opposition. He must work rapidly when and where he pleases, but he can work at the same time painstakingly, as indicated in the length of all his fingers. The hand of Henry Hadley is that of a seeker of the new, the new which he brings into the fold of the known and approved.

Edwin Franko Goldman, creator, shall I say? of Goldman's Band—for that seems a proper term—is a man of action, with an original twist and the ardor of a zealot. His handshake tells you at once that here is a man who "does." His zeal is indicated in the high development of the lower mount of Mars above the thumb just under the life line. The original twist grew out of several factors. He has a great deal of executive ability and a lightning-like perception, shown in the length of his first fingers and their pointed tips; these combine with the power of diplomacy indicated in the length of the fourth finger, show him to be an opportunist.

Frederick A. Stock

Frederick A. Stock

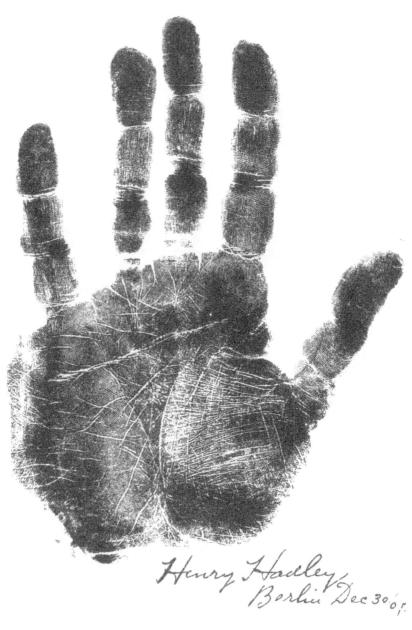

Henry Hadley
Berlin Dec 30 '05

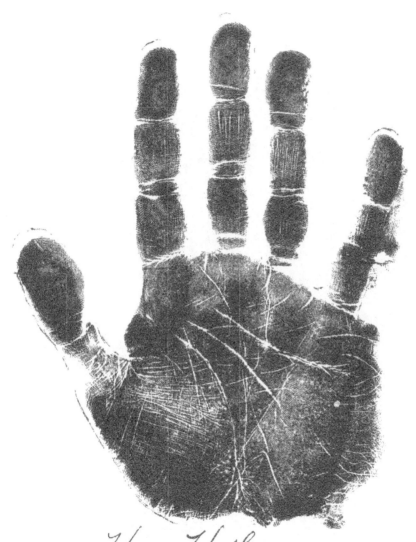

Henry Hadley
Berlin Dec 30/1907.

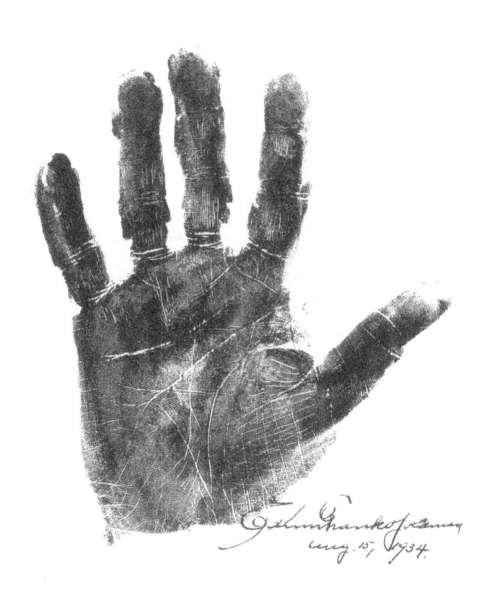

G. Klimkanko v. aumay
aug. 15, 1934.

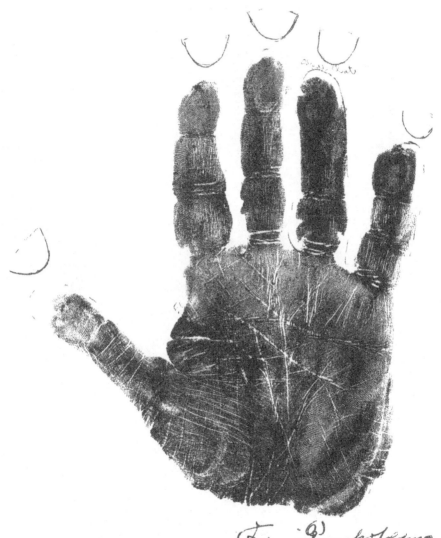

Sannikrankofedm
aug. 15th 1934

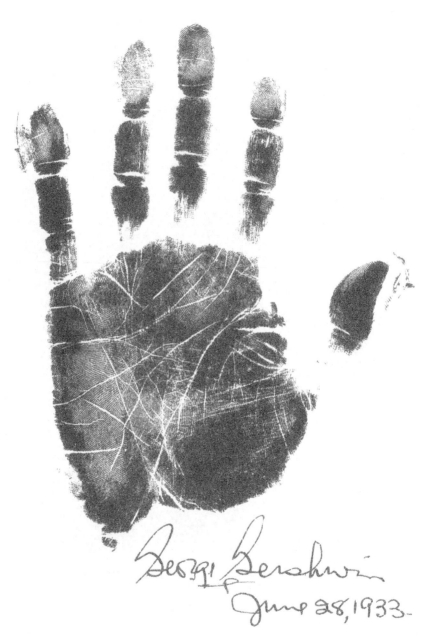

George Gershwin
June 28, 1933

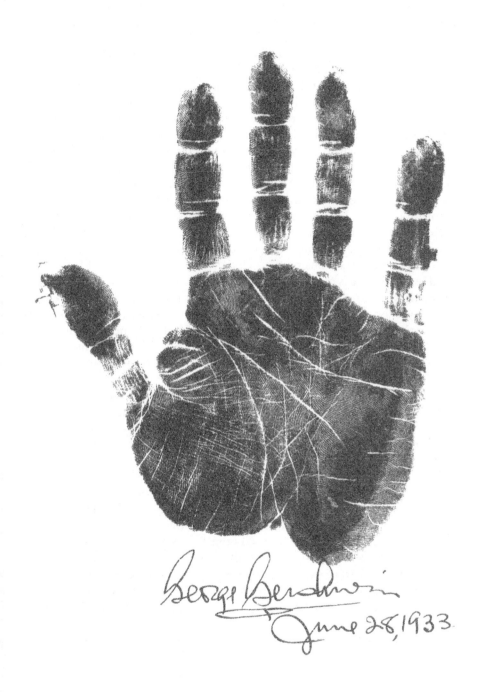

George Gershwin
June 28, 1933.

However, he does not wait for the door of opportunity to open. He opens it. The space between his life line and head line under the first finger show Goldman to possess great independence of thought and action, and the spatulate tip of his third finger shows that he possesses decided originality. The result we know in his "symphony band," an innovation which has been extraordinarily successful.

His is a dynamic hand, again the hand of a man of action. The mount under the heart line on the outside of the palm is well developed, showing bravery and courage that seeks an opportunity to show results. The rather square tip of his fourth finger shows a desire for reason as a basis for expression, while the length of the nail phalange reveals his ability to teach or show others how he wants a thing done.

He possesses an inflexible will; the first phalanges of his thumbs are long and stiff, so stiff that having once determined upon a course of action it is as the laws of the Medes and Persians—unalterable. He may take time to arrive at such decisions; he possesses power of logical thought, but once having made the decision he will see no reason why he should retrace or reconsider.

He has the nails of the critic, both of art and of work; they are broader than they are long, and taper almost to a point at their bases. This critical faculty may often make him unhappy when it is applied to personal relationships, but in his work it is a great asset. His head line, in its depth and clearness, shows efficiency, and this efficiency plus his critical faculty have enabled him to build, man by man, a band whose members play as a unit, with no misfits and no evident weakness.

As a musician, Edwin Franko Goldman's place is unique, and his own. He works hard and his compositions reflect a charm of personality which is also shown in his hands. Even in these impressions you can get the feel of the man's sincerity, and despite his critical power, his good will towards you.

George Gershwin brought jazz up to the level of the musical intelligentsia—or if you prefer, brought the musical intelligentsia down to noticing jazz. In either event he did something for music which is going to last a long, long time. I met George Gershwin in 1933, and when I shook hands with him—no, that is incorrect—when he shook hands with me, I felt as if I were experiencing one of his dramatic flashing climaxes. There was nothing half way about that handshake. Gershwin was so direct you felt you must respond at once: tell him what you wanted and why you wanted it.

The decided development of the third phalange of the thumb, the mount of Venus, together with the development of the mount of the Moon just opposite, are accentuated by the markings of the capillaries on the mount of the Moon. The character of this whorl indicates an intensification of the imaginative faculties, and definitely placed Gershwin's talents as musical. His originality is shown in the rather spatulate development of the tip of his third finger, Apollo.

The palms of his hands were firm, and the nail phalanges of his thumbs, longer than the second. Together these meant great will power. If he allowed the pride shown in the development of the mount under the first finger, Jupiter, and his supersensitiveness as shown in the high cushions on the nail phalanges of the fingers, to govern him, his great will power might have aroused opposition and antagonism and erected barriers to his progress. When he controlled his pride and sensitiveness his will power was an asset enabling him to persevere against the odds he had to meet. He was sincere in his work; the length of the nail phalanges of his first fingers shows that, and the middle phalanges of his first fingers are of a length equal to that of the first, indicating a sense of justice which was as uncompromising in his attitude of criticism towards his own work as to that of others.

Chapter 15: *The Thing as He Sees It*

To "Paint the thing as he sees it
For the God of things as they are,"

must be a joy to any artist. To Lions among painters, there must come a supreme felicity. For they know, through the appreciation of their fellows, that what they see and depict rings true. William Merritt Chase, whose prints head this chapter, was for many years one of the few great American painters. Honored so greatly in Europe that he was asked to stay there permanently, he decided to return to his native land. For years after, he not only painted but taught. Few Americans are not familiar with what are his best know works, "Lady with a White Shawl" at the Metropolitan Museum in New York City, the portrait of his daughter at the Chicago Institute of Art, and the famous codfish that graces the Corcoran Art Gallery in Washington, D. C.

Among living artists there are hundreds who recall with gratitude his efforts for them. First at the Art Students League and later at The Chase School of Art, he worked hard as a wise counselor, a generous critic. Long and successful as was his career, and as rich as were its rewards—for Chase achieved both fame and fortune—none grudged him any fragment of his achievement. Chase was popular as man, teacher and artist.

The most striking characteristic of the prints shown here lies in the wide flares between thumbs and palms and between the fingers. The first flare indicated a tendency to spend a disproportionate amount of time upon unimportant matters, and then, in order to meet a demand, to work with a grand rush. When the mood was on he would work day and night, and when reaction came he would loaf with complete ease. The same flare showed the extremist in economy and extravagance in the use of money. He was either, by turns. The wide stretch between first and second fingers showed independence of thought, based upon moods and not upon logic and reasoning. The almost equally wide flare between second and third fingers revealed his disregard of the future. William Merritt Chase was a man who would let the morrow care for itself. Between third and fourth fingers the great flare showed independence of action and, when considered with the flare of the thumb from the palm, was a sign of additional "artistic temperament." He was famous, in some circles, not only for his work, but also for his personal idiosyncrasies.

The third finger is of especial interest; it is known as the "art" finger, and it shows some of the qualities that helped to make him one of the great artists of his day. The long first phalange of this finger was a sign of the love of truth in art; the middle phalange disclosed in its length a genius for color. Added to this was the imagination shown in the developed mount of the Moon, and the warmth and ardor shown in the high mount of Venus. Anyone who looks at a Chase painting will find the fidelity of a realist blended with the imagination of the idealist. The third phalange of this finger in its length revealed his understanding of the commercial value of his art, but the shape told his tendency to allow his moods rather than his financial needs to direct his action.

Dominating even the flares and this art finger was the perfect circle of intuition beginning under the little finger and running down the hand to end on the mount of the Moon. Such a circle, plus the plainly visible whorl on the mount of the Moon, indicated a power of insight that was a never failing source of inspiration. William Merritt Chase was a seeing artist, whose vision was not limited by the power of the human eye.

Among the rarest of my treasures are these prints of the hands of Vasili Verestchagin, soldier, painter of scenes of carnage, propagandist of peace. Verestchagin was a Russian and met his death at Port Arthur where he had gone to be at the front of hostilities. The battleship on which he embarked was torpedoed. In many countries his paintings will live forever. Perhaps the best known are those of Napoleon's Retreat from Moscow and, to Americans, the large canvas showing Theodore Roosevelt leading the Rough Riders in the charge up San Juan Hill. These hand prints were made shortly after that famous charge. Verestchagin had a large hand with a remarkable length of palm in proportion to the fingers. The width of the palm under the fingers and at the wrist, together with its firmness, showed him to be a soldier at heart, not a soldier of aggression, but one with a recognition of authority, and acceptance of the discipline necessary to an end. Despite his short fingers which revealed a dislike of detail, this discipline was strong enough to overcome his tendency to be impulsive in speech and action—as is signified by the space between head line and life line. He was further aided by a stiff thumb, with a long first phalange indicative of a strong will and an equally long second phalange, a sign of a balance of logic and reason when applied to will power. The stiffness of his thumb was a sign of tenacity; he could endure and hold on when he had an end in view.

The long nail phalanges of his short fingers revealed that he was almost a religious zealot in his work for peace. Like Chase, he had the rare circle of intuition running down from the base of the fourth finger into the mount of the Moon, an indication of the gift of insight. The long

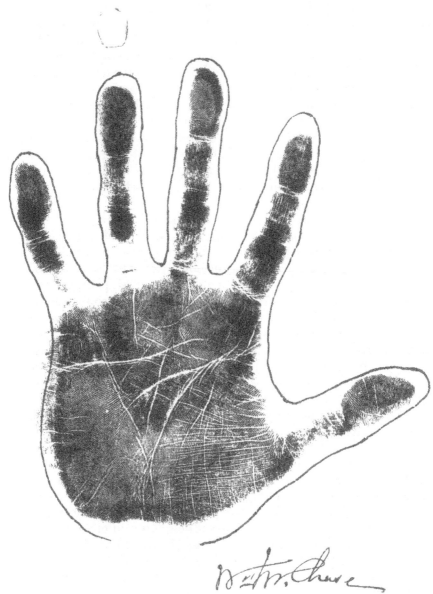

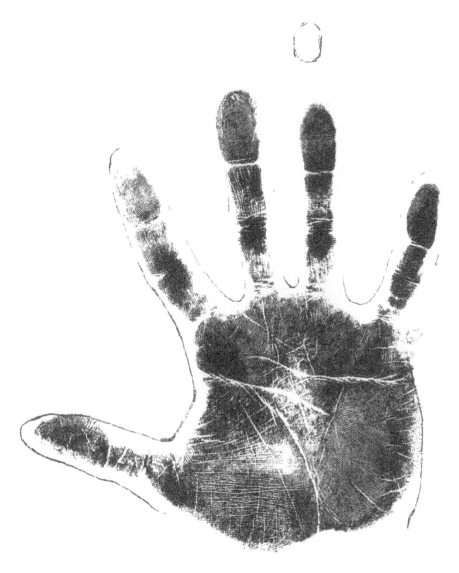

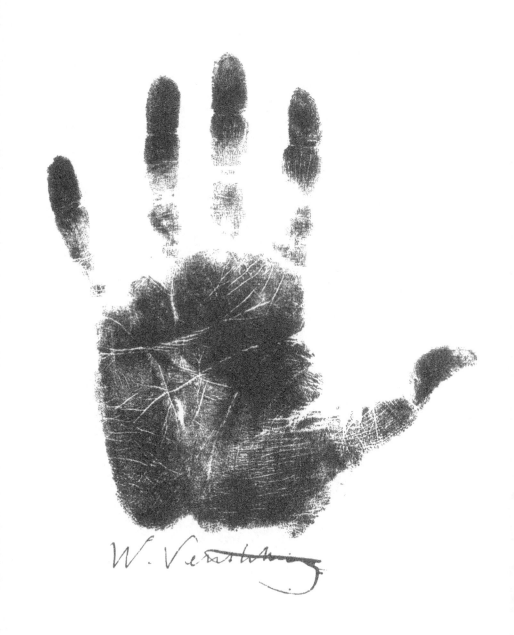

middle phalanges of his fingers showed a strong mentality; his head line in its depth and clearness disclosed again that strong mentality and a remarkable memory. The middle phalange of the art finger was a sign of a never failing understanding of the use of color, and the high mount of Venus revealed his ardor for his cause. Verestchagin was both artist and preacher, and as long as war endures his work will carry its deathless message of the horror of war.

My interest in Wayman Adams goes back to the time when he was climbing over the rocky road of financial worries towards an unknown future. Like William Merritt Chase, he was born in Indiana, attended art school in my home city in Indianapolis. Since then, Wayman Adams has climbed steadily and surely, and his honors have been many. At the Sesquicentennial in Philadelphia he was awarded the silver medal; a year later he was awarded the first Altman prize at the Academy. In 1933 he was awarded the medal of the Holland Society of New York.

Wayman Adams has the double jointed thumb of the man with a strong dramatic instinct, and he has the flexible thumbs showing a surface adaptability to people and environment. The wide stretch between thumbs and fingers and between the fingers themselves reveal him to be an extremist, a man willing to take a chance. Contradicting this sign is that of the close joining of the life line and head line in both right and left hands. Wayman Adams loves adventure, but this sign of caution will keep him from risking much.

His art finger, the third, has a spatulate tip which evinces decided originality and individuality in art expression. In the length and breadth of the first phalange is shown the dominating influence of line, form and technique in his work. The middle phalange of this finger is about equal in length to the first phalange, which indicates that color balances form. The width of the middle phalange reveals a love for pet animals. The love of color is further indicated in the full development of the mount of Venus, at the base of the thumb, which in an artist would mean that the warm glowing tones will be superseded by richer, more sombre hues, as the imagination shown by the mount of the Moon deepens and adds subtlety to the more primitive emotion. The third phalange of this finger in the length shows an appreciation of creature comforts and a recognition of the commercial value necessary to obtain such comforts. He may "dream dreams" but they are visions which he works to realize.

On all the fingers are developed cushions on the finger tips, a revelation of sensitiveness and tact in approach to his work. In his right hand, running from the base of the palm to the third finger is a well-marked talent line which terminates in the fork of brilliancy, a definite sign of achievement.

The different shape of the tips of his fingers shows a versatility that has led him to experiment in various phases of art. The rounded tip of his first finger indicates a quickness of perception; the square tip of his second finger a natural leaning towards architecture or construction engineering. The long middle phalange of this finger shows the wisdom and prudence he uses in meeting his personal problems. The length of the fourth finger indicates a diplomacy expressed in actions rather than words since the caution mentioned and the analytical trait, which the small nail indicates, leads him to make the gesture but withhold the expression in words. He prefers to make the entente cordiale through his art expression rather than discuss it.

When I made my first impressions of the hands of J. Scott Williams in 1910 he had acquired a reputation as an illustrator of the first rank, and was one of the outstanding teachers of the Chicago Art Association. When I made the impressions shown here, in 1934, he was working as a mural artist upon the walls, and as a designer of the stained glass windows of the State Library in Indianapolis.

Nothing is more fascinating to a reader of hands than to see what has happened to them during twenty years. In 1910 the first thing that attracted my attention was as perfect a circle of intuition as I have ever seen, the curved line running from the mount under Mercury, the fourth finger, down into the lower part of the mount of the Moon. In the impressions made in 1934 the circle is not so perfect. The unusual intuitive faculties that are his by right of his Scotch ancestry had their influence in Williams' youth. At the base of the palm you can see that the life line and the line of destiny are united for a space, a sign of duties and restrictions imposed by home ties, a condition that might easily have uprooted his desire for art expression and turned him to readier ways of financial gain. But that intuitive faculty impelled him to hold on; he knew that art was an integral part of his life, to be cherished at all odds. The change in the formation of the line making the circle of intuition marks the issuing of J. Scott Williams' personality from a nebulous land where the flood light of intuition was his only guide, into a charted area where the light still glows but where today he can see plainly his goal. His analytical, argumentative tendencies shown in the shape of his nails, broader than they are long, and the tenacity of purpose which the long first phalange of his thumb indicates, have lifted his vision into clear objective. He still makes use of the intuitive qualities indicated by that circle, but he

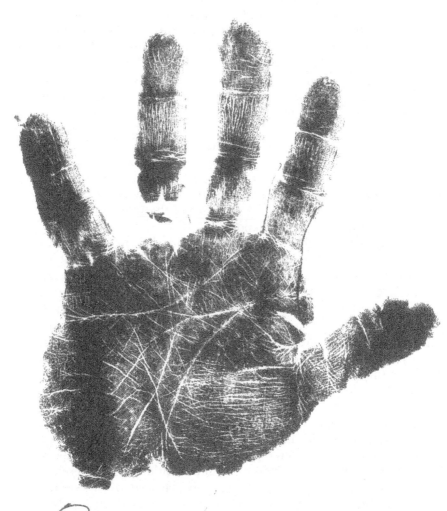

Jayne Adams
November 22ᵈ 1933

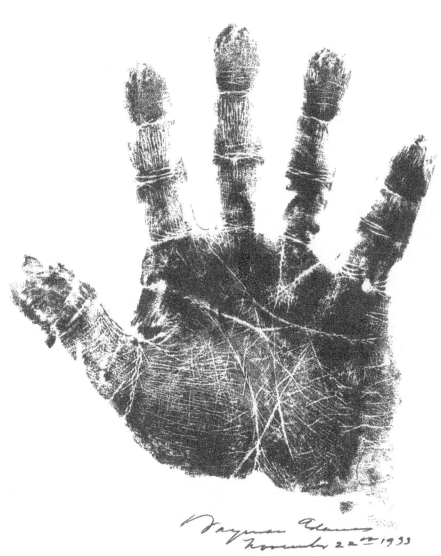

Wayman Adams
November 22nd 1933

J. Scott Williams
Sept. 16th. 1934

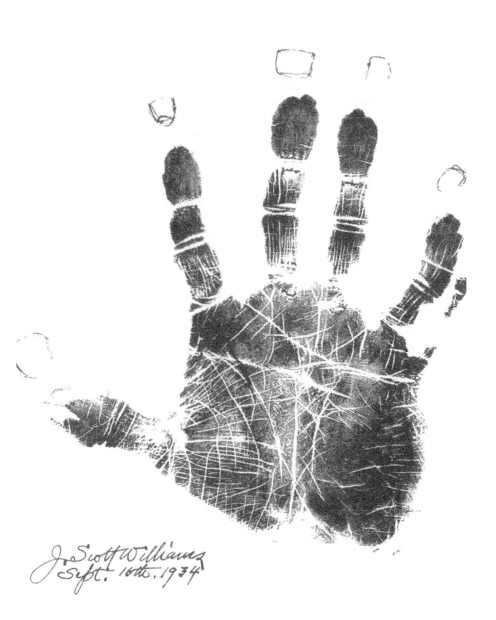

J. Scott Williams
Sept. 16th. 1934

now uses them as a flashlight when the way is dark for a little time; in the main it is bright and clear.

The length of the third finger indicates, first, his love of taking a chance. The long first phalange of this finger shows that lines and construction dominate his interest in art expression, and this phalange is influenced by the definitely spatulate tip of the second finger which is a sign of a zest for research. A second influence is seen in the definite curve of the fourth finger towards the third finger. Such a curve is a sign of a definite interest in science and art.

Under the third finger of his right hand is a distinct talent line with a less noticeable secondary line. J. Scott Williams has made a name for himself in two fields of art expression, with pen, pencil and brush on the one hand, and by surmounting the mechanical problems involved in the designing and making of stained glass windows. His line of destiny indicates a continued financial success through art, while the star of ambition realized, marked upon the mount of Jupiter, shows that public recognition is and will be his. J. Scott Williams' mental make-up is a wonderful combination of the scientist, mathematician, research analyst, and the artist.

Chapter 16: *Inspired Paws*

More intimately than with any other form of artistic expression, the hands of a sculptor are a part of his work. The painter has his intermediary in the brush, the writer in his pen, the musician works through the limitations of a mechanical device, and the actor employs his whole personality in getting his effects. The sculptor who models in clay has his two hands. If he uses tools they are probably of his own devising. The skill of his hands in direct contact with his medium is responsible for the result.

The inspired paws of Lions among sculptors have, therefore, an added significance. One would expect large well-formed sensitive looking hands. Look at those of one of the greatest sculptors of our time, the hands of George Grey Barnard. They are small, rather stubby, almost childlike in shape, if it were not for the power suggested in the huge thumbs and the solid, fleshy look of fingers and palms. George Grey Barnard has earned that look of power. One of the many young, struggling artists who managed somehow to get to Paris and to study at the Beaux Arts, Barnard so impressed his personality and his gifts upon others that in recognition of his potential power. aid was given him to complete his studies. As an artist he needed no gratitude to force him to his best. But through all the years since, he has freely expressed his thanks to those who freed him from privation and who made it possible for him to begin the making of a remarkable personal history. Honors both in this country and abroad have been heaped upon him. Two museums, one in Madison, Indiana, and another at Swarthmore, Pennsylvania, have been named for him, and the latter contains some two hundred pieces of his entire work. In the garden of John D. Rockefeller at Pontiac Hills, N. Y., is his famous "Adam and Eve," while all across his native country from the Metropolitan Museum in New York to the marble shrine containing the bust of Lincoln at Redlands, California, as well as in Norway, France and England, his work is cherished.

Small hands, but mighty ones! According to scientific palmistry these hands run true to form. People with small fingers and small palms like to tackle big things. If they cannot execute them personally they like to plan large undertakings for others to work out in detail. Under George Grey Barnard's first finger you can see a star, an unusual marking, which indicates the realization of ambition and unexpected honor. About this star is a lined square which is a sign of preservation from excess ambition. He is free from arrogance and excessive pride. The first and second fin-

George Grey Barnard

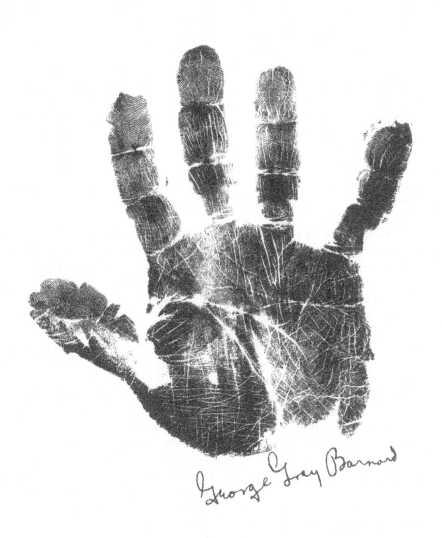

George Gray Barnard

gers are much closer to the third than in the ordinary normal person. They lean toward the finger of art expression. His fourth finger is beautifully formed and has an unusual flare from the hand, a sign of rapidity in thought and action. The gift of expression is shown in the length of the nail phalange; it is the gift of words, but of verbal expression. George Grey Barnard prefers to talk rather than to write. The shape of the tip reveals tact in management of his affairs. In the right hand the head line droops to the mount of the Moon, the mount of imagination. In the left hand running straight from the head line to the base of the third finger and ending in a clear trident of fame, fortune and honor, is a perfectly formed talent line with what seems an unnecessary strengthening line running by its side. In the right hand the trident is in process of final formation. Incredible as it may seem from the recognition already accorded him, there is ahead of him a crowning masterpiece of his art life—these impressions are dated May 20, 1934.

The shape of his nails denotes an analytical nature and one much given to argument. There is also a saving sense of humor as is disclosed by the short line ending in a fork in the center of the mount under Mercury, sometimes called "the merry thought mark."

Gutzon Borglum's hand is that of the born fighter. He welcomes obstacles, more than that—he seeks them. In his career this love of combat is shown in his selection of work. The forty-two figures in the colossal monument entitled "Wars of America," at Military Park, Newark, New Jersey; the Confederate Memorial begun upon the face of Stone Mountain, Georgia; the first national memorial federally authorized, built by the State of South Dakota on the face of the Black Hills with funds appropriated by Congress, are all indicative of Borglum's desire to meet the unexpected, the difficult, well nigh the impossible, and to grapple and conquer it.

Look at the aggressive qualities his hand reveals. A high development of the mount called lower Mars, on the upper part of the mount of Venus under the life line. Short broad fingernails, indicating mental impatience and irritability; palms broad under the fingers, showing a driving force that is physical as well as mental and that urges him into action; a hard palm revealing an equally hard mentality; stiff, unyielding fingers, those of a man who holds steadfastly to his course of action; stiff thumbs that show an utter lack of adaptability to people whose views and outlook upon life do not coincide with his; short fingers, as in the case of George Grey Barnard, the fingers of a man who wants to tackle big things—all of these are aids to the man who sets out to conquer.

109

He is an honest man and an honest worker. The long first finger, indicative of executive ability, is topped with a long nail phalange. This shows the underlying sincerity and honesty of purpose that animates his desires. In the length of his fourth fingers is evidenced considerable power of diplomacy. Borglum scorns to use this to adjust his personal problems, since for them there is no better viewpoint than his own. But when he has others working with him in his huge endeavors, he does use this diplomacy and the executive ability shown in his first fingers. His intense interest in what he is doing is also a happy factor in securing his aids. He opens the door of opportunity to those who seek to work with him. If they wish to ally themselves with his work, they must be a part of the same struggle.

The first phalange of the second finger is also long, as is frequently the case in the hands of sculptors. In the second finger it suggests the carrying of a mental vision sufficiently strong to act as a lodestone urging him on to the creation of his dreams. The third finger, the art finger, has a long first phalange with a rounded tip. Its possessor likes form, and has an innate ability to handle the constructive problems that accompany art projects. The extreme length of this third finger, almost as long as the second, tells of a liking for risk or chance. The flat third phalanges of his fingers, with the wide space between the fingers at their bases, speaks of an indifference to the luxuries of life and social contacts, and a like indifference to hardship when a necessary part of his work.

Under Jupiter, the first finger, the mount is high. Here is a natural desire for approbation and commendation. However, his short broad nails are critical. This man will be apt to question what he desires. He will doubt the sincerity of the praise given him and look for a hidden motive. In the center of the mount, directly under the third finger, is a star of celebrity and, since it is the third finger, of "art" recognition. In Borglum's right hand this third finger of Apollo leans towards the second finger of Saturn, showing his tendency to inject a sombre, almost tragic, note into his selection of subject matter for his art work. From the line of destiny there are two definite lines of success—based chiefly on financial recognition because of artistic merit. Gutzon Borglum will live to see greater acclaim of his great talents if he employs the ability and diplomacy he possesses in such large measure.

Four years ago I read Paul Manship's hand in his wonderful studio in East Seventy-Second Street, New York City. Long before this I had known Manship's work, both abroad and in this country. Two years after, he was to add to his record of notable achievements a piece of work

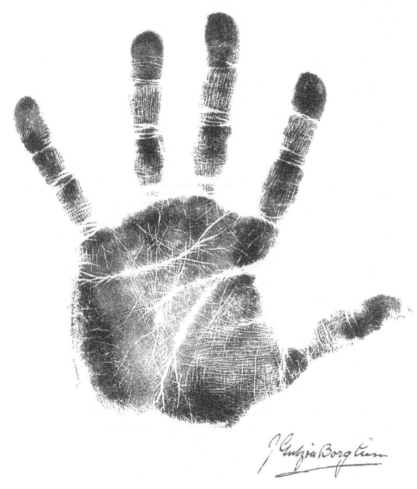

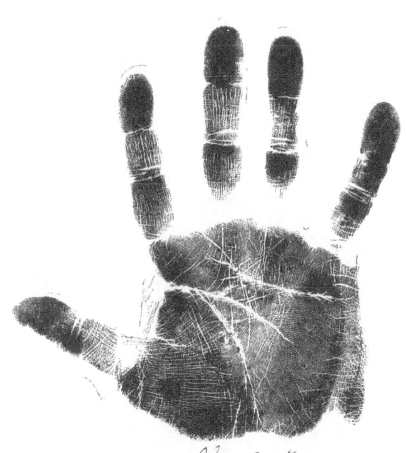

Gutzon Borglum

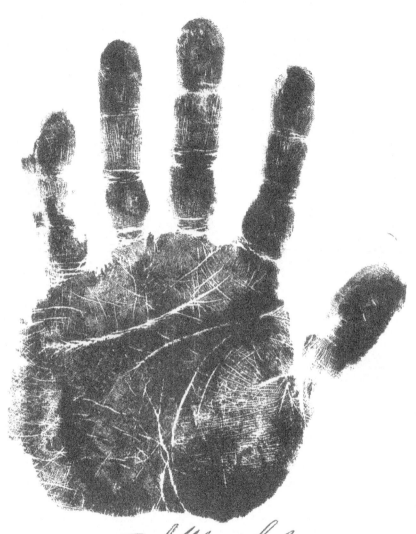

Paul Mauskopf Apr. 8, 1931.

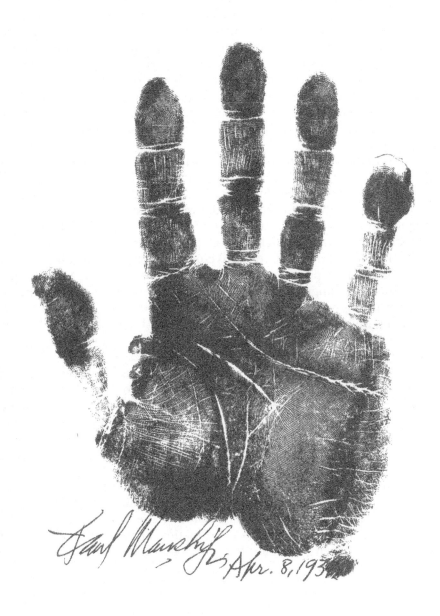

Karl Menninger, Apr. 8, 193_

which connoisseurs of art travel many miles to view. It is the bronze statue of Lincoln as a young man, at Fort Wayne, Indiana.

Like George Grey Barnard and Gutzon Borglum, Paul Manship has the square, firm palm of the out-of-doors man. In the case of Paul Manship an extraordinary vitality is also shown in the clearness and depth of the life line. The firmness of the palm reveals tenacity of effort, which is strengthened by the determination shown in the long first phalange of the thumb. Manship may not welcome opposition, but when opposition comes, whether it arises from material limitation or technicalities to be mastered, it serves as an incentive to greater effort. The shape and firmness of the palm coupled with the rounded tip of the fourth finger announce a man who prefers to express himself in achievement rather than in words.

Originally this man was a slow thinker, and, according to the short head line in his left hand, inclined to a single track of thought. The right hand indicates development. The space between the head line and life line is much greater than in the left. He has developed breadth of view and the power to think in more than one way. The mount of the Moon in this hand is highly developed and has upon its surface that whorl of the sixth sense, indicative of imaginative power, in sight and foresight. These powers are sustained by the shape of the first phalange of the second finger. It is moderately spatulate, and together with its length is a sign of interest in psychology and the workings of mentality which borders upon mysticism. And yet, Manship's is a practical nature, in the main. The development of the mount under Saturn shows a power of adjustment of his practical and mystic urges, so that he can safely steer his work and his acts. The art finger shows, as we would expect, the long first phalange that denotes form, a quick eye for lines, and a love of activity in their use. A love of color is shown in the second phalange of his third finger and, together with the high development of the mount of Venus, brings warmth, tenderness and ardor that produce the seemingly impossible in marble and bronze, and makes his sculpture glow with life.

Upon the center of the mount of Jupiter under the first finger is a star, a sign of recognition by the public, and of honor and elevation. In addition, there is a star of celebrity under the third finger in the left hand, which is still in process of formation in the right. Although his rewards have been great, Paul Manship has ahead of him the culminating honor of his career.

III

Frederick W. MacMonnies has but recently passed on leaving behind a long list of achievements which reveal a rare gift and appalling amount of energy. Both here and abroad MacMonnies received honor upon honor.

Of his later works perhaps the best known are the statute of "Civic Virtue" in City Hall Park, New York, and the colossal group erected upon the battlefield of the Marne in France. His hand prints show the same powerful characteristics as those of the sculptors we have met, plus longer and more significant fingers. Physical restlessness and love of physical activity are shown in the breadth and firmness of the palm. The long fingers indicate a devotion to detail, and their smoothness, great inspirational quality. In addition, MacMonnies had a whorl on the upper part of the mount of the Moon, a whorl with a definite center, almost like an eye. Not only did he possess the sixth sense of intuitive insight, but he possessed it in superlative degree. Such a mark meant genius.

Unquestionably, Frederick MacMonnies could have been a painter. The middle phalange of those long third fingers, the fine development of the mounts of Venus and of Luna evidence all the qualities needed. But his love of physical activity and the development of his long straight head line indicate the forces that took him from the field of painting to that of sculpture.

The flare of his thumbs from his fingers was so great as to indicate the extremist, between the first and second fingers it showed excessive independence of thought, between the second and third fingers his disregard for the responsibilities of the morrow, and between the third and fourth fingers quickness of action which with his tendency to extremes might have wrecked his career. However, the latent prudence and wisdom indicated in the long middle phalange of the second finger and the keenness of judgment in that powerful head line were sufficient to arrest his tendency to extremes. Add to this the strong will shown in the first phalange of the thumb, and you will see how MacMonnies kept his powerful impulses within his control. His will dominated the logic and reason of the second phalange of the thumb, but it did not dim or dominate the intellectuality and clarity revealed by the head line. This man fought his battle of life with clear vision. At times he chose to allow his will to govern his reason, but he had the power of choice. He knew the penalty and paid the price.

The spatulate formation of the tip of his third finger is a sign of the originality which helped to make his work famous. The long nail phalange of that finger showed his fidelity to detail. Despite his independence, he had an ingratiating suavity and ready adaptability to circum-

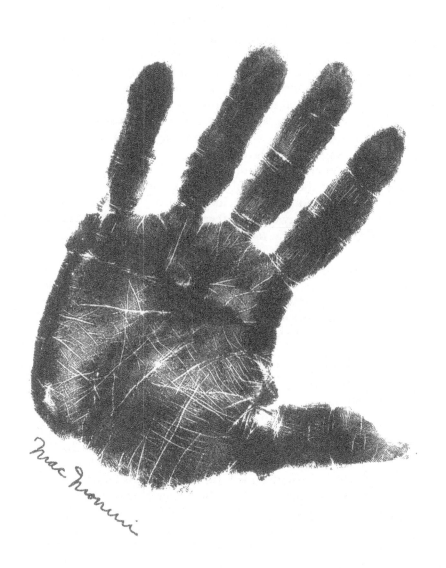

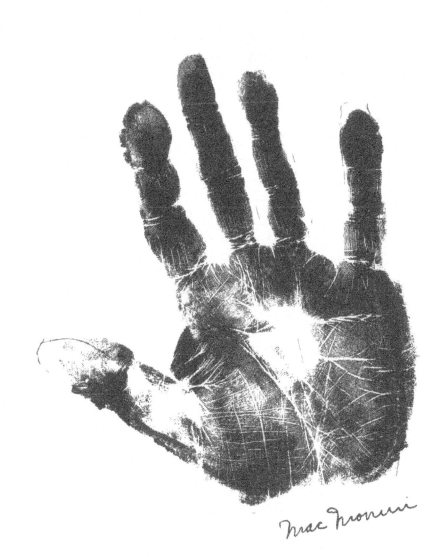

stances and to people, indicated both in the flexibility of his thumbs and the diplomacy in his long fourth finger. The narrowness of the space between his heart line and head line in both hands suggests a certain intolerance of advice or suggestion towards efforts to lead or direct him, either in his work or in his personal affairs. Again his power of diplomacy acted as a saving factor. He was a strong character; all of his traits were manifested in intense degree. In the right hand under the third finger was the fork of brilliancy in art expression. In the left hand this had become the three forked mark of fame, fortune and honor, well won.

Chapter 17: *Their Eyes See Far*

Dear to our hearts are our everyday artists. They come into our homes in our newspapers and magazines; they are with us and of us. The Lions whose Paws appear in this chapter are known all over the country, some of them all over the world.

Dean of them all is Charles Dana Gibson, honored as National Academician in 1932, an artist whose work has been familiar to Americans for almost forty years. Who does not know the "Gibson Girl," from the full-bosomed, large hipped damosel of the nineties to the modern slim miss of today? "The Education of Mr. Pipp," "A Widow and Her Friends," "The Social Ladder," books whose stories are told in a succession of drawings, are classics of their kind containing what, too often, classics lack, a superb sense of humor.

As you can see by the prints, Charles Dana Gibson has very long hands and very long fingers. His palm is of the conic type, broad under the fingers, sloping decidedly towards the wrist, the sign of a love of beauty. His nails, which these prints cannot show, indicate again in their length and shape, a love for beauty, for poetry, music and every form of art, and a love of harmony in life and everyday surroundings. And again the long first phalange of the long third finger with its rounded tip speaks of beauty and of art, of a quick eye for line and for structure. On the mount of imagination—the upper part of the mount of the Moon—in the left hand is a deep talent line that forces its way through varied obstacles owing to ill health and ill-fortune, upward on to the mount of Apollo under the third finger. Such a deep, strong line shows a single minded desire, and its termination under the art finger suggests that this desire is for art expression. Running parallel to this dominating art line is a second line indicative of ability in another medium. The long fourth finger with its long second phalange showing the gift of words, and the long sloping head line dipping towards the mount of imagination upon which, in both hands, is the whorl indicative of the gift of foresight and insight, show that this second gift is literary—he can express himself in words.

Between the beginning of the life line and the beginning of the head line is a wide space; Charles Dana Gibson has independence in thought and action. His right hand shows a wide flare between thumb and fingers, the flare of an opportunist. His thumbs are flexible. He is adaptable to any phase of life's activities, and mentally he has never been bound. The width between head line and life line through their entire stretch shows

114

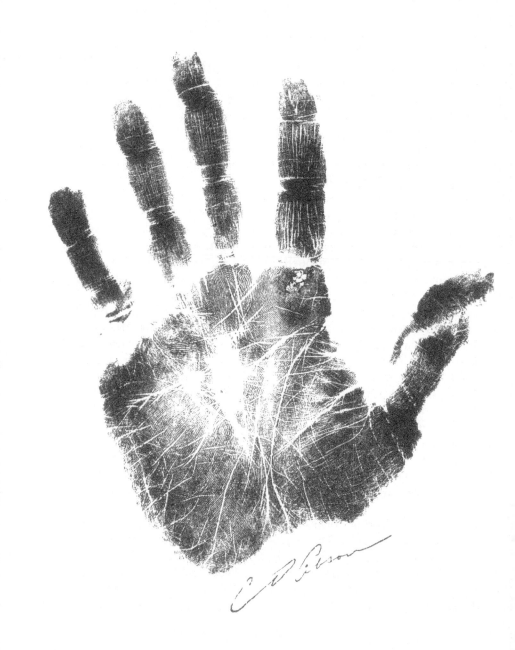

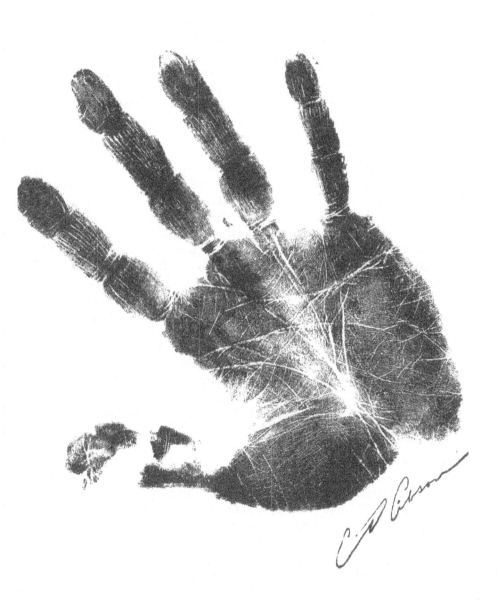

a tolerance that obtains towards all acts of others. For himself, the long first phalanges of all his fingers declare a rigid conscience that will accept no subterfuge or makeshift in art or in life.

The long first finger with the high mount beneath is that of the born leader. His fourth finger shows great assets,—its length, diplomacy; its pointed tip, tact; the length of the first phalange, the gift of expression or oratory; and beneath the finger the height of the mount declares that gift of humor that has made so much of his work famous.

Charles Dana Gibson lacks the aggressive physical and mental restlessness that might drive him to commercialize his great talents to the utmost. The star of celebrity in his left hand under his third finger is not realized in his right. He has never exhausted his gold mine; he has used and enjoyed it.

James Montgomery Flagg has acquired distinction as an illustrator, as a humorist—you recall his work with "Life" and "Judge"—as a portrait painter, author, and a writer for motion pictures. This differentiation in achievement is indicated in his flexible fingers and in the flare between them and the thumb. The slight curve of his palm towards the wrist shows the general appeal of beauty in nature or in art. The breadth of the palm under the fingers shows a restless nature, while his stiff thumbs indicate that wherever his restlessness leads he is prepared to put unflagging persistence back of the effort. In the earlier part of his life there was a disposition to throat and bronchial trouble, which is shown in the shape of the nails of the little finger and of the thumb, together with the islanded formation at the joining of his head line and life line. This difficulty was aggravated by impatience—shown in the shape of the nails —over the interference of ill health with his plans. That he has learned caution even to the point of over-caution is indicated in the much straighter head line in his right hand, and in the very close joining of the life line and head line in that hand.

James Montgomery Flagg's smooth fingers are those of a man who works through inspiration. He has a multiplicity of ideas crowding for expression. Between the second and third fingers is a mark like a finger print. This intensifies the wisdom and conservatism indicated in the long second phalange of the second finger, and carries that wisdom to the art finger, preventing over-production at the expense of art demands.

The rather square tip of the third or art finger indicates the ability of James Montgomery Flagg to see the technical value of line in the expression of form. The length of the middle phalange and the fullness of the mount of Venus show a love of color. The length of the fourth finger signifies a much needed diplomacy to enable him to extricate himself from situations into which his restlessness plus his irritability and impatience, as shown in his short broad nails, plunge him. The rather short third phalanges of all of his fingers disclose an indifference to the luxuries which money can give. He does desire comforts, since that means freedom from worry over financial limitations. While the development of the mount of Venus is a sign of a strong emotional nature, his stiff thumbs show a great degree of self-discipline, and his acquired caution in speech and action acts as a barrier to his tendency to be demonstrative.

The unusually straight head line in the right hand is a sign that James Montgomery Flagg has learned to don the armor of indifference and to present a humorous cynicism towards the world in general. His attitude conceals a depth of feeling, with tenderness and gentleness towards those he loves.

The line of fate or destiny, rising from the base of the palm, and in his right hand beginning on the mount of imagination, reveals imagination as the basis of his success. This line continues without interference until it passes the heart line. Then there is shown a necessity for guarding financial resources. The flow of income lessens and one source seems to vanish, although the main channel, evidently fed by the active earning art capacity, continues unchecked.

Under the fourth finger are straight lines which are signs of an ability in some form of scientific research. Ordinarily they are known as the "medical stigmati" and are a sign of an aptitude for the profession of physician. They do not indicate a love of that profession. He could have been a successful physician, but I doubt whether he would have liked the work.

Beneath the third finger in the left hand is definitely outlined the fork of brilliancy. In the right hand this has developed into the trident of fame, fortune and honor. These lines are not so deeply marked as in the left hand and indicate that James Montgomery Flagg has greater distinction awaiting him than any he has as yet achieved.

I now present the prints of the hands of a left-handed person. As I have stated, there is no mysterious significance to the palmist in the use of a left hand in place of a right, but the reading must be reversed, that is the right hand becomes the "natural" hand, and the left hand shows developed characteristic. Howard Chandler Christy's portraits of President Harding, President and Mrs. Coolidge, Mussolini, Amelia Earhart, Eddie Rickenbacker, and the many beautiful women who have graced

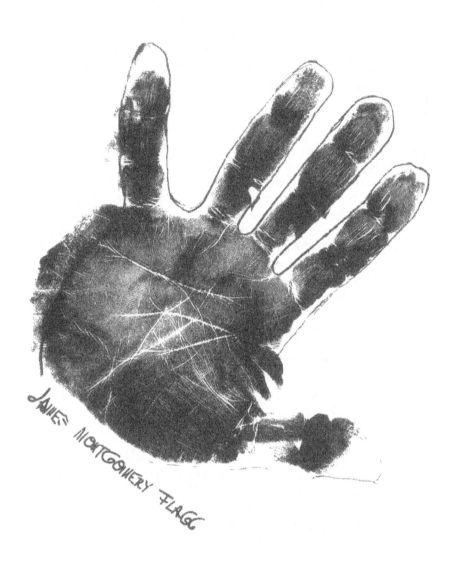

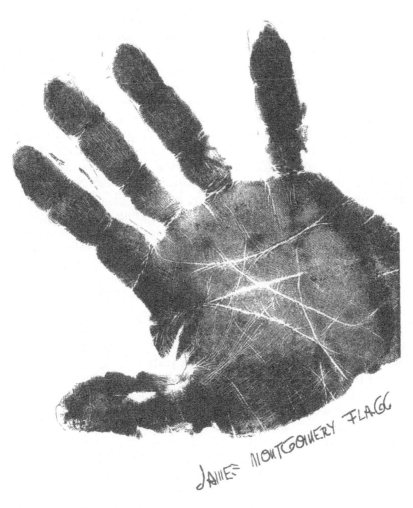

James Montgomery Flagg

the pages of hundreds of magazines and books are all the work of his left hand.

In the print of his left hand shown here are to be seen unusual and arresting lines of destiny, fate or success. Tracing these lines from the base of the palm next to the life line you can see that the first is joined to the life line itself, a sign that necessity for earning influenced his early years of work. Then the first line ends and there comes a definite advance in his career shown by two different lines. One of these travels close to the first and carries definite success, although somewhere in the fifties the financial stream seems to lessen. From this second line of destiny a third line runs to the lines of talent under the third or art finger, a sign of financial success through art expression.

Howard Chandler Christy's finger nails, broader than they are long, show him to be analytical, and with the developed joints of his fingers, to have an inclination towards fussiness, especially when he is not feeling quite up to the mark. Also, he becomes introspective, and this is an asset unless he exaggerates his mental introspection and worry about minutiae, thus avoiding bolder lines of action. In both hands his head line droops to the mount of the Moon showing a tendency to allow his imagination to bias his judgment. The length of his fingers reveals care in detail, and their smoothness to the second joints indicates inspirational qualities. The long first phalange of his middle finger shows an almost morbid desire to be absolutely fair and to give full value in all that he does. The wide flare between the third and fourth fingers is a sign of independence of action, and he has the saving grace of humor, as shown in the development of the high mount under Mercury, the fourth finger, which acts as a check to some of his morbid tendency to depreciate himself and his talents. His heart line, rising between his first and second fingers, reveals his loyalty and devotion to his friends, the kind of man who holds them through long years.

The third finger, the art finger, has all three phalanges about equal in length. The almost square tip of the nail shows a fidelity to technique; the first and second phalanges his ability in line and color, and the third phalange that trait unusual in an artist, the power to make a commercial success of his work.

The squares on the plain of Mars in the right hand, made by cross lines running from the mount of Venus over the line of destiny and his talent lines, disclose preservation from dangers that might threaten to end his earning capacity, by wiping out the ability to express his talents. In his left hand those talents become definitely deeper and stronger, and his art expression shows no dimming with the passage of the years.

Such a tiny person and such a tiny hand to hold within it the hearts of hundreds of thousands of dog lovers who follow with joy the adventures of "Sinbad" and "Tippy" and "Cap Stubbs." "Edwina," as she signs herself, Edwina Dumm, as she was christened, is one of the very few women who have made a place for themselves in the front ranks of cartoonists.

In her hands one would expect signs of a sense of humor and of love of animals. In the print shown here you can see the high development of the mount under Mercury, the fourth finger, indicating wit and humor, and in the right hand there is an additional mark, termed the "merry thought mark," an open triangular formation in the center of the mount. Her love of animals is indicated by the dominating size of the middle phalange of her third finger. The phalange beneath this one is remarkably short. It is the phalange that concerns itself with a desire for personal glory—Edwina must have none, or next to none.

She is a painfully shy person. The close joining of the life line and head line in both hands suggests that at first this was because of health conditions. In order to work as hard as she liked she had to become something of a recluse. The clearly marked "square" enclosing the island at the joining of the life line and head line, and the lines running parallel with the life line show that her health has definitely withstood the attacks upon it, but the habit of shrinking from publicity has become firmly fixed.

Between the second and third fingers is a very wide space, one of the signs of originality, and this is fed by the imagination shown in the sloping head line terminating on the upper part of the mount of the Moon.

Her thumb is stiff in both hands. She is a persevering young woman, and her will power is directed intelligently by the well developed second phalange of the thumb, the sign of a sense of logic and a power of reason. Her firm palm is an additional asset: it indicates the reserve she maintains in order to dominate her physical limitations.

The plainly etched whorl into which her head line dips, tells of a gift of insight; in her case used to understand and explain through the double media of art and wit, animals and human beings.

Despite her shyness she is a very definite person. Edwina has decided views as to her activities; the flares between her fingers show independence of thought and of action.

In her right hand under her third finger is a decided trident of fame, fortune and honor, developed from the fork of brilliancy in the left hand. There are four other definite lines in her hand that have especial

118

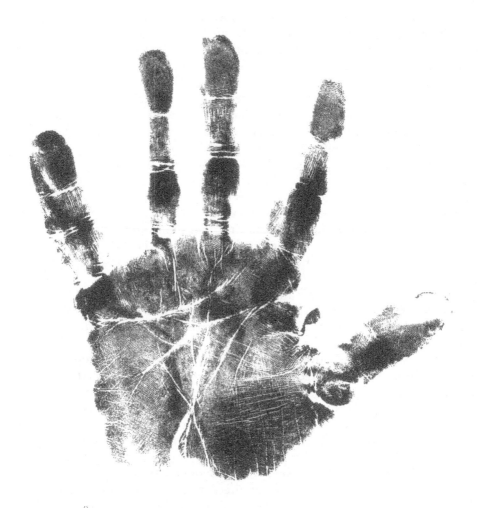

Howard Chandler Christy

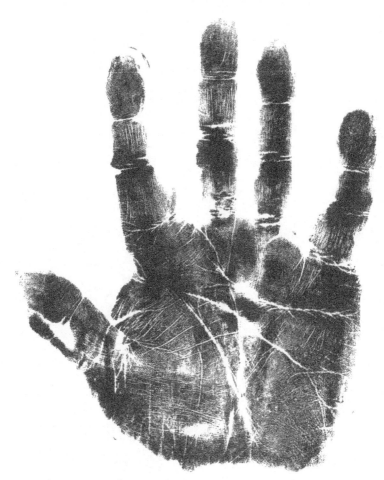

Edwina Dumm

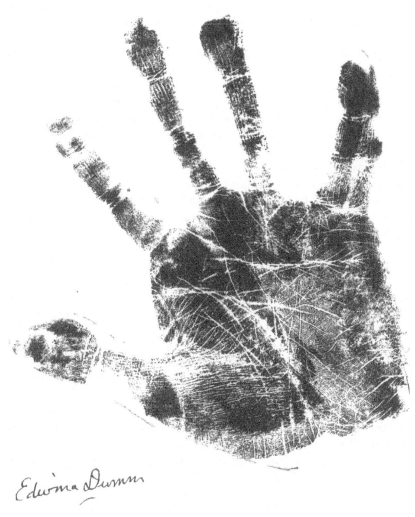

Edwina Dumm

significance. First, the line rising from the life line and running to the second finger indicates success coming from her own exertions; second, the line rising from her head line and running to the mount of Saturn shows recognition coming from the fancy of the public; there is an indication of success in the line of destiny that, nevertheless, shows home ties, obligations and duties; and fourth, an unusual line runs from the life line to the center of the mount of Jupiter under the forefinger and ends in the star of ambition realized and unexpected honor. Edwina has realized a great deal. She is to realize much more in the years to come.

Some of my readers may have experienced the thrill of walking through an Art Gallery or museum and finding a picture or some phase of art expression signed by one whom they had met or knew intimately.

That was my experience when I visited Kensington Museum in London, sauntered through the room devoted to representative lithographs of outstanding commercial artists, and found one signed by Ervine Metzl.

"It was the only American work deemed worthy of a place in the collection" the custodian explained.

This was all the more surprising because I had heard nothing from the artist about this honor, though I knew him well enough for him to have spoken to me about it.

When I say that his hands show amazing contradictions, the incident I have just cited helps to prove my statement.

His palm shows audacity and conservatism. First, in the wide flare of the thumb from the hand indicating a spendthrift of time, strength and money, counting the cost afterwards, yet with the conservatism of a square palm in which practical results come from sober realization. In his square palm he obeys the laws of the community following its rules and requirements. In the breadth under the fingers, there is shown a liking for activity which in this case is evidenced mentally rather than physically, since the palm is flexible and resilient.

Short fingers show his dislike of detail and the tendency to take things in their entirety; to absorb experience, expression and result as a whole and analyze afterwards.

In its length, the first finger indicates his ability as a leader, director and executive who can plan work for others. The rather square tip reveals his hesitancy in accepting first impressions without submitting them to the analysis which his nails, being shorter and broader than they are long, indicate.

In his second finger the long first phalange discloses a semi-mystical characteristic directly at variance with the square palms, denoting his demand for realism. The wisdom and prudence shown by that middle phalange is an additional balance acting as a deterrent to his tendency to expend energy unnecessarily.

The third finger with its almost spatulate tip denotes his liking for the unusual, the out-of-the-ordinary in any phase of art expression. In the length of the first phalange is shown his interest in line, form and construction rather than color.

A much needed asset is the evidence of diplomacy shown by the unusual length of the fourth finger. It serves to smooth out contention, resentment and hurt feelings which his impetuous speech has created. His long first phalange shows the gift of verbal expression and the pointed tip reveals that much needed tact in the management of matters where the driving force of his executive ability has failed to take cognizance of the limitations of those working under his direction.

In all fingers the third phalanges are rather full though of varying lengths. First, there is the liking for the comforts of daily living. He can see nothing gained by the endurance of physical hardship or limitation if there is no need of taking cost into consideration.

The long third phalange of the fourth finger indicates the commercial acumen which he can apply to the value of his own work as well as to judge the value of the work of others. The wide flare between his first and second fingers denoting excessive independence of thought and between the third and fourth, the equal independence of action, show him to be an extremist. Fortunately his thumbs indicate the qualities that act as a restraining power or guiding force. The long first phalange indicative of will is directed and guided by that long second phalange of logic and reason. It is finely formed in the balancing of a determination which could degenerate into dogged obstinacy if it was not directed by the brilliant mentality—logic and reason—capable of seeing all sides of a situation denoted in the waist-like formation of that second phalange.

One of the outstanding characteristics shown by the lines in Mr. Metzl's hand is the beautifully shaped trident of fame, fortune and honor under the third finger of the left hand. This indicates the natural expression of idealism. The drooping headline in this hand shows an imagination which biases judgment, and creates a world of dreams rather than concrete results.

Notice too in the left hand, the whorl like a finger print on the lower part of the imagination. The genius who could dream dreams, but who needed development in practical fields of expression to acquire an un-

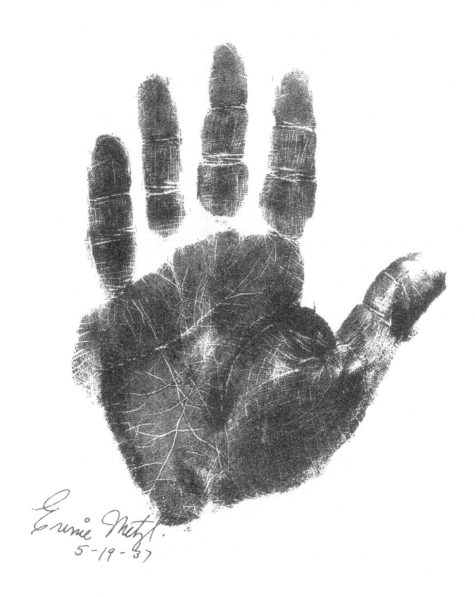

Ernie Metzl.
5-19-37

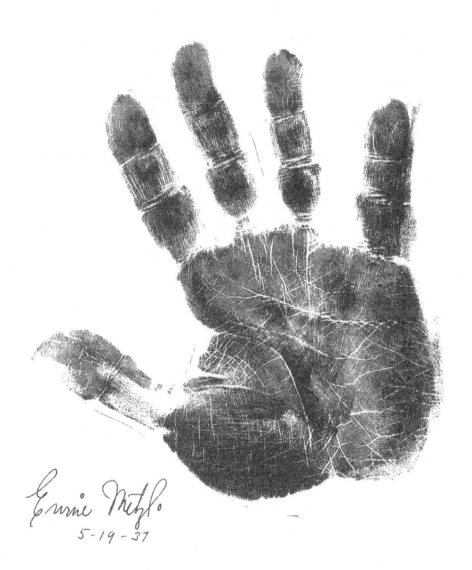

Ernie Metylo

5-19-37

derstanding to use the tools necessary to carve out and make his visions real.

Turn to the right hand, and note first how that strong will directed by logic and reason, has developed a straight head line dealing with facts rather than dreams. It has required persistent plodding effort to overcome the dislike of detail and the innate mental irritability over delayed results. Note too how the wonderful talent line in the right hand in place of being the trident of fame, fortune and honor as in the left, has developed into a definite line of one continuous effort in art expression.

Mr. Metzl has wisely garnered his forces and turned all of his gifts into an intelligent development of one phase of creative art requiring not only the finest of technique, but the use of other qualities—imagination and daring experiment—indicated in the general flare of the fingers and thumbs and the spatulate tip of the third finger.

His head line shows the developed intelligence by means of which he can use the warm glowing colors contributed by the Mount of Venus and the imagination lighted by the whorl of inspiration, which places his work under the expression of creative art rather than cold commercialism.

Chapter 18: *On Unknown Trails*

"How," demanded an Editor who was considering the publication of some of my work, "do you get people who are scientists and great men of affairs to lend themselves to a thing like hand reading? Do they believe in it?"

"Many of them do not," I replied dryly, "and they have their hands read for that very reason."

"But I don't see that."

"Scientists," I informed him, "and inventors, as well as men and women of great affairs, are and must be open minded persons. Most of them know nothing at all about the—as I believe and call it—SCIENCE of hand reading. They know something of the work of charlatans, but they also know of charlatans in medicine, in general science and in all affairs. Rather than cast a doubt upon a possible science of which they know nothing, they have extended their hands to me and have allowed me to read them. The very qualities that sent them out upon unknown trails and returned them as Lions made it imperative that I, as a hand reader, should have the opportunity to demonstrate my work. Some of these people have been impressed by my readings to a point where they have made a further investigation of the subject. But the most of them withhold judgment, in perfect courtesy to a possible fellow scientist upon a trail unknown to them, but not a false trail until it is proved to be false.

Dr. Roy Chapman Andrews, recently appointed head director of the Museum of Natural History in New York City, a scientist whose years of work have been crowded with honors, was perfectly willing to have me come to his office and read his hands. He readily made an appointment. After that I had to wait with patience. For the whimsical character who roamed the oceans from the Arctic to the East Indies in studies of whales, and who after that led the largest expeditions ever sent to Asia into the Gobi Desert, opening up that unknown region of the earth to motor traffic and bringing back to us knowledge of wide and varied character, from fossils to gold, proved to be a bit elusive. I kept three appointments before I saw Dr. Andrews, but it was not from lack of interest on his part or indeed on the part of the people who work with him. As I began the reading, the group grew in numbers. Dr. Andrews as a real sport of a scientist, did not mind. What I found in his hands I might shout to the listening world. But I felt a bit disturbed in making a frank reading. I said so, and the crowd melted away.

I was looking at the hands of a man of power—I think that the reader

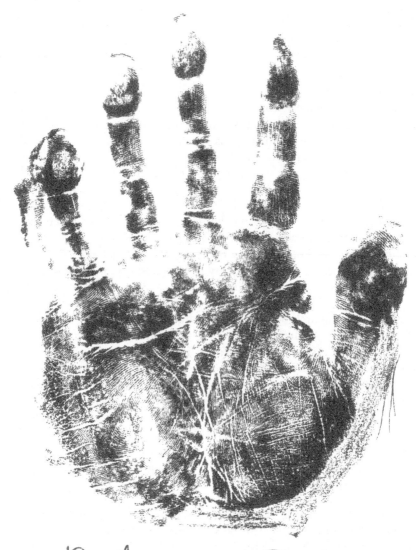

Roy Chapman Andrews
June 27 1933

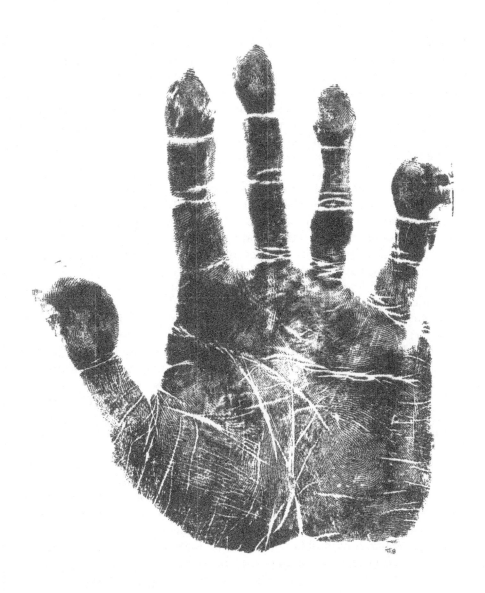

Roy Chapman Andrews
June 27, 1933

will know that by the prints shown. They are hands with many conflicting characteristics but dominated by few: firm hard square palms, the palms of the man who sees the necessity for a practical foundation for what he does, and who will work out the plans essential to that foundation. Great independence in thought and action is shown in the wide flare between the third and fourth fingers, and coolness and courage in time of danger is disclosed in the high development of upper Mars, just under the heart line on the outside of the hand. Add to these a definite whorl shown upon the Mount of the Moon, into which the head line dips—indeed the whorl seems almost an obstruction to the head line in the left hand—and you have a man whose foresight is pronounced along intellectual lines. And top this with the most significant sign of all, the spatulate tip of the third finger, that certain indication of originality, and the double joints of the thumbs, an equally certain indication of love of the dramatic, and you have a condensed picture of Andrews, a courageous, independent, practical character with a gift of prescience and decided originality which will develop along dramatic lines. Certainly Andrews' expeditions have been dramatic.

There are less obvious traits that speak more intimately of the man himself. The thick, long first phalange of the thumb is that of a possessor of the power of iron discipline. The practical palms indicate a love of order; the short fingers show that he wants someone else to maintain that order. But if he must maintain it himself, he can. The length of his first finger shows a strong sense of responsibility and the length of the nail phalange of that finger adds integrity and a high sense of honor. Andrews will always live up to all responsibilities he undertakes, even against mighty odds. The length of his fourth finger, Mercury, shows tact, and the length of its first phalange, the gift of words. He prefers talking to writing. The nails are broader than they are long. Andrews is argumentative and introspective, sometimes mentally irritable, and apt to become belligerent. However, he has a very flexible thumb, and suavity comes to his aid accompanied by a delightful sense of humor that has saved him again and again, a sense of humor which is shown in the development of the mount of Mercury beneath the fourth finger.

On the hands of most famous men and women are definite lines under the third fingers. There are none in the hands of Dr. Andrews. But upon the mount under the third finger is a less usual sign, a circle upon the mount of Apollo, an indication of glory and of lasting success.

From the heat of the Gobi desert it will be refreshing to plunge into the sea with William Beebe, Director of the Department of Scientific Research for the New York Zoological Society, and best known to us because of his having explored the depths of the ocean to a degree never before achieved by men. Beebe's studies of birds and of insects and animals are, from the scientific standpoint, equally or more important. But there is something alluring and challenging in assailing the hidden darkness of great depths, and the imagination insists upon examining this long, lean man, not only in the light of scientific, but of physical achievement. William Beebe has hands so sinewy, so hard that it was with great difficulty that impressions could be made to show anything of the centers of the palms. His palms, square and firm, are much leaner, but not unlike those of Andrews. His liking for physical activity because of a definite purpose is indicated in their breadth and firmness just under the fingers. Ceaselessly active, there always is another task waiting. His life line is that of a man of great vitality and endurance. The long, middle phalanges of his fingers at once places him in the ranks of those whose lives must be dominated by mentality. The length of the first phalanges of all his fingers, and the disconnected and broken line of fate or destiny running from the base of the palm to beneath the second finger tell of the idealist. Beebe will follow what he feels he must follow, even if he wrecks his personal fortunes in so doing. The length and shape of the third phalanges of his fingers are those of a man who is quite indifferent to comfort when there is an end in view. The long first finger is that of the true executive, and the development of upper Mars between the heart and head lines toward the outside of the palm shows courage and coolness plus resourcefulness in time of danger. Again, as in the hands of Andrews, we find the spatulate tip of the third finger which shows his interest in originality in art expression. The length of that third finger, however, adds another quality. Beebe has a keen appreciation of beauty in detail, in the markings of the wing of a bird, the gleaming hues of the scales of tropical fish or the grace of a wild animal. He loves color, form and line, through whatever medium they may be evidenced.

On the first phalanges of his fingers and thumbs Beebe has small whorls, an indication of a man who is not swayed by the acclamation of the public, a marking which is sustained by the similar whorls under the third finger in each hand. His idealism prevents him from responding much to the admiration of people even when he feels he has earned at least a part of it. These marks are found in the hands of men who are curiously detached in their personal attitude towards people. They realize that their work is of little value unless it is brought to people, hence in that sense they need people. But they are continually absorbed in new activities on unknown trails leading to fresh discoveries—their

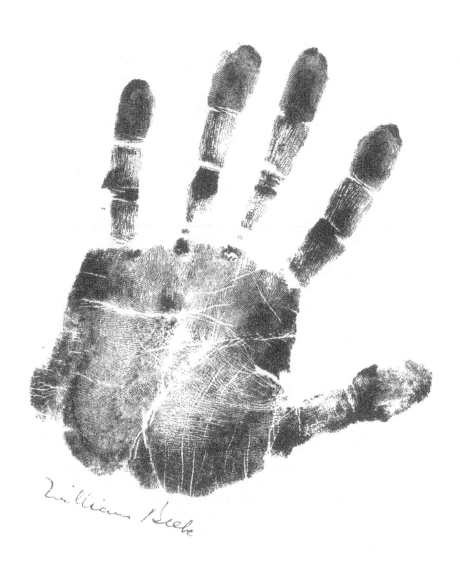

William Beebe

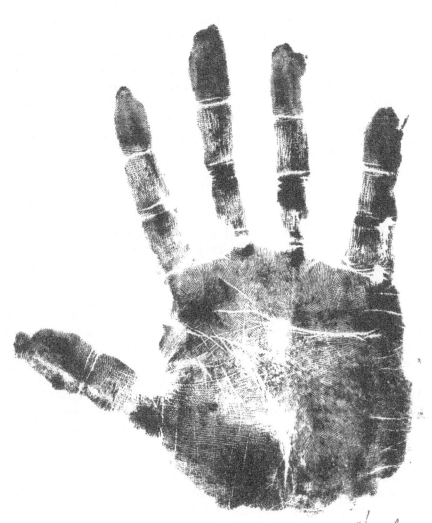

William Beebe

15-12-'34

appreciation of the plaudits of the public is because of definite results based on the use of these scientific facts placed before them.

This independence of thought is again indicated in the flare between the first and second fingers. Beebe is a law unto himself. The long nail phalange of the second finger with the high development of the mount of Saturn under that finger, shows a strong sense of responsibility and of prudence that help in forming his personal law. Between the second and third fingers is a flare which, with the long first phalanges of those fingers, indicates the idealist who almost literally "takes no thought for the morrow." The wide flare of the fourth finger signifies quickness of action in emergency, an instant reaction between hand and brain. He has the gift of words in the long first phalange, a gift eagerly attested by readers of his delightful books, "Edge of the Jungle," "World's End," "Exploring with Beebe," etc. The length of the fourth finger shows diplomacy, and tact is further evidenced in its pointed tip.

William Beebe's hands then show him to be a man filled with idealism, a gifted man of high mental ability, able to direct his activities and highly sensitized to the manifestations of form, line and color, who follows his own ideas in his life and who likes people and their admiration but is not swayed by them. The long first phalange of his thumbs adds that his highly developed will power is quietly forceful, and backs and sustains him to the limit.

I must confess that when I went to see Dr. Raymond Ditmars it was with a great curiosity not unmixed with fear. I am so afraid of a snake that I run from a dead one, and here I was calling upon a man who not only knows and understands snakes, but who has sought them all over the world in many hazardous undertakings and has become their interpreter to man in many writings, "The Reptile Book," "Snakes of the World," etc., etc. It was with much interest that I went to the New York Bronx Zoological Park where Dr. Ditmars is Curator of Animals. I was surprised when I was greeted by a soft voiced, scholarly looking gentleman with a strong cordial hand clasp, that gave one confidence in his sincerity and integrity. When you look closely at the powerful hands of the accompanying impression you will notice that the palms have a most unusual number of whorls upon its surface—on the mount of the Moon, between the first and second fingers, the second and third fingers, and the third and fourth fingers. It could be called a "seeing" hand, that is, its owner has foresight in many directions and can apply, indeed he must apply, his qualities in the light of that foresight. I will try to show you how this works out in the man's life.

Ditmar's palm is square, firm, broad under the fingers, and about as broad at its base. It is the palm of a man who likes to work both physically and mentally, a man who has respect for law and order in life and his own surroundings. The long head line indicates a certain methodical form of procedure as well as great intelligence. His thumbs are flexible, a sign of adaptability, and the flare of the thumb shows an indifference to creature comforts—that he can endure deprivations if necessary to his ultimate success. Hunger, hardship, fatigue count for little with Ditmars, but the short broad nails show that he can be mentally irritated when indifference, opposition and carelessness upon the part of any of his associates interferes with the success of definitely laid plans.

The highly developed upper mount of Mars on the outside of the hand under the heart line shows quiet force, coolness in danger and physical bravery—great assets in the hands of all followers of "unknown trails."

Now it is time for the whorls. Many hands show a whorl—looking like a thumb print—on the mount of the Moon. This I have termed the sixth sense because it usually denotes a gift of prescience. Dr. Ditmars' palms show an unusual number of like markings on the mounts under the fingers. These denote foresight in the application of the traits denoted by the fingers and the mounts under them. While the length of the first finger shows executive ability, ambition and a desire for leadership, the length of the long first phalange reveals a certain modesty, almost a desire for self-effacement because of what seems to him the great difference between the things he wishes to accomplish and the results which he has been able to attain and which are acclaimed by the public. The whorl beneath the finger opens his mental eye to the recognition that the public as a whole would fail to grasp his point of view and misconstrue his modesty as a weakness and so invite misunderstanding and unjust criticism. His only course, therefore, is personally to show the public his activities, the grave dangers and hazard to health and life entailed on his expeditions. The plain recital is but doing justice to his co-workers and assistants. Another whorl almost under the second finger is another "lamp unto his feet" enabling him to avoid mistakes. For in the middle phalange of his second finger is indicated a strong characteristic of wisdom and prudence. His innate tendency would be to play safe and feel justified in allowing his past work to speak for him. This mental searchlight enables him to use his wisdom and prudence in safeguarding not only his own life but the lives of those associated with him. The length and shape of this second finger show a serious mind, deeply absorbed in his chosen work, fully cognizant of the danger and the hazards, and en-

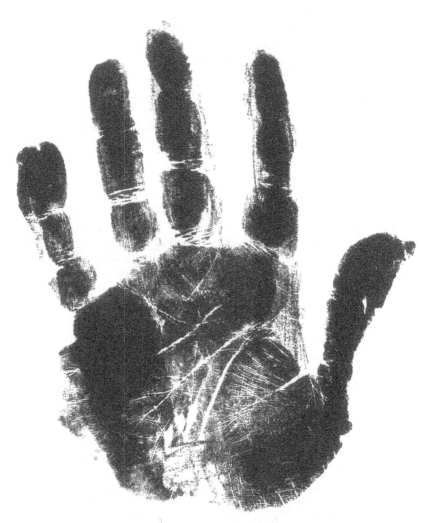

Raymond L. Ditmars
June 29, 1933

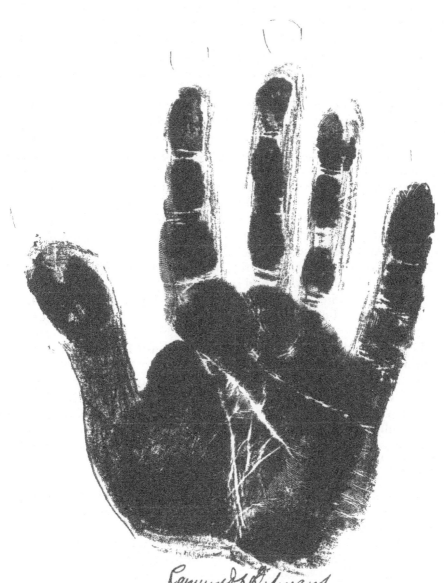

Raymond L Ditmars
June 29, 1933

abling him to plan and work out the details necessary to insure a safe return.

The whorl between the second and third fingers, toward the base of the second finger, is the flashing light of encouragement and faith in himself which enables him to overcome the naturally somber side of his nature and gives him the impetus to "count his mercies" and by so doing forget his "miseries." It lights the path of safety between the over-caution shown in the second finger and the over-confidence indicated in the third finger.

The third finger is somewhat longer than the first, indicating a natural tendency to take a chance—after using wisdom and caution in preparation—while the spatulate formation reveals the originality and resourcefulness both physical and mental which he brings to meet any emergency in his varied activities.

Doctor Ditmars' hands disclose a nature with many contradictory traits, but the development of those qualities leading to success is shown in the definite trident at the base of the third finger in the left hand, indicating the fame, fortune and honor which are his by right of achievement. At present there are two defined lines in his right hand—the absence of a clearly developed third line shows that the future holds for Dr. Ditmars additional honor and recognition.

Vilhjalmur Stefansson came to my home under the friendly piloting of Kenyon Nicholson, the playwright. I am quite certain that Stefansson did not want to come, nor did he want his hands read. But he came, and he gave me the prints of his hands because, as I have said in the beginning of this chapter, a real scientist and explorer never decries an unknown trail as false until he has so proved it. You know Stefansson as an Arctic explorer, an associate professor of anthropology at Harvard University, and a writer of such books as "Life with the Eskimo," "The Friendly Arctic," "The Northward Course of Empire." To spend months battling the ice and cold, year upon year, demands not only strength of body but strength of purpose. The long, clear, deep life line shown in both hands testifies to the abundance of vitality needed, and this line is the more significant in that the various cross lines indicate that in the early part of his life Stefansson had certain health obstacles which he has definitely overcome. His strength of purpose seems to date from the very acute break in the line of destiny running up the middle of the palm next to the life line. This line, in both hands, starts not at the base of the palm, as is usual, but from the middle of the hand on the plain of Mars. Lines starting at this point tell of a man who achieves success from his own personal exertions, not from any chance or opportunity nor from

127

the assistance of others. These may, of course, be contributing factors, but the man himself makes his career and his work.

Stefansson's palms are square and hard, rather unyielding, indicating the man who demands facts as understood by him. He grinds statements presented to him through his own mental mill. The firmness of the palm indicates an unyielding tenacity of purpose. The palm is broad under the fingers, showing a liking for out-door life and its rugged activities, and a dislike of enforced inactivity necessitated by desk work. The writing of Stefansson's books must have been real drudgery to him.

In his left hand the thumb has a wide stretch from the fingers; in the right it is closer. This indicates, first, a natural ability to act quickly in an emergency or to avail himself of opportunities that may advance his aim. The restriction and added stiffness of the right thumb are signs of a caution deliberately developed and an added ability to take command of a situation from a mental standpoint. The length of the fourth finger shows a considerable power of diplomacy, but it is the kind of diplomacy used in the ironing out of difficulties encountered, not that which makes meeting people an accomplishment. On the contrary, the square tip of the fourth finger shows a lack of tact, only softened in the eyes of the just by the integrity and honesty of purpose shown in the long first phalange of the first finger.

Again in the right hand we see changes definitely and deliberately made by the man himself. The first finger of that hand is a little longer than that of the left hand. Stefansson has developed his executive ability through the necessity of assuming responsibility, and has become a fine leader. The length of the third finger, which is longer than the forefinger, reveals another most unusual characteristic. This length shows he has an abundance of zest and enthusiasm in tackling a problem sufficient to induce him to take a risk despite the caution shown in the close joining of his life and head line, while the spatulate tip of this finger discloses his originality in meeting an unexpected necessity.

Under the first finger is a star, a sign of recognition and honor and of ambition realized, and under the third finger in each hand is the star of celebrity.

When on a brilliantly sunny day in April, 1930, I made the impressions of the hands of Dr. Harvey W. Wiley, he was eighty-five years of age. The entire history of those years was there for me to see—the history of a search for truth and of the spread of that truth as an aid to all humanity. Dr. Wiley will perhaps be longest remembered for his work in behalf of pure food and for the better understanding of the value of food to man. All of his life he was a fighter; from the early years when, as a pioneer in

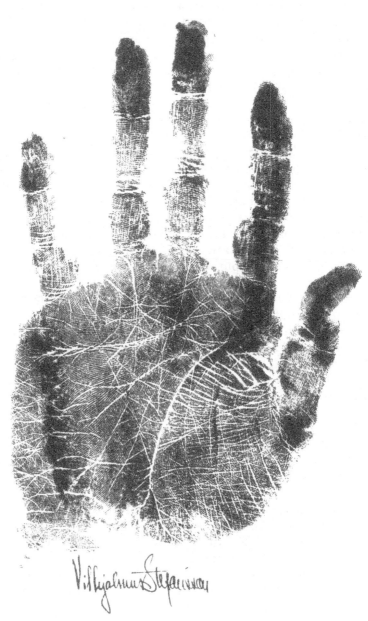

Vilhjalmur Stefansson

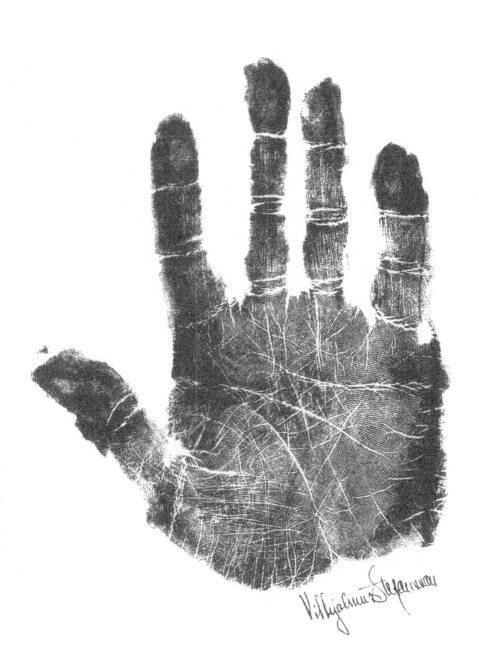

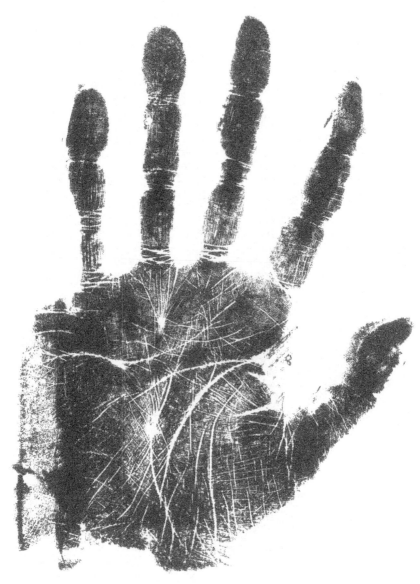

Harvey W. Wiley.

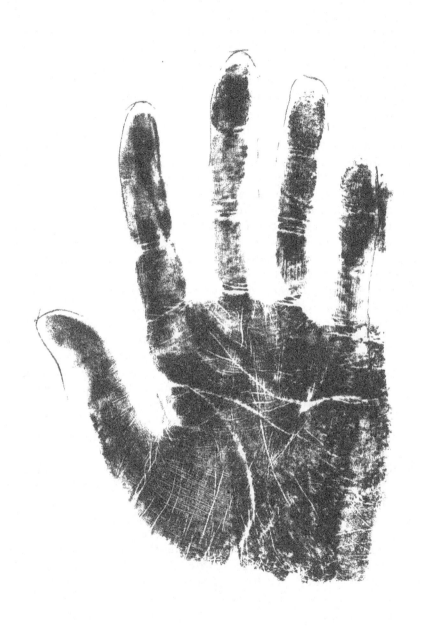

Harvey W. Wiley

the "barter and swap" exchange of physical work for mental food, he managed to fight his way through Hanover College and thus acquire an education which he enlarged and enriched as his work necessitated. Dr. Wiley's adventures on unknown trails explored not physical but mental ignorance. His hands, however, in many aspects were very like those of the explorer of natural phenomena.

The square palm was that of the man who deals with facts, and the breadth of the palm under the fingers shows his love of out-of-doors activity. The long fingers, all except the third showing the rounded tip, belong definitely to the man who was interested in a mental quest. They mark the explorer of the intellectual. That long third finger, longer than the first, testified to the lure of the unexpected, and in Dr. Wiley s hands was strengthened by the love of the dramatic element in life shown in the double jointed thumb. But the tip of this long third finger was square, not the usual spatulate tip of the explorer. Here is an essential difference in character. The spatulate tip shows the seeker of the unknown; the square tip is that of the seeker of truth. The true explorer seeks the new, the man of Dr. Wiley's type seeks truth new or old, perhaps truth that has been at our doors through many years, a prosaic form of truth and without glamour, unrecognized.

Few things could be prosaic to Dr. Wiley. His fingers, smooth to the second joints, showed decided inspirational qualities, and at the base of the palm was the well-developed mount of imagination crowned with the whorl of the sixth sense. Thus was shown a power not only of insight, but of insight plus imagination which could glorify the commonplace. Dr. Wiley was a true executive, as revealed in his long first finger, with a love of power and ambition indicated in the developed mount of Jupiter at its base. His heart line, starting between the first and second fingers, sent a fork toward the center of the mount. Heart lines like this are found in the hands of those whose affections and ambitions are centered in a selfless desire towards all mankind. The long phalanges of all his fingers denoted an almost over-development of conscientious effort. But Dr. Wiley was not a gloomy character. His natural buoyancy, shown in the rounded tip of his second finger, and the enormous physical vitality which his life line disclosed, made it impossible for him to recognize defeat. Whatever his trials, he came through smiling.

In the left hand under the third finger you can see a fanlike formation of many lines indicating possibilities of recognition in many lines of work. In the right hand these have merged into two lines, the lure of the unknown trail and the love of humanity; these are his lines of honor.

The hands of Bernarr Macfadden are those of the man who possesses such an abundance of vitality that he must, perforce, make his mark upon his generation. As you can see, the hands are definitely spatulate in formation, broad under the finger, sloping somewhat towards the wrists, a type that in a less vigorous development would be that of the artist. In a hand of such vigor, this is the type of palm which indicates the man of almost unlimited physical and mental energy with an excess of independence in thought and action. Compared with the ordinary run of human beings such a man is a human dynamo and usually he is the possessor of many devoted friends and many active enemies, the former admiring and the latter bewailing the very excess of his activities. Palms of this type also show a practical outlook upon life and an ability to be methodical and persistent along a definite course of action. The length of his first finger reveals a naturally limited amount of executive ability and a dislike of assuming responsibility for others. The dominance of the nail phalange, however, shows a conscience which often forces him to assume responsibilities. The rounded tip of the first finger shows a power to readjust his mental attitude and to use the diplomacy indicated in the length of his fourth finger to meet and disarm opposition.

Under the first finger is a high mount revealing a great love of approbation. The rounded tip of the second finger is evidence of a natural optimism. "Hope springs eternal" in Bernarr Macfadden and this naturally sunny outlook is backed by the fighting quality shown in the development of upper Mars on the outside of the hand under the heart line.

The amazing vital quality of the man is shown in many ways, but more significantly in the development of the huge mount of Venus. Very few hands have such a great development, the only one I have so far examined in these pages is that of Lawrence Tibbett. Macfadden literally cannot shut off his high powered engine; in many ways it runs him, rather than he, it. He must act; he must go on. In his early years the frayed life line shows serious impairment of health. But even then, that amazing vital force and the buoyancy shown in the round tip of the second finger, plus the fighting power indicated in upper Mars, helped him to continue fighting and believing in what he was able to accomplish—a complete establishment of health. In such a fight the wisdom and prudence indicated in the first and second phalanges of the second fingers enabled him to overcome obstacles; later they helped him build his strange and highly successful personal career. Bernarr Macfadden's deep and straight line of destiny, fate, success or financial line, beginning in the right hand low at the base of the palm, showing need for work early in life, then joining the life line indicating that he was held down by home ties and duties, and

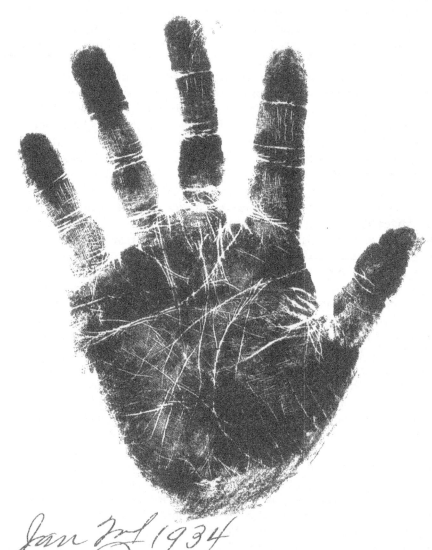

Jan 7rf 1934
Bernarr Macfadden

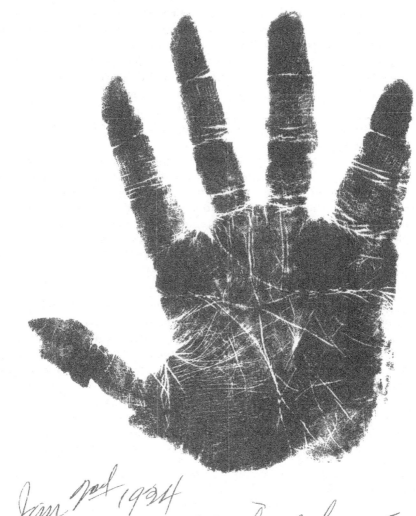

Jan 1st 1934

Bernarr Macfadden

then separating and going directly up under the second finger, shows success won in whatever course he was pursuing.

The long deep head line in the right hand reveals his ability to see his way clear even when the path of his progress is apparently barred. In the rounded tip of his thumb is indicated his impatience over slow returns, but with the strong will shown in the first phalange of the thumb and its flare from his hand, is revealed an almost reckless determination that, by its very intensity, sweeps obstacles out of his path.

Like almost every man in this chapter he has the long third finger of the born gambler. As in the other men this instinct is curbed by the practical palms, so that instead of being gamblers in the ordinary accepted sense, they "take a chance" on the unknown trails. The square tip is like that of Dr. Wiley and indicates a love of truth and a desire for reason in all things.

In addition to the diplomacy mentioned, the pointed tip of the fourth finger shows tact, and the length of the first phalange the gift of words: the man is never at a loss in speech or in writing. The strongly marked sixth sense on the mount of the Moon has helped in all his undertakings—in the establishment of his great publishing business, in his work on health and a better understanding of man's physical needs, in the building of his sanitarium, and in the "penny" restaurants which year after year have ministered to the wants of the needy in New York City. Usually his gift of prescience has known the moment at which to start a new enterprise, but when it has failed—or he has failed to recognize its promptings—his recovery has been so rapid that his financial equilibrium has never been seriously threatened. The clear markings of talent lines in the hands of this gifted man are many. But they are dominated by two, and the hand indicates that these two are financial ability and his gift of words.

These Lions who have ventured afar upon unknown trails have endeared themselves to me through common possessions—high courage, conscientiousness and willingness to take a chance. I am sure that these qualities, shown plainly in their hands, will likewise endear them to my readers.

Chapter 19: *These Lions Must Roar*

Diverse as are the Lions whose hands are read in this chapter, they have one common and striking bond. All of them place a great value upon the spoken word. Nearly all of them write, and write well, but this does not satisfy them. They must express themselves vocally to find real satisfaction.

Had William Norman Guthrie lived in the twelfth century, he would have been among the Crusaders. In this, the twentieth century, he is rector of St. Marks in-the-Bouwerie, in New York City, and from this conservative stronghold his vitality leaps forth in the name of the cause to which he has devoted himself.

Dr. Guthrie is a brave, even a belligerent man. On the percussion of the palm above the mount of the Moon there is a great development of the mount of upper Mars. His stiff thumbs show strength of will, and persistence. The unusually long nail phalange of his second finger, longer than the second phalange, reveals a religious zeal so intense that it tends to push aside the powers of logic and reason shown in the length of the second phalange of his thumbs. His long fingers show care in detail, and his square palm indicates recognition of authority and of law and an insistence upon order in all things. His first finger is a little longer in his right hand than in his left. He has developed his executive ability. In the long third phalange of his first finger is shown a desire for approbation. This is a sincere desire to be worthy of his calling; he is extremely conscientious in all things as is shown by the length of all of the nail phalanges.

Dr. Guthrie is a mixture of the practical and mystical. The rounded tip of the second finger is not that of the optimist, but of the man who cannot admit defeat. The long and broad first phalange is that of the mystic, but the level head line of his right hand shows an acquired ability to keep to logic. His third finger reveals a love of line and of color, while the extremely long fourth finger discloses a great diplomacy, an asset to a zealot. The tip of the fourth finger is rounded and further emphasizes his tact, while the long first phalange of this finger shows fluency in expression. The fullness of the mounts of lower Venus and the Moon reveals his love of music, of melody and rhythm, and at the base of the mount of the Moon on each hand is a very large whorl. William Norman Guthrie is Scotch, and this whorl, according to the Scotch tradition, shows that he is attuned to the still small voice of wisdom that resides within every man if he can but hear it.

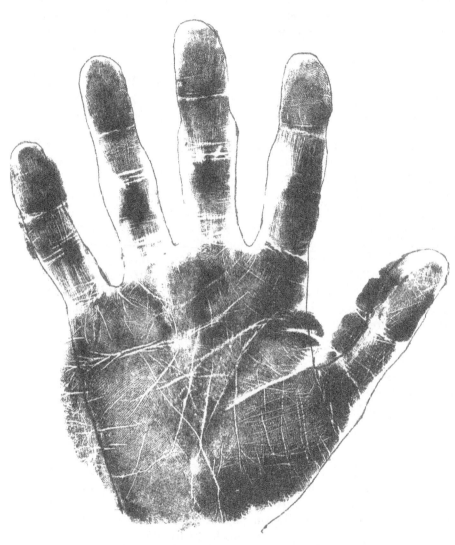

Wm Guthrie
Nov 3ᵈ 1934

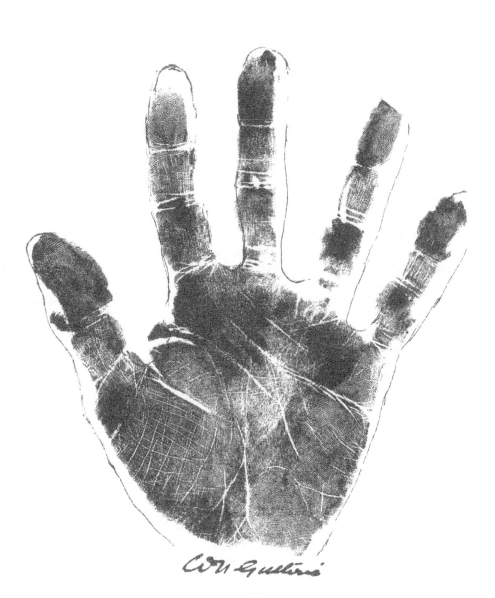

In the early part of his life, the life line shows lines of interference that suggest that he drove himself beyond his physical powers. Dominated by his zeal he has successfully strengthened his physical resistance, and the life line is both deep and clear. His is the hand of a man who is driven by a force that seems greater than his personal will; at times he succeeds in emerging and becoming more of what he thinks of as "himself." At other times he is submerged and loses all sense of personality in the work with which he has identified himself.

Stephen S. Wise, Rabbi of the Free Synagogue of New York, has a voice familiar to listeners all over the world. Rabbi Wise, like Dr. Guthrie, has the full development of upper Mars that indicates bravery and belligerency against opposition. The full mount of lower Mars, situated on upper Venus, indicates also aggression and resistance. His palm is conic, the shape usually found in the hands of those interested in art expression, and the fine texture of the skin shows that he is a man with great powers for absorbing knowledge and for discrimination as to the use of knowledge that will most ably serve his ends. His strong thumb indicates tremendous will power, and the relative length of the thumb phalanges shows that his will is a force directed by his logic and reason. The long first phalange of his first finger shows conscientious integrity, and its rounded tip a quick perception. The long third phalange and the full mount of Jupiter beneath show his liking for power, while the length of the whole finger indicates decided executive ability.

The second finger is square-tipped. This is a sign of restraint, and when considered with the close joining of his life line and head line at the beginning, an indication of caution, reveals that Dr. Wise is by no means reckless in his fighting. The third phalange of the second finger discloses in length and shape his desire for a home and for those he loves about him. His third finger with its rounded tip shows a great appreciation of idealism in art, and the fourth finger tip, also rounded, reveals tact. The length of the nail phalange shows his gift of expression in speech; the second phalange tells of his gift both in speech and writing. Like Dr. Guthrie, his fourth finger is very long, and is a sign of his diplomacy. He has gained in initiative as the flare of his thumb from his hand, greater in the right than in the left, testifies.

His heart line starting from the mount of Jupiter is that of a man loyal to his family and friends. The full development of the mount of Venus adds warmth, tenderness and sympathetic understanding, and shows a great love of music. He is not only a highly gifted man, but a man with a great appreciation for almost any phase of human endeavor, par-

133

ticularly in the art world, with a response that is so whole-hearted to any human appeal that his friends must be legion, and his admirers, even those who have never seen him, must regard him with a warmth that approaches affection.

The name of John Haynes Holmes is as well known because of his conservative radicalism as is that of William Norman Guthrie for his radical conservatism. Dr. Holmes is now pastor of the Community Church in New York City. He is innately a philosopher with his interests wholly in humanitarian projects. His hands affirm this, first in the long fingers with their developed joints, and again in the long nail phalanges. His flexible thumbs indicate an easy adaptability to all sorts of people, as well as to all kinds of surroundings. This is a curious hand.

While the long nail phalanges proclaim the zealot, the unusually long third phalanges of all the fingers denote the appreciation of the material and the practical. Without lowering his standard of spiritual thinking, Dr. Holmes recognizes the imperative need that man must live. His nails, broader than they are long, are those of the analyst; he waits and considers conditions before acting. His head line, only slightly sloping, is that of the man of common sense, and this modifies the excessive independence of thought and of action suggested by the wide flare between the fingers. The first phalange of the thumb shows a strong will, but the longer second phalange indicates that this will is directed by reason. The rounding tip of his first finger reveals an almost inspirational quality to sense conditions and to follow through to the heart of the cause. The square tip of the second finger and the long first phalange belong to the religious philosopher who demands truth. This demand for truth is repeated in the long nail phalange of the third finger, truth in art, in science, in living. His heart line, beginning in a fork under Jupiter, again reveals idealism in a love of humanity. The mount of Venus is full, and in this man suggests a much needed vitality that is, however, not always sufficient to sustain him when he overdoes—and possessors of those great flares between thumbs and fingers and the fingers themselves, always do. His attitude towards money is reckless; for himself it is a negligible factor, for others it is essential as a means to better living.

Under the third finger in the right hand are lines of talent and ability absent in the left. Dr. Holmes has developed them there by sheer hard work.

Like Rabbi Stephen Wise, S. Parkes Cadman, radio minister of the Federal Council of Churches of Christ in America, was known to hundreds of thousands of listeners who never met him.

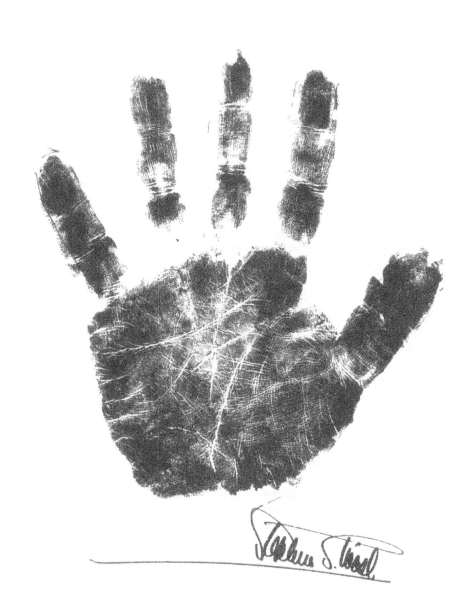

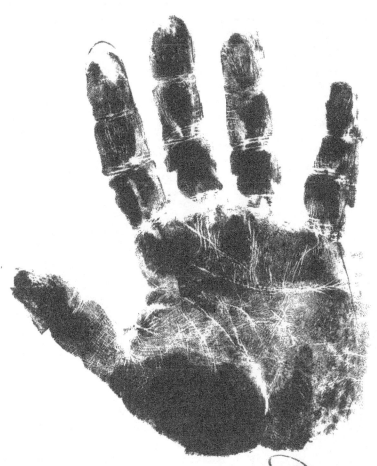

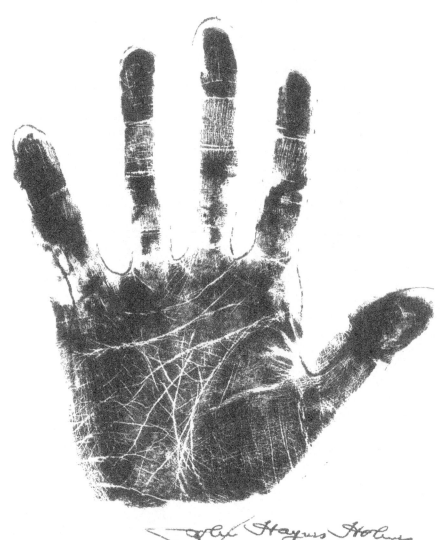

John Haynes Holmes
November 15, 1953

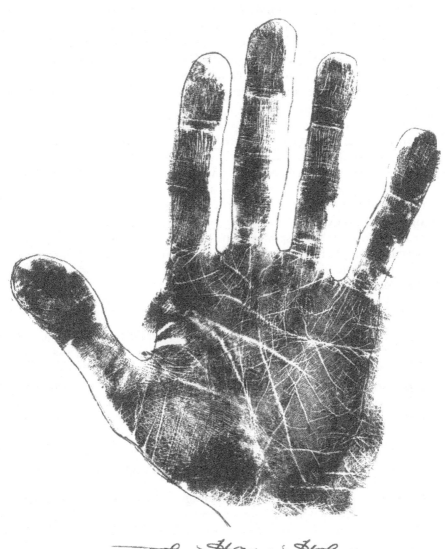

John Haynes Holmes

Nov. 15, 1933

Like Rabbi Wise, Dr. Cadman had both mounts of Mars, lower and upper, well developed. He, too, could and did fight for his beliefs. Notice in his right hand how his long head line runs over the mount of upper Mars, suggesting an intellectual and not a physical fighter, and that his mental growth was strengthened by victories won. His was a mental hand. The long middle phalanges of all his fingers reveal that mentality dominated his emotions. His head and life line were joined at the beginning: he was a cautious man. His thumb was long and showed both considerable will power and power of logic and reason which directed that will. Add to this the clear common sense indicated in the long head line, and you have a complete picture of a man of poise and balance well fitted to conduct his affairs.

Dr. Cadman had his obstacles. His fingers, shorter than his palm, revealed a dislike of detail. He tended to grasp a problem in its entirety, and the length of the executive finger suggests that having grasped it he could direct others to aid in handling its minutiae. The rounded tip of his first finger shows a quick perception, and the first and second phalanges, representing the qualities of mercy and justice, are balanced. This balance was a check upon his tendency to give extravagantly of himself and of all he possessed in response to the calls made upon him. The spread between his fingers is that of the giver, the extremist, but the characteristics of caution and common sense balanced this tendency and reduced it to the practical.

Dr. Cadman liked appreciation, as the long third phalange of his first finger and the full mount beneath, clearly show. The rounded tip of the second finger declares him to have been an optimist, and the length of the third phalange of this finger indicates his love of home as a haven of peace and understanding. The third finger has a spatulate tip, a sign of a gift of originality. The middle phalange is longer than the first; his love of color made its appeal before he analyzed the technique. The first phalange testifies to Dr. Cadman's integrity. The third phalange of this finger discloses an understanding for the need of commercial returns for his work and a recognition that material success has a value in potential power. The fourth finger has the pointed tip denoting the man of tact, its length denoting diplomacy and the first two phalanges the gift of speaking and writing. Upon all the fingers the cushions on the tips are well developed, a sign that their owner shrank from voicing unpleasant truths even when they might have been needed to defend himself against unwarranted criticism.

Under the third finger in the left hand is the trident of fame, fortune and honor, but in the right hand this developed only the two-pronged fork of brilliancy.

No one who has fallen under the spell of that genial talker, Sigmund Spaeth, can doubt the value of the spoken word. Dr. Spaeth might have been a serious savant. His mentality and his attainments fit him for any of what we term the more intellectual occupations. Spaeth prefers to laugh as he goes along and to have millions laugh with him. His work for the better understanding of music, well cloaked under his famous title of "Tune Detective," has done much to debunk the trash talked about music and to bring to thousands of radio listeners understanding of the masters. Dr. Spaeth's palms are broad under the fingers and taper towards the wrist, a shape one associates with art appreciation. He is an instrumentalist of no mean ability. The flesh of his hands is moderately firm, and with the fulness of the third phalanges of all the fingers, suggests that the owner likes ease and luxury and would be idle—only something keeps pressing him to work. Ahead of him are many, many things he really wants to do, and do them he must. His long first finger shows that he is a man who can plan his time, and the long nail phalange shows a man of conscientious qualities that force him to fulfill accepted obligations when he would much prefer loafing.

The second finger has a spatulate tip. This is the sign of the explorer, and with his only moderately firm palms, signifies the seeker upon mental trails. He must either find the new or make new relations for the things already discovered. The slightly spatulate tip of his third finger shows originality, and like all the men in this chapter, he has the long fourth finger of the diplomat.

One of the difficulties of Dr. Spaeth's career has been his ability to do many things well. His head line shows intellectual brilliancy, but drooping as it does, and in the left hand ending in a fork on the mount of the Moon, there is a chance that imagination may bias his judgment. His nails show a power of analysis and of criticism, but when considered with his drooping head line, they also show an introspection that may at times cause an exaggerated sense of too heavy responsibilities. His nails also show his gift of humor, a gift which enables him to pick himself out of his own doldrums and, more important, to give to the public a fund of good cheer.

His flexible thumbs show his adaptability to people and surroundings. The long nail phalanges, signs of a strong will, overshadow the logic and reason of the second phalanges and indicate that he is prone to make desire rather than judgment his master. However, the close joining of life line and head line at the beginning reveal caution, and the long nail

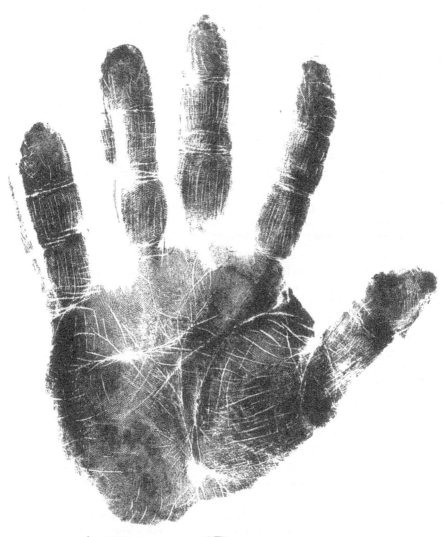

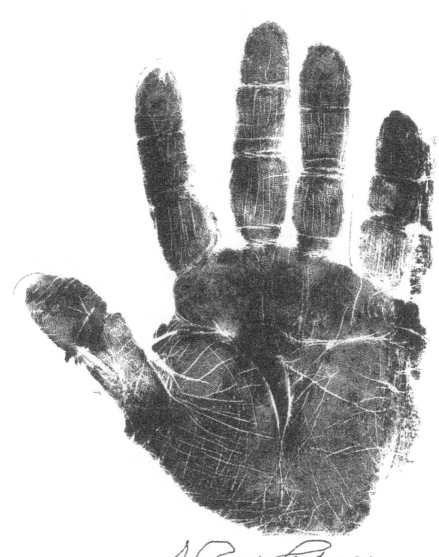

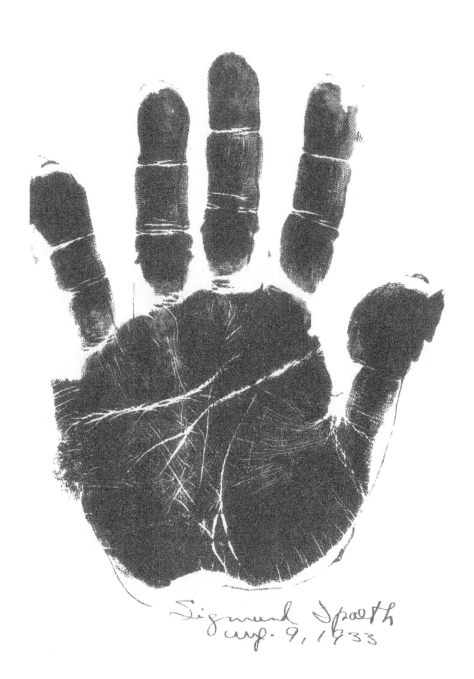

Sigmund Spaeth
aug. 9, 1933

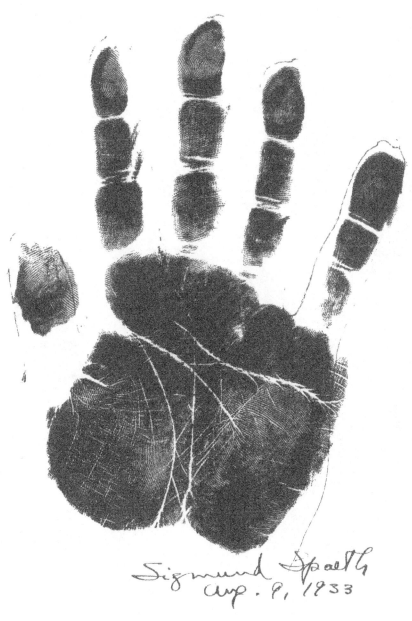

Sigmund Spaeth
aug. 8, 1933

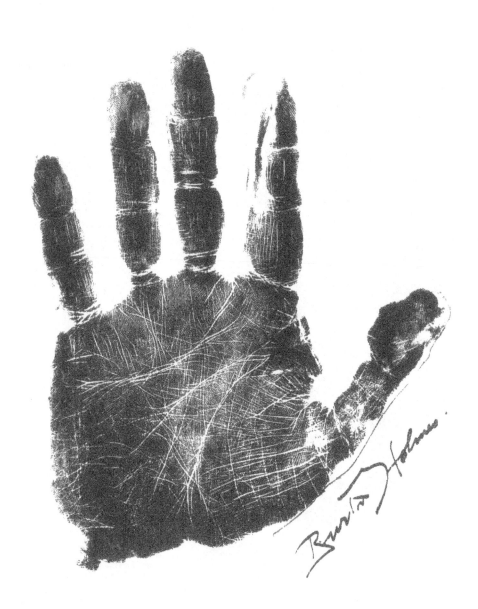

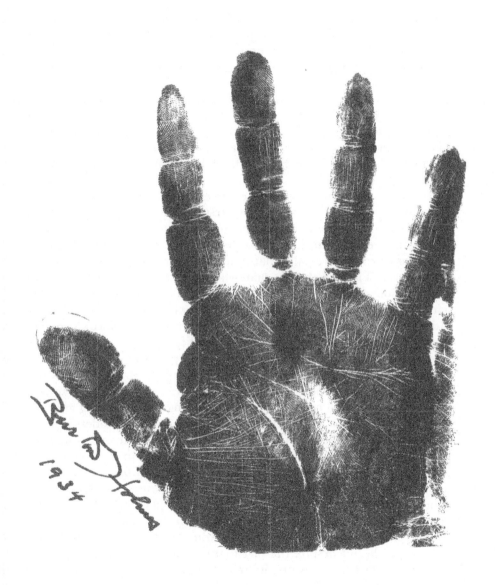

phalanges indicate conscience. He has realized some of his gifts, but not to their utmost. His fourth finger shows in the first and second phalanges his gift of speaking and writing. His ability in music is revealed by the development of the lower part of the mounts of Venus and of the Moon, especially with the memory suggested by the mental concentration evinced in his head line. Under the third finger in his left hand are varied lines of ability; in the right hand under the third finger is the trident of fame, fortune and honor, hardly fully defined as yet, but traced, waiting for the achievement that will make it plain.

In many ways Burton Holmes was the forerunner of our modern radio talkers. Long before that instrument had brought the world into our homes, Burton Holmes was doing his best to arouse us to the knowledge that the world is a wonderful place and that our little part is not nearly all of it. A pioneer in his particular field, he remains a leader of a host of imitators and followers.

Burton Holmes chose to talk. He writes well, as the fifteen volumes of "The Burton Holmes Travelogues" testify. But he likes best to be in personal contact with an audience, and for forty-five years he has been talking all over the world, except as he modestly says, "South Africa."

He has a firm square palm that indicates tenacity of purpose and force of character. It is the palm of a man who can face facts and adjust himself to limitations within himself, or those imposed by outside authority. The width beneath the fingers shows a liking for physical activity, in his case satisfied by travel and lecturing. The width of the mount of Venus towards the wrist is a sign of a strong vitality, and the well-developed mount of the Moon opposite discloses a good power of imagination. His thumbs are double jointed; here is the lover of the dramatic, to whom life itself seems a drama of the greatest intensity. His fingers are smooth and reveal inspirational qualities. The forefinger is both long and flexible, again a sign of activity, this time in connection with leadership. The flares between his fingers show independence in thought and in action.

The second finger is square-tipped. It is a tip that, in connection with his powers of inspiration, shows judgment. He recognizes the lure of the mystical, the mysterious and the fascinating, but uses the wisdom and prudence indicated by the length of the middle phalange of this second finger to avoid any activity arousing criticism.

The space between life line and head line is wide. He could be impulsive in speech, but despite the fact that his thumbs are double jointed, they are rather stiff in the first joint and imply that such impulse is kept under restraint.

In the length of the first phalange of his third finger is shown his eye for line and form, a gift which has made for his success with camera and, the days before motion pictures, lantern slides. The middle phalange shows a love for and an ability to handle color, and this too has been a factor in his remarkable career, while the long and wide third phalange indicates a realization of the value of the commercial element and when added to the practical common sense shown in his head line reveals one of the fortunate individuals who can turn their imagination and inspiration to practical service and so insure commercial returns.

Again we find the long fourth finger of the diplomat—which makes this one hundred per cent for this chapter—and the gift of tact in the rounded tip.

Under the third finger in his left hand are many ability lines; in the right hand these have become three, possibly indicating his ability as lecturer, writer and critic. He has added to the value of these different expressions by a magnetic touch disclosed in the large whorl on the mount of the Moon. This is the hand of an intelligent, balanced personality, one which has used its excesses and deficiencies so that an equilibrium is reached. Burton Holmes well deserves his great success.

Chapter 20: *Lion Trainers*

The title of this chapter may seem a bit confusing. How can a Lion be a Lion Trainer? Yet among our human Lions there are some who seem especially fitted to lead and to help younger Lions to develop themselves —and no more suitable title has occurred to me.

Dr. John H. Finley, associate editor of the *New York Times,* has had a long career as educator, editor and writer. His numerous and bewildering activities extend to many parts of the world. He is honorary vice-president of the Boy Scouts of Scotland, and has received decorations and orders from Japan, Italy, Norway, Denmark, Greece, Czechoslovakia, France. He is President of the New York Adult Education Council, the American Geographic Society, and of the National Child Welfare Association. And these are but a part of his activities.

As I shook hands with Dr. Finley and recalled this imposing list I felt that the big powerful hand that grasped mine was characterized by one signal gift. It was the handshake of a tolerant man, of a man who lives and lets live.

On the hands themselves the most arresting characteristic is the circle of intuition in the right palm—a line curving from under the fourth finger to the base of the mount of the Moon. In addition there is a very clearly marked whorl on the centre of the mount of the Moon. These two markings, indicative of ability to read beneath the surface and to see into the future farther than the average man, are great assets in the work undertaken by Dr. Finlay. His palms are of the square type. He is orderly, methodical and practical. The character of the flesh of the palms with their shape indicates that he has great tenacity of purpose, a tenacity that is free from pugnacity or aggression.

The lines of the palms reaffirm Dr. Finley's tolerant handclasp. The wide space between head line and heart line in the right hand is a sign of lack of prejudice, while the close joining of the life line and head line shows caution and conservatism in speech and action.

The fingers are dominated by the third, which is extremely long, somewhat longer than the forefinger. This is an indication of a man who finds zest in tackling odds and pitting his resources against them. The first finger, although overshadowed by the third, is long enough to mark the executive, and its pointed tip adds quickness of perception. The nail phalange of the second finger, Saturn, is unusually long, showing a mental attitude of serious consideration motivated by high ideals. This finger leans towards that long third finger, and so indicates a feeling of security based upon an assurance of knowledge. Dr. Finley's belief that there is healing for every sorrow, a solution for every human problem, is never failing.

The stiff thumb with its will phalange directed by the second phalange of logic and reason, is that of the intellectual, while the fourth finger, Mercury, is long enough to indicate the gift of diplomacy. He has the gift of expression in the length of the first phalange of this finger, but he prefers to write his words before speaking them.

The long, middle phalanges of all his fingers show again the dominance of the mental world. This man is a gifted intellectual, with great tolerance and a deathless hope in the ability of man to solve his destiny.

The name of James W. Gerard has enjoyed a double fame. First, as our Ambassador in Berlin during the stormy days preceding the World War, and second, because of his world-quoted statement that "fifty men rule America," and his naming those fifty men!

In September, 1934, Mr. Gerard permitted me to make the impressions of his hands. It was a gracious gesture upon his part, as he had no belief in scientific palmistry. His palms, firm and pink, indicate the grim firmness under the outward affability, just as the thumbs by their stiffness, reveal the positive stand he takes when he has made a decision. While he is able to meet people of all kinds, the stiff thumbs also show that he maintains his own personal standards during the meeting; if there is adjustment, the other person makes it. In the length of his fourth finger, Mercury, is shown diplomacy and in its pointed tip, tact in planning for the aid of others. But, although he uses these qualities they are always under the reserve of a conscious holding to his determined standards.

One of the interesting studies of the hands of James W. Gerard is that of contrast between the two. The left or "natural" hand shows a close joining of the life line and head line, indicative of over caution and conservatism. In the right hand, in the space between these lines, is shown the development of the much needed trait of initiative. In the left hand the space between heart line and head line is not nearly as wide as it is in the right. Gerard has made a decided gain in tolerance. In the center of the palm in both hands is a unique marking, a square taking in the life line, the head line and the line of destiny. Such a mark is known as a "square of preservation on the plane of Mars." It does not necessarily imply preservation during warfare, but from any disaster. It signifies that its possessor will survive great danger, and come through in safety.

On the mount of the Moon under the head line is a whorl, large and

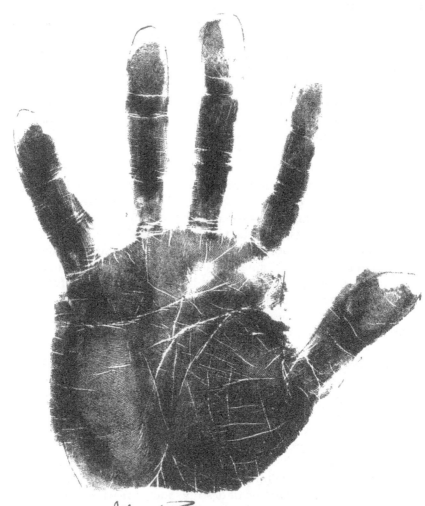

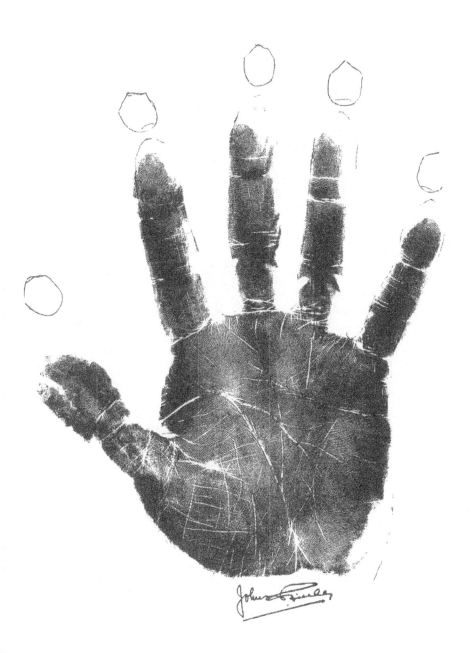

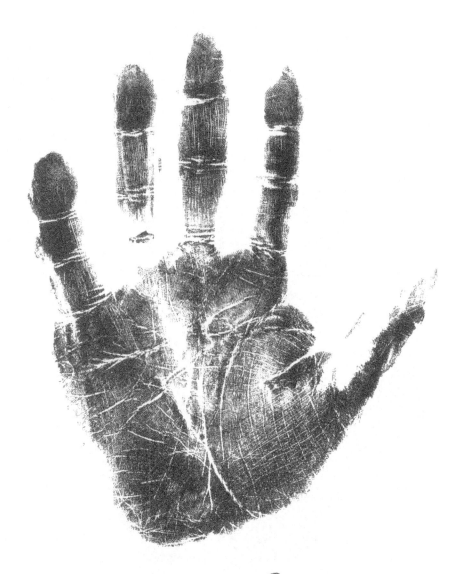

James W. Parent.
Sept. 6th 1984

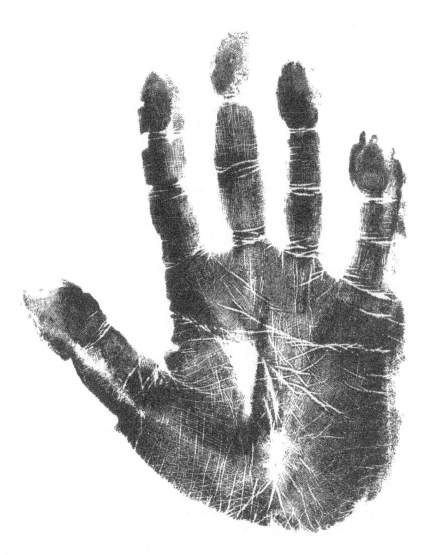

James W. Pearsall
Sept. 6 ᵗʰ 1934

well defined, the sign of the "sixth sense" that is the guide of so many of our Lions. And upon the mount of Jupiter under the forefinger is a star, a sign of unexpected honor and elevation, a sign which has certainly been justified in view of James W. Gerard's history.

The independence that led to that remarkable statement concerning the "rulers of America" is seen in the stretch between the first and second fingers, and between the third and fourth fingers, independence of thought and action.

It was in the House of Representatives at Washington, D. C., that I met Ruth Bryan Owen, at that time a member of the House, representing the state of Florida. Since then, Ruth Bryan Owen has made history for women as our first female ambassador, appointed by President Franklin Delano Roosevelt to the country of Denmark.

As I examined her hands I became convinced that in some respects Mrs. Owen resembles her gifted father, William Jennings Bryan. The wide stretch between the thumb and fingers in her left hand reveals that she is always tempted to fly off at a tangent and to give unstintingly and unnecessarily of her time, strength and money to others. This wide flare has been a little modified in the right hand, but Mrs. Owen is still inclined to be blind to her own interests when her enthusiasm is aroused. The phalanges of her thumbs are equal, a sign of clear judgment and ability to size up a situation. The rounded tips of her thumbs are indications of impatience over delayed results. Her fingers are flexible, the kind of suppleness that marks the person who gleans knowledge from everything, from all contacts and observations. Her short nails are those of the highly critical, introspective, mentally irritable individual, but are indicative as well of a quick sense of humor that makes her a good sport when opposed or defeated.

She has the long nail phalanges of conscience and a sense of duty, and the length of all of her fingers discloses a care in detail that extends from her professional duties to fastidiousness in dress and personal surrounding .

Ruth Bryan Owen is an optimist. While her forefinger shows executive ability and the length of the second finger a recognition that life is real and earnest, the rounded tip of that finger is that of the buoyant person who rises above sober and sordid care with a sublime faith in an unknown future. The square tip of the third finger, Apollo, marks an appreciation of originality in the work of others, but such work must be practical; nothing visionary appeals to her. The pointed tip of the fourth finger reveals tact, and the first phalange shows a power to express herself, especially in the instruction of others. Her conscientious quality is shown again in the length of the nail phalange of this finger. Ruth Bryan Owen could easily be led to become an extremist in her zeal for an individual or for a cause, but it would never be for personal gain.

I met Booker T. Washington in Indianapolis. He had come to us to speak of the work of the Tuskeegee Normal and Industrial Institute of Alabama, of which he was the founder. At that time the negroes of Indianapolis were jealous of one of their own race who had won recognition, and the negro waiters of the Hotel English threatened to strike if asked to serve Dr. Washington. Certain of the white professional and busines men entertained Dr. Washington in order that trouble might be averted. It was shortly after this incident that Theodore Roosevelt, recognizing greatness in individuals regardless of "race, color or creed," received Booker T. Washington at luncheon with him at the White House.

I was, of course, deeply interested in the impressions of Dr. Washington's hands. There was the square palm of the practical man with the recognition of need for obedience to law and order and control of self. The well placed stiff thumb showed the keen tenacity of purpose—not deterred but rather strengthened by obstacles or opposition, when the logic disclosed in the second phalange backed up his determination. His long nail phalanges evidenced his conscience and sense of duty. The fourth finger again in length revealed the diplomacy common to leaders, and showed in the rounded tip his tact in the management of matters, while the equal length of the nail and middle phalanges disclosed his ability as an orator or a writer. His forefinger was comparatively long indicating executive ability, and had the pointed tip of quickness of perception.

His head line indicated that his mentality was used in furthering one particular line of work, rather than diversified interests—a one-track mind. His heart line showed him to be undemonstrative, but faithful in affection to the few, and with ear attuned to the call of distress.

As I look at the impressions of the hands of Lewis E. Lawes, Warden of Sing Sing, I am relieved to find one man in this chapter of Lions who are Lion Trainers, who does not succeed through diplomacy. As you can see for yourself, that fourth finger is very short. His signs of success must be sought elsewhere. Look now at his forefinger. It is exceedingly long, the finger of the true executive who knows how to wield authority. Mercy and justice are indicated in the equally balanced first and second phalanges of this finger. The rounded tip is a sign of understanding, a comprehension that is aided by the "sixth sense" whorl on the mount of the Moon. The fullness of the mount of Jupiter under the first finger shows

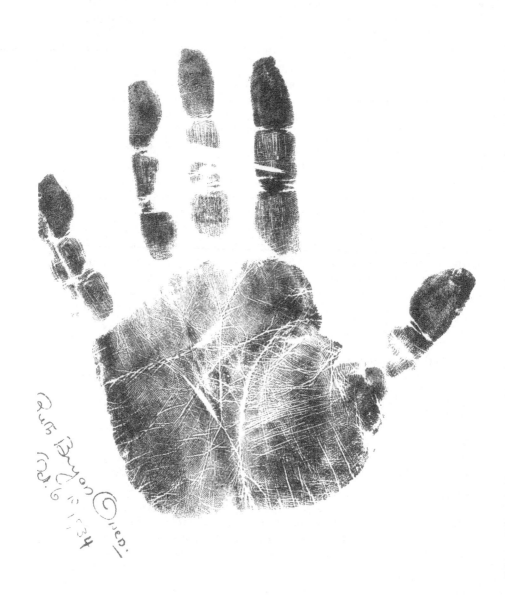

Ruth Bryon Owen
(Mrs.) 6-18-1934

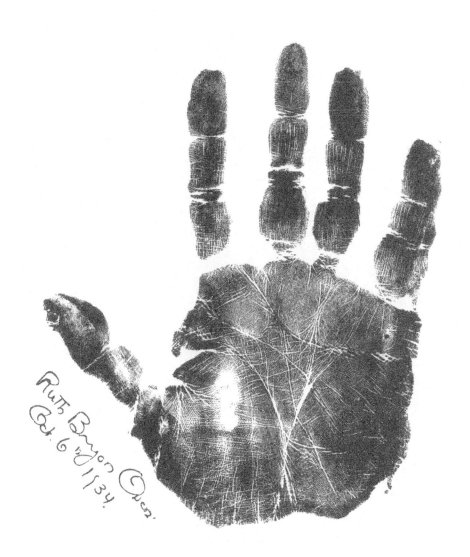

Ruth Bryan Owen
Oct. 6 / 11/34.

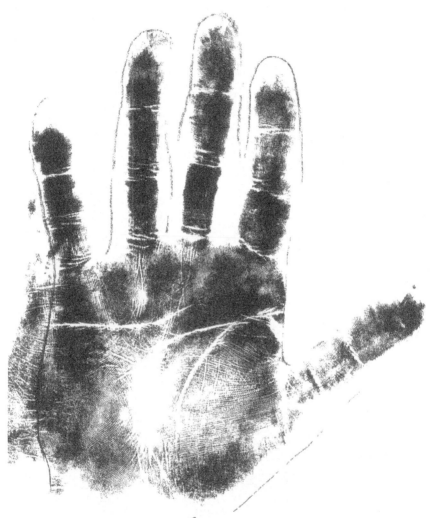

Booker T. Wasshigtn

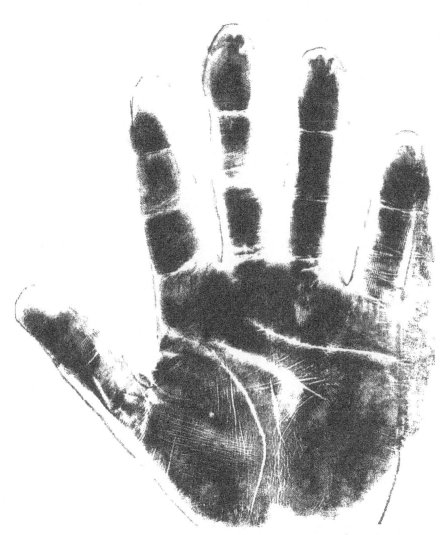

Booker T. Washington

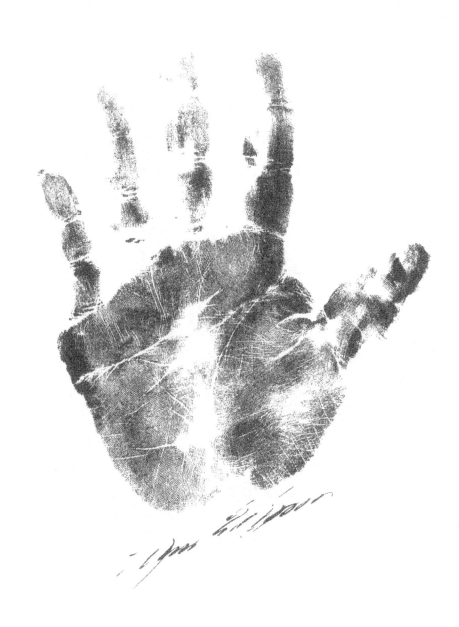

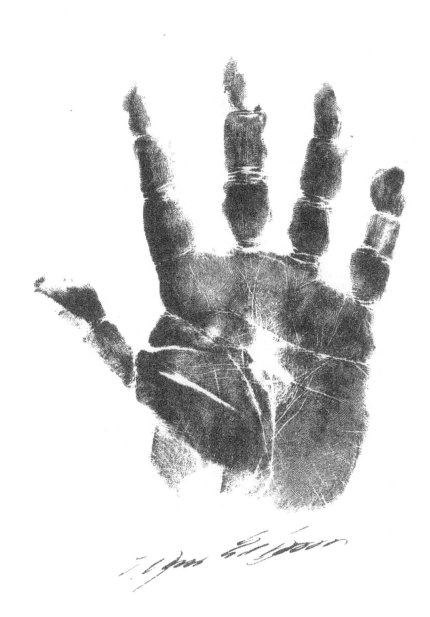

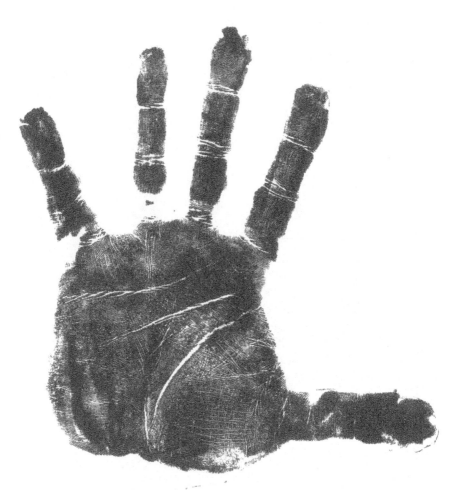

Alfred Smith

that Lewis E. Lawes has his full share of ambition and likes recognition.

The square tip of the second finger discloses an unbiased power of judgment. In the length and breadth of the first phalange is shown honesty of purpose and a desire to be impartial. The long middle phalange declares that here is a man who uses his wisdom with prudence.

His third finger shows a genuine love of beauty which inclines to the practical. Utility has the first consideration. He likes warm glowing color, as the middle phalange shows, and in music he prefers rhythmic and melodic composition. The shortness of the fourth finger does not interfere with the long first phalange telling of Lewis Lawes' gift of expression. He is a very brave man; see the high development of the mount of upper Mars, on the outside of the hand above the head line.

He has the courage of his convictions as well as physical courage; he is able and ready to meet attack, because he has faith in his honesty of purpose. He is not immune to mistakes, as the wide flare between the fingers, indicating independence in thought and action, shows, but he is immune to any weakening in his principle.

The long second phalanges of all his fingers show the dominance of mentality in his life, and the full third phalanges declaring that he has a full appreciation of the comforts of life, are subservient to those phalanges of mentality. His square practical palms are those of a disciplinarian but not those of a martinet. The long first phalange of his thumb declares his perseverance and again this is under the mental—the reason and logic of the second phalange. His thumb is flexible; although he is persevering, he is not stubborn, he can take advice.

His head line again shows fixity of purpose in its depth, and its straight course almost parallel with the heart line reveals his dislike of altering his decisions.

Lewis Lawes is so filled with a desire to be just and "on the square" that any question as to his sincerity arouses the decided aggression shown in the development of the mount of lower Mars on the mount of Venus just under the life line. He will make a fight to have people understand his motives and continue to fight until he has established that understanding.

When I shook hands with Alfred E. Smith, I said,

"I like your handshake."

"That is one thing I ought to do well," he replied with a ready smile, "I have had plenty of practice. I am the man who shook hands with every man, woman and child in the United States in 1928."

Al Smith's palms are firm but not very hard. They are the palms of a man who uses audacity rather than sagacity in arranging his affairs. They are self-reliant palms and evince a good deal of independence. In the slope towards the wrist there is an innate liking for mental and material harmony. The wide flare of the thumbs from his palms and the flares between the fingers disclose his impulsiveness and uncurbed generosity. His left thumb is stiff and shows his natural tendency to be stubborn. In his right hand the thumb is quite flexible, revealing a gain in ability to persevere without stubbornness. He has the tendency to let his heart and emotions rule his head, as is shown in the rather narrow space between heart line and head line at their beginning. To counteract the effect of this, there is the wisdom of the long middle phalange of his second finger which guides the diplomacy of his long fourth finger.

The length of his nail phalanges discloses honesty and fair dealing, while the development of the mount of upper Mars on the outside of the palm under the heart line reveals the kind of courage that endures when the battle is on, and through the time of defeat. The high mount of Jupiter under the forefinger indicates love of approbation justly deserved, since those long nail phalanges show integrity of purpose. On the mount of the Moon is the whorl which, in his case, evidences what is termed "personality plus." It accentuates those outstanding characteristics of sincerity, sympathetic understanding, and quick appraisal of opportunities.

Chapter 21: *On the Path of Progress*

The two women who head this chapter are known all over the world as representative of woman's advance in man's field, the field of business. They have capitalized their feminine accomplishments, the one, Elsie de Wolfe, as an interior decorator, the other, Alice Foote MacDougall, as the builder of renowned restaurants.

Elsie de Wolfe, now the wife of Sir Charles Mendl, I have known since 1902 when I made these impressions of her hands. A high spirited, vivacious woman, she appeared on the stage, tackled and won success in a big decorating business, and has just written a book which is having a good sale, a feminine book—"Recipes for Successful Dining." All along the way, be it rough or smooth, she has enjoyed herself. Her double-jointed thumb indicates not only her ability to dramatize, but her love of such dramatization. The wide space between life line and head line at their beginning shows excessive independence in thought, an independence amounting to daring. This quality has stood her in good stead; she has assailed the projects into which she entered with considerable originality and much drama, and as a result always succeeded in attracting attention. Once they are attracted, she has the power to hold people. Her thumbs are flexible, she is suave and adaptable; her fourth finger is the long one of the true diplomat. Her smooth fingers show decided inspirational quality; she can visualize the completion of what she undertakes and so work towards a well-defined goal. The flares between her thumbs and fingers and between her fingers, again show independence mixed with enthusiasm and spontaneity. Add to these, inspiration qualities and dramatic ability plus suavity and diplomacy, and you have a personality that is sure to be effective. But Elsie de Wolfe has a gift that is greater than any of these. In both hands is seen the rare circle of intuition, starting under the fourth finger and ending on the lower part of the mount of the Moon. This signifies her ability to seize upon the opportune moment, and her deep belief that what she does at a particular time is not only right but the only thing to be done. She knows that she will succeed, and she does succeed; in fact with this gift she is herself, success.

The most striking characteristics first seen in the hands of Alice Foote MacDougall are the sloping of the palm to the wrist and the fulness of the lower parts of the mounts of the Moon and of Venus. Add to these the deep drooping head line of the left hand, and you wonder how this woman ever entered the business world. For these signs proclaim her to be of the world of creative art, with a love of music, a highly developed imagination, and her short smooth fingers add a dislike of detail, and strong inspirational qualities.

To find the motivating power forcing her into a business life, look at the lines running from the heart line crossing the lines of ability under the third finger, especially in the right hand across the lines ending in what is known as the fork of brilliancy. Such lines show her desire for art expression turned into business interests because of the needs of those she loves. Add to these the height of the mount below the heart line on the outside of the palm, the mount of upper Mars. There is courage of the kind that never admits defeat, hence never gives up. The first phalange of her thumb shows a strong forceful will that is directed by the logic and reason indicated by the long second phalange. Her optimism is repeated in the round tip of the second finger; she does not lose hope, because she cannot. The long third phalange of her first finger and the mount beneath show an ambitious woman, and the third phalange of the second finger is that of the home lover; she wants a home that is her own. Her third finger with its rounded tip shows idealism, and in the length of the nail phalange is seen an eye for construction, lines and form, while the middle phalange reveals a love of color. Those who have visited her restaurants know that even the tiny shop at Grand Central Station gleamed like a many faceted jewel amid its commonplace surroundings. The full third phalange of the third finger shows plainly that Mrs. Mac-Dougall understands the commercial advantages of using her art gifts in her business.

Here then is a fighter who cannot be daunted, who fights for those she loves, who is essentially an art lover and a home lover and who has a fair complement of artistic gifts. To back her she has a strong will, powers of logic, honesty and integrity as shown in the nail phalanges of all the fingers, diplomacy as shown in the length of the fourth finger, independence and impetuousity in the flare of her fingers. Her nails show her to be mentally irritable, but the fullness of the third phalange of the fourth finger reveals a saving grace of humor. The breadth under the fingers, together with the firmness of her palm, reveal a liking for much activity both physical and mental.

Her success is based upon the use of all these qualities, but in greater degree to her unfailing courage.

Otto H. Kahn was a banker, one of our most distinguished and successful financiers, yet it is not as a financier that I recall him, but as a lover of the arts. I met him through William J. Guard, well known and

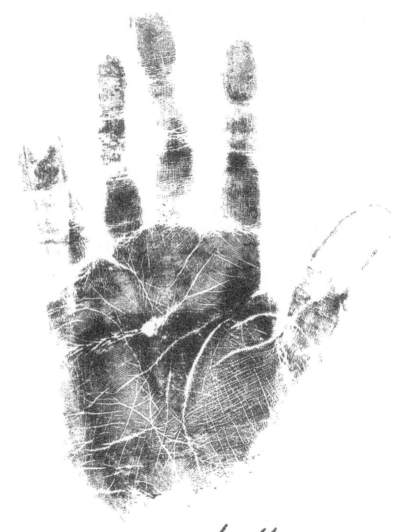

Elsie de Wolfe

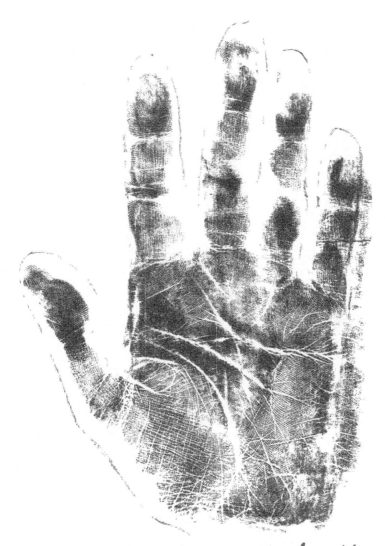

Eric de Wolfe

Quin Forth MacDougall
December 2nd, 1933

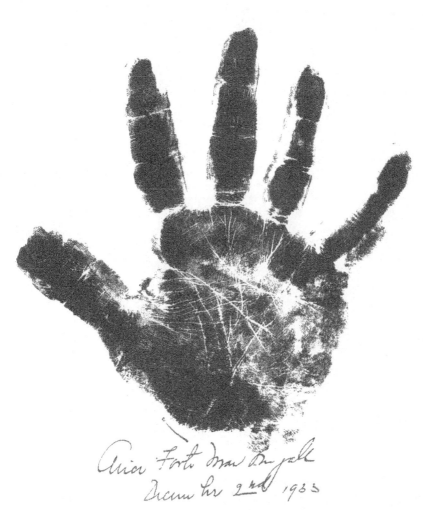

Alice Forte MacDougall

December 2nd 1933

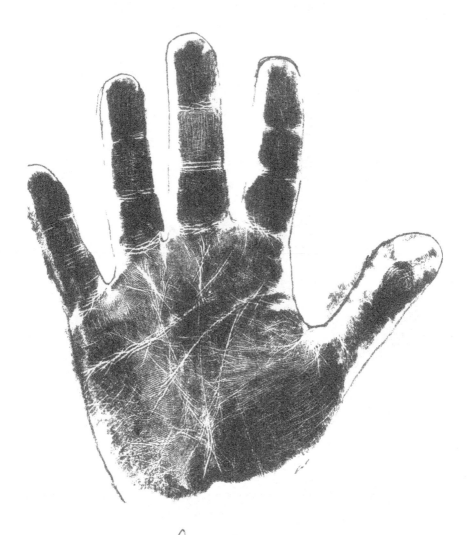

Albert Einstein

December 17 1933

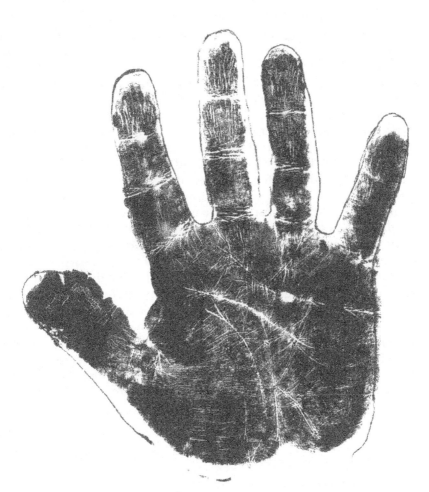

Otto H. Kahn

December 17ᵗʰ 1933

much loved press representative of the Metropolitan Opera House, and it was because Mr. Kahn wanted to frame the impressions I had taken of Billy Guard's hands that he consented to allow me to take those of his own. Looking at these impressions—again we have the square palm, the palm of the man of order and of method who recognizes authority and the need for discipline. His fingers were short but beautifully placed and smooth, and showed an ability to grasp quickly a situation, the smoothness indicating an inspirational insight. The shortness of the fingers was a sign of a dislike of detail, but in this hand it is over-balanced by the mentality indicated in the length and depth of the head line and the wisdom revealed in the long middle phalange of the second finger. In his left hand the close joining of his life line and head line at their beginning was a sign of his natural caution and a tendency to be overly conservative in personal activities. In his right hand these two lines were decidedly apart. Otto Kahn had acquired independence. As his life advanced, he was no longer afraid of criticism. The thumb in his left hand was much stiffer than that in his right. Again, the change testified to the change in the man himself; he had begun with his will forcibly on the alert against possible interference, as he achieved success he relaxed, and his personality became suave and agreeable.

His gifts are indicated in the length of his forefinger, that of the natural leader, the mentality shown in the depth and clarity of his head line, the power of expression as revealed in the length of the nail phalange of the fourth finger, and the insight denoted by the smoothness of all his fingers and the whorl on the mount of the Moon. This insight directed his mentality. It made Otto Kahn a man who was more than a banker; many who remember him with admiration forget that he was a banker. It showed Otto Kahn where his great joy in life lay; in the artistic world, to which he gave freely of himself and his money, he found that his sixth sense had led him to the Mecca of his desire.

Chapter 22: *Can the Leopard Change His Spots?*

When a reformer or a radical succeeds in becoming a recognized Lion, he is under deep suspicion. A business man does not have to justify the making of money; an actor or artist or writer is not expected to explain what impels him to do what he does. But any man or woman who works for the improvement of society in general suffers from the suspicion that a personal ax is being ground. In this day it is still out of the ordinary for an individual to work for anything save to express and to capitalize his personality and his gifts.

If a reformer or a radical makes his living in the very work of reform, he is doubly suspect; if he makes no money, he is believed to be seeking notoriety, honor, distinction. Do the hands of reformers and radicals sustain this suspicion? Here are the impressions of the hands of seven of them who are real lions in their particular fields. What do these hands tell?

I met Norman Thomas only once. To my surprise this man, who heads the Socialist Party, and who is so audacious in his assailing of our "status quo" both in government and economics, gave me what I class as a diffident handshake. Thomas is a sensitive personality. The long nail phalanges of all his fingers show an active conscience. The medium length of his first fingers shows a moderate amount of executive ability with little personal ambition. The decidedly rounded tips of these fingers, together with the length and character of the nail phalanges, indicates the power of and desire for self-abnegation. Thomas wants to surrender his personality to something.

The length of his third fingers, which are longer than the first, reveals a quality of willingness to risk personal liberty, health and financial assets in order to prove his sincerity. The tips of the third fingers are rather spatulate. Thomas is an extremist, but not a fanatic. These fingers are his driving power: an extremist must act.

The length of his fourth fingers show diplomacy. The pointed tips show the gift of expression, and this is helped by the quickness of thought and action shown in the flare between the third and fourth fingers.

That Thomas has climbed his hill of Gethsemane at times is shown in the drooping of his head line toward the mount of the Moon, which shows imagination. But coupled with those phalanges of conscience, it is an imagination prompted by the flagellations of a conscience which permits little, if any, complete relaxation. Regardless of one's personal reaction to the view that Norman Thomas holds and preaches, his hands

148

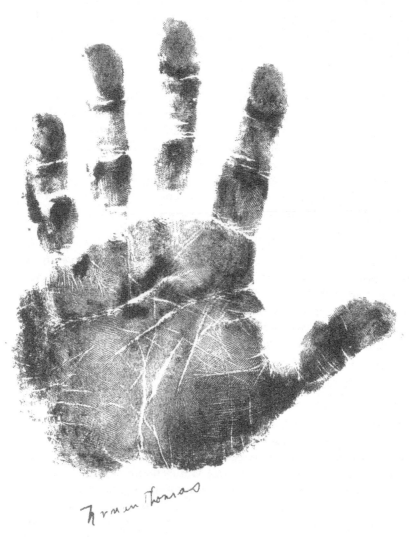

Norman Thomas

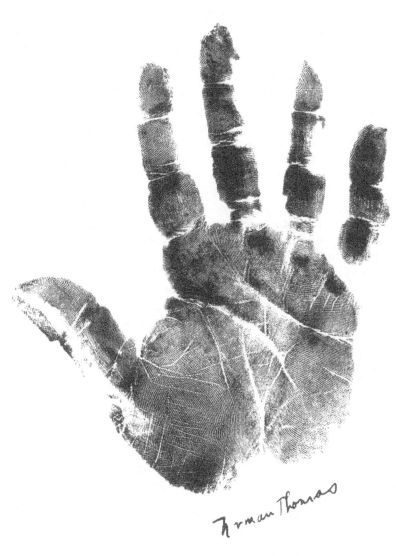

Norman Thomas

show that he meets the test of the true reformer. He is working not for himself, but for what he believes to be right. He is literally giving his life to his cause.

In the past twenty years no woman in this country has worked under such a storm of abuse and misunderstanding as Margaret Sanger. Through it all she has never swerved from her one purpose, to make the children of tomorrow the conscious products of informed parents. When she came to my hotel I knew the work to which she had given her efforts and her personal history. As a girl she had seen her mother overwhelmed by too-frequent child bearing.

As I looked at her palms I understood why she, of many women who had gone through a similar experience, had begun her work. If you will look closely at her hands you can see the circle of intuition in both, that is, the curve which leads from under the mount of Mercury, the fourth finger, and extends to the percussion of the hand on the mount of the Moon. The whorl of the capillaries form what I call "thumb" or "finger" impressions on Luna, as if fingers had just rested upon the spots. These are found not only upon the mount of the Moon, but between the second and third fingers and the third and fourth fingers. These are all signs of intuitive gifts. Margaret Sanger does little conscious planning. She receives impressions and makes plans without knowing that she does anything. Suddenly a course of action lies open before her. It is plain and direct; the only course she can possibly follow.

As she shook hands with me I felt in that sincere firm grasp, an immediate reaction to my personality. The resiliency of her palm is remarkable, she literally feels a person's mood and opinion, as she touches the hand.

The development of the mount of Venus coupled with the drooping of her head line in the left hand to the mount of the Moon shows her sympathy with the problems of others together with an imagination that at times interferes with her clarity of judgment. She has suffered periods of great depression because of lack of progress in her work The straight head line in her right hand shows that she gained confidence as she went on. The development of the mount at the base of the first finger, Jupiter, shows that she has some love of approbation, but not enough to be a motivating force. Her motivation comes from impulse, sympathy with others, and her rare intuitive qualities. There is no self-interest in it. Her driving power again is impulse, backed by intuition. She is a true reformer in that she is not a self seeker, but she is a reformer of a rare type, and her success must be explained by her intuitive qualities. Hard as her struggle has been, she seized upon the propitious time to launch her cause.

It was late in the life of Susan B. Anthony that I read her hands, a time when most of life lay in the past, and little in the future. No one who met her would call her a sentimental woman, her intellectual qualities and her barbed arrows of wit were too much in evidence. But her heart line, forked at one end and running to the space between the first and second fingers showed idealism. She was easily touched by sorrow in the lives of others, broad and generous in the affections, loving humanity rather than the individual. This heart line, together with the long nail phalanges and the long nails, brought her sentiment under the rule of her conscience. Her palm, square with what is called a "tendency to the spatulate," a rare form, told of considerable practical ability with a restlessness that demanded she be up and doing. The mount at the base of the finger of Jupiter was flat, she cared nothing about approval or disapproval of others. The rounded tip of this finger, together with the long nail phalange, showed power of self-abnegation, but the strong branch line running from the life line up to the mount of Jupiter and crowned there by a star denoted intense ambition. Susan B. Anthony knew the struggle between that ambition and fidelity to the work which she had set herself. Her motivation was not always selfless, but her conscientious qualities drove her to plan a course that minimized her personal desires and turned her efforts towards her great work for womankind. She was a true reformer because she was able to direct her ambition to her cause. At times it might be woman suffrage and Susan B. Anthony, but it was never Susan B. Anthony and woman suffrage.

Ben B. Lindsey first came into public notice through his work in the Juvenile Court. An undeserved notoriety is his because of the title his publishers selected for his book, "Companionate Marriage." When he came to see me in Los Angeles I knew at once by his handshake that his quality of high courage was not impaired. He will die fighting with his back to the wall. The shape of Ben Lindsey's palms, broad under the fingers and sloping towards the wrist, and the texture of the skin, shows him to be a mental and not a physical fighter. But he is a defender and not an aggressor. The development of the lower mount of Mars, which is the mount just under the beginning of the life line below the first finger, shows that he will stand by his own beliefs at any cost. The development of the mount of Jupiter under the first finger shows that he likes approval, but it is the approval of his friends or of people who are sufficiently discriminating to appreciate honesty of purpose. He does not care at all for the plaudits of the mob.

150

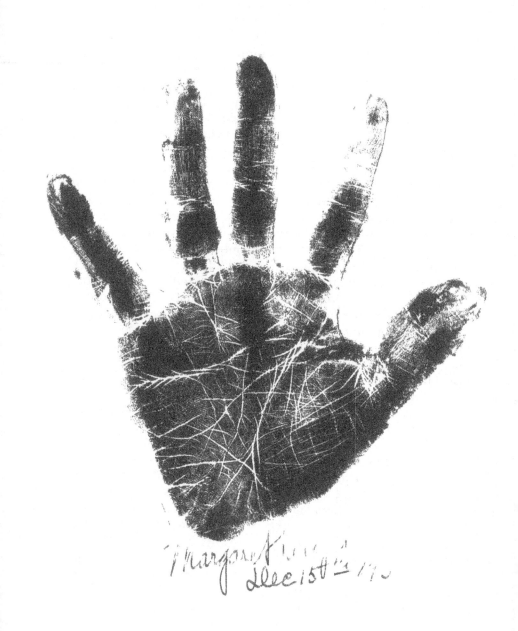

Margaret
Dec 15th '75

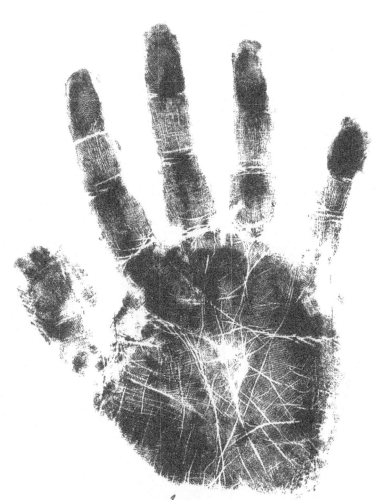

Margaret Sanger
Dec 15th 1933

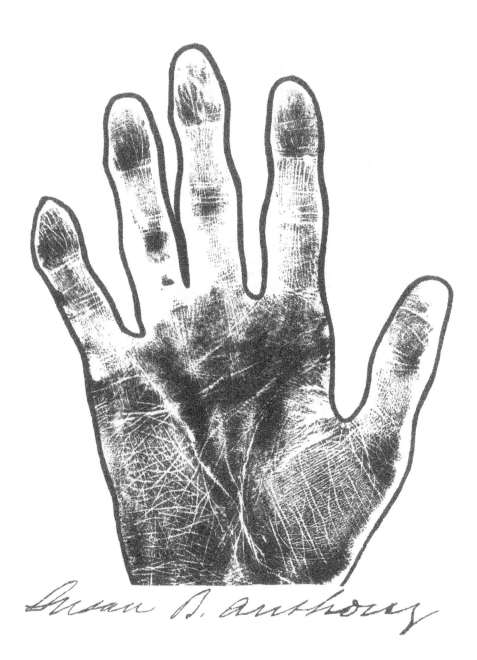

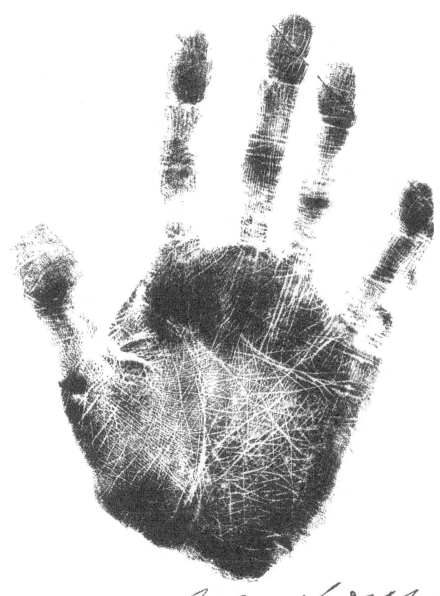

Susan B. Anthony

Dec. 9. 1899

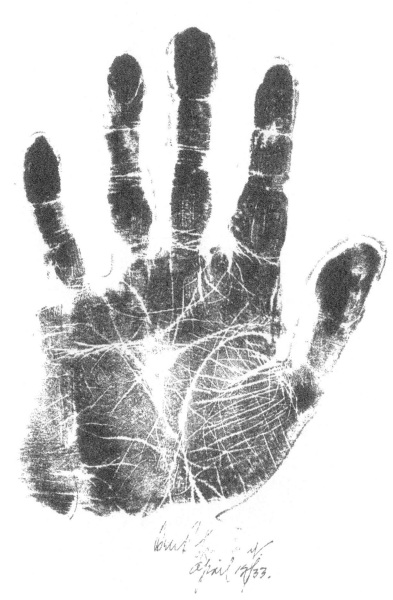

Under the third finger, Apollo, is the star of brilliancy. Lindsey is a gifted man. In his right hand his gifts have merged into the fork of brilliancy; he has gained distinction as a writer and as a reformer. He is better at writing than at speaking, if the speaking is extemporaneous, as is shown in the long fourth finger. He has the gift of expression, but the shape of the tip shows that the gift of expression is not spontaneous, he applies his mentality and works it out. He has the long nail phalanges of conscience, but he is no extremist. He became a reformer because at some time he was moved to the defence of a belief, of a person or persons. Challenged in that defence, his keen sense of justice came into play, a sense shown in the development of the first phalanges of the first fingers.

He remains a reformer because that sense of justice has not yet been satisfied, and his fighting qualities will not let him rest. He is a true reformer in that he fights for the rights of others and not against injustice to himself.

In the reading of thousands of pairs of hands it is seldom that any two pairs are sufficiently alike to arouse my interest. Whatever personality may be, it is expressed in the hands. Not all of our machine age or our mass education or anything else we may invent to make life more uniform serves to alter that expression. It is therefore remarkable that the hands of Jane Addams had a strong likeness to those of Susan B. Anthony. The impressions of the hands of both show practical ability, the lengths of the first fingers show a high order of executive ability, the third fingers show an appreciation of the artistic, and the fourth fingers of both have unusually long nail phalanges which indicate extreme conscientiousness and honesty in every phase of living. Both impressions show a life line that at times is weak and broken, and both have thumbs in which the first phalanges show a tremendous will power. There are many other similarities—with certain differences. Both impressions show heart lines that reveal sympathy for others, but Susan B. Anthony's heart line is that of a woman, who, drawn by suffering in general, fights for a cause bringing relief. This is shown in her heart line rising under Jupiter, while Miss Addams' heart line, running deep and clear, rises between Jupiter and Saturn and dominates her hand, showing that her love has been more for individuals.

Jane Addams had the forefinger denoting self-abnegation. Her natural conservatism, shown in the stiffness of her thumbs and fingers, and the firmness of the palm which indicates caution exercised in even what seems to be unimportant details, mark her as one of those rare individuals who can blend self sacrifice and common sense. The length of her first finger showed not only a strong sense of justice but a great deal of mercy. With her, the immediate need of the individual would be more insistent than the more general effort to help all individuals. Jane Addams had no personal ambition. She lived to receive fame and almost boundless admiration, but achievement for others was at all times her motivation.

Carrie Chapman Catt, to whom Susan B. Anthony resigned the sceptre of leadership in the cause of woman, lived to see suffrage an accomplished fact and later transferred her efforts to the cause of world peace. She is an idealist, as her third finger, Apollo, shows in the rounded tip. The mount of Jupiter shows that she has some love of approbation, although not enough to make it a dominant quality. An interesting marking on this mount is a well-defined star which indicates that ambition will be realized and that honor and distinction beyond all personal expectation will be hers. The impressions shown here were made by me thirty-five years ago. The star is no false prophet.

The interest in Mrs. Catt's hand is in its balance. Rarely have I seen a more even development of natural gifts and potentialities with thumbs in which will and logic are equal. Her long straight head line shows a clarity of intellect, the depth a mental ability to grasp the details of facts that are necessary to any work upon which she is engaged. Her mind is far from being single track, but she can concentrate at will and bring all her powers to bear on one objective until that is attained, whereupon she can at will turn them to another. The rounded mount of Venus shows sympathy for others. Hers is a hand dominated by her mentality. Her outlook is clear, and she can see for some distance ahead. She appreciates approbation, but when she is engaged in a campaign she never thinks of herself, the campaign alone counts. Her long smooth fingers reveal inspirational qualities, and the forefingers are those of a born leader. Is Carrie Chapman Catt a true reformer? Perhaps no true reformer is as purely a mental type. But she is not working for personal fame or glory, neither would interest her sufficiently. She is more of a leader than a reformer, and when she becomes allied to a cause which she is convinced is one which she can further, she will give of herself until there is nothing left to give.

Jacob Riis demanded results of himself. It mattered little what any one else thought if he could maintain his self-respect based on approval of his own actions. His hands showed that in their long nail phalanges and rounded finger tips, together with the very firm palm. His third finger, Apollo, with the length and square tip of the first or nail phalange dominating the second phalange, denoted his demand for truth. Riis wanted truth as a basis before he acted. His right hand thumb was double-jointed; Riis had a flair for the dramatic. Both in his own **personal** experience and in writing and talking, this quality was an enormous asset. The length of the nail phalanges of his second finger, Saturn, with the square tip of that finger, showed common sense as well as the urge of conscience. Riis wanted practical results to follow his efforts at reform, and he wanted them quick. He got them.

Any resident of New York City should know that to him more than to any other person is due the building of Croton Dam, and so the first pure water for the city, better housing conditions, and playgrounds for the children of New York. He had the long phalange and the rounded tip of self-abnegation in his forefingers, but I doubt if he ever recognized them. He would enjoy, through his dramatic sense, even a personal loss. He was a true reformer, not even knowing or missing what he might have been, had he used his undoubted abilities for self exploitation. His entire being was focussed upon his self-imposed tasks.

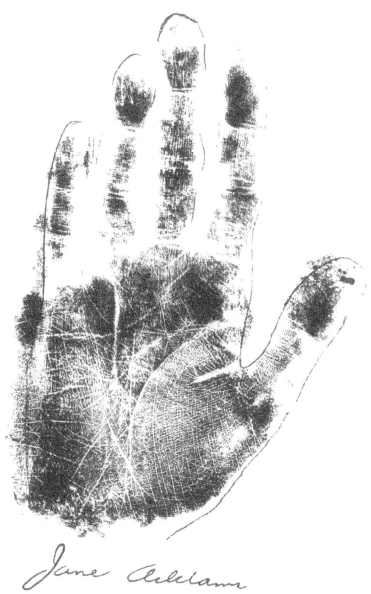

Jane Addams

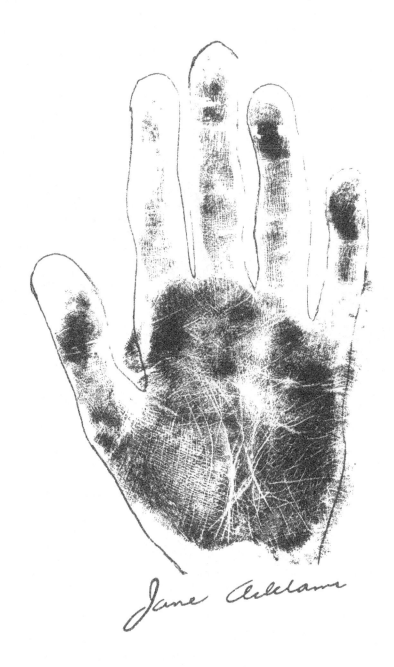

Jane Addams

Eanie Chapman Catt

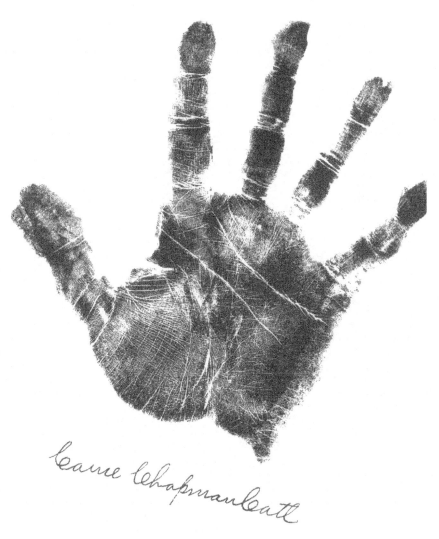

Carrie Chapman Catt

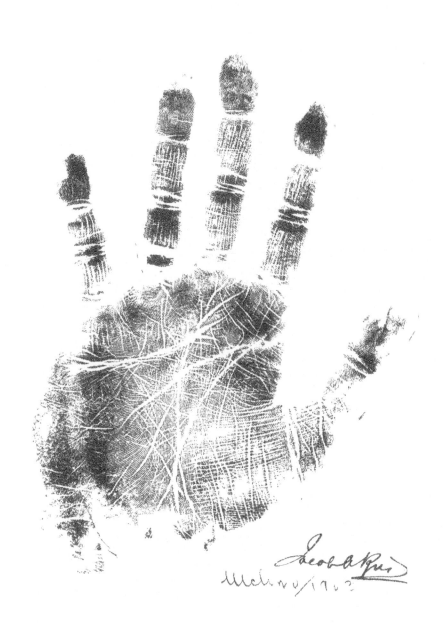

Jacob A. Riis

March 10 / 1903

Chapter 23: *He Who Walks Alone*

In the course of a long and interesting life—if not to others, it has been so to me—I have met both in this country and abroad, certain men and women who have made a unique place for themselves in the world. They are of two kinds: first, those who by force of character, circumstance or opportunity have stood out against the mass of humanity but who have no particular occupational label attached to the very real work they have done; the others belong to professions, but they are unique in those professions, so much so that even in their particular group they, like Kipling's cat, "walk alone."

Look at the impressions of the hands of William Fortune—you may not know him, but that is your distinct and great loss. William Fortune is that rarest of human beings, one who gives of himself to his city, his state, his country and the world, an example of what a man of gifts can do for others. He began as a newspaper man, and it takes an entire column in "Who's Who in America" to follow him to the point where the late President of the United States, Calvin Coolidge, commended him for his outstanding public service as, if you please, a "citizen." His later work has varied through many phases of Red Cross relief work in war and peace as a member of national committees appointed by Presidents Coolidge and Hoover, to the directorship of the Boys' Club of his home city, Indianapolis. A man who receives recognition from his President, his state, and, most remarkable of all, his own city, must of necessity be something of a Man!

You can see that William Fortune's palms are square, with short, smooth and what are termed "mixed" fingers, that is, fingers with variously shaped tips. His palms are soft, thus showing a liking for mental rather than physical activity.

The development of the third phalange of his first finger shows ambition, and the fulness of the mount beneath, a liking for praise which acts as a curb to the mental irritibility which the shape of the nails, broader than they are long, indicates. The long nail phalange of the first finger with its rounded tip reveals a quickness in grasping the crux of a situation and an innate integrity that sets his standards for personal action. In the right hand the first finger is slightly longer than in the left; William Fortune has developed his executive ability. This executive ability, coupled with the mental concentration disclosed by the long, deep, slightly drooping head line in the right hand, is backed by the force of will shown in the first phalange of the thumb and the gift of diplomacy revealed by the length of the fourth finger, a combination that has enabled him to accomplish his outstanding achievements.

The rounded tip of the second finger indicates his interest in the investigation of that which is beyond ordinary human knowledge—the mystic, or so-called supernatural. This interest is somewhat balanced by the length of the middle phalange, indicative of prudence, and by the decidedly conservative spread of the fingers of the right hand, and the developed caution shown in the close joining of the life line and head line in the right hand.

The third phalange of this second finger signifies a love of home and of the land. You can see the decided leaning of the finger towards the third finger, Apollo. The serious and somber strain in William Fortune's nature has been lightened by the buoyancy and sunshine of Apollo. His third finger has the square tip of the man who requires that creative art shall have a reason for its existence. The rounded tip of the fourth finger shows tact, and, coupled with the length of the first phalange, reveals a gift of expression in writing and speaking. Under the finger the full mount of Mercury discloses a sense of humor, strengthened by the width of the third phalange.

William Fortune is a man who respects and wants order, who has disciplined his tendency to extremes and developed prudence and caution, whose natural gifts are those of speaking, writing with wit and diplomacy, ability in mental concentration and a will power that expresses itself in tenacity of purpose.

Although Walt Disney has spent little time in making a fitting background for his personality, nobody can dispute the right of the creator of "Mickey Mouse" and "The Three Little Pigs" to walk alone.

The "Mickey Mouse Studio" is quite ordinary, not at all in the "Hollywood manner." Disney's own office building is unpretentious, much like that of a small town newspaper.

I climbed a wooden stair which led to a door with "OFFICE OF WALT DISNEY" in plain back letters on the glass, and entered a small room sparsely furnished with desk, chairs, tables and floor loaded with drawings, paper, odds and ends. Someone swept off a chairload to make a place for me near Walt Disney who was busily engaged in working out another Mickey Mouse story.

His thumbs are double jointed, disclosing his liking for dramatic episodes and the ability to create them in life. His palms are square and very firm, an indication of tenacity of purpose and the practical side of his nature that makes him a worker and not a dreamer. His thumbs are

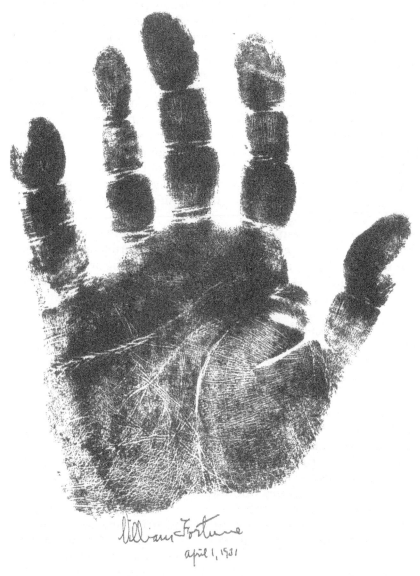

William Fortune
april 1, 1931

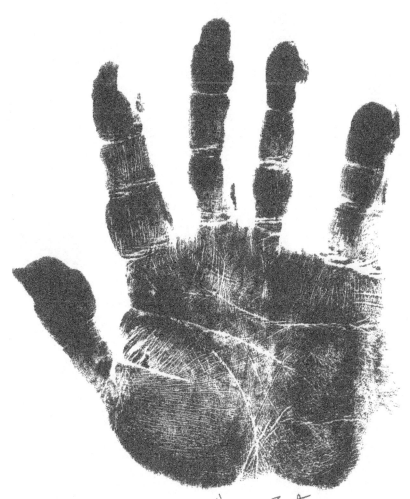

William Fortune
April 1, 1931

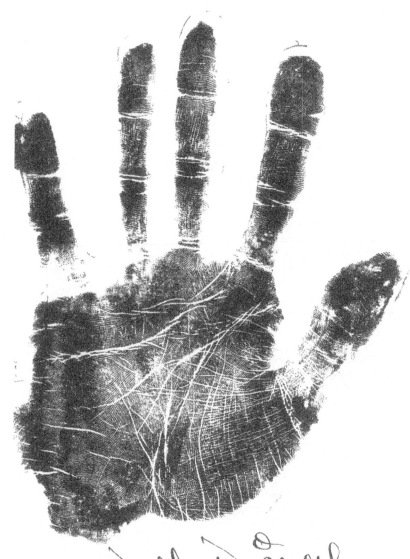

Walt Disney

4·14·55

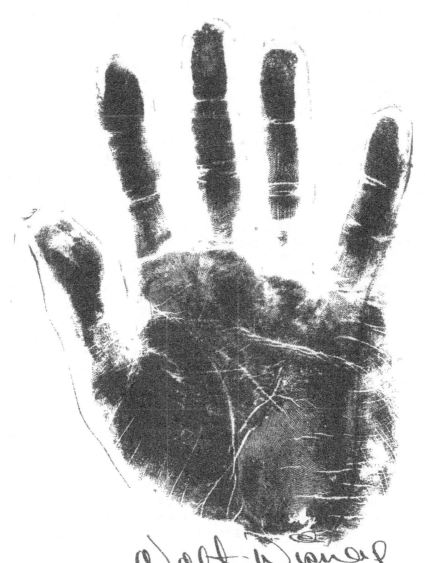

Walt Disney

4-14-33

very flexible; he adapts himself easily to all people and all circumstances; no background is necessary for his work, the work alone and the drama of the work count. The flare of his fingers reveals his natural tendency to fly off at a tangent, not a fortunate quality for him. Disney has developed the motto "curb that impulse" because experience has convinced him of the necessity of conserving his time and his strength for his work. He has made use of the wisdom and the deep seriousness shown in the long, heavy, second finger, Saturn, to accomplish his purpose.

The mount of the Moon in Disney's hand has a high development, indicating an active and original imagination. The mark of intuition leading to genius is there, and, coupled with the development of the mount, makes a bottomless well of joy upon which he can draw.

His fingers, curiously enough, are rather short, which indicates a natural dislike of detail; but the nail phalanges of the third fingers are long, showing a quick eye for line and form, and with the square tip, a recognition of the necessity of practical preparation for successful results. The second finger, Saturn, shows in the shape and length of the first and second phalanges the sober second thought and the prudence which are essential to his progress, and the length of the first finger indicates executive ability and great initiative. The first phalange of the third finger is longer than the second, revealing Walt Disney's liking for lines, form and construction and, with the square tip, his appreciation of technique. Color, shown in the second phalange, is therefore subservient, and he prefers black and white as his medium of art expression.

His fourth finger is unusually long, extending above the first joint of the little finger. Disney is a real diplomat; he has rare tact in management of his affairs. This finger also shows a great gift of expression in the length of the nail phalange. The long nail phalanges on all of his fingers reveal the innate conscientious qualities that make those who deal with Disney trust him wholly.

Charles Holman-Black was one of our noted singers. Today that distinction is almost overwhelmed by his record during the World War. At its close he was decorated by France and her Allies as having done "the most stupendous and long continued one man relief work," a record which alone would entitle him to a place in this chapter. I made the impressions of his hands when we were living in Paris.

As you can see, his palms lack the usual slope to the wrist that characterizes many of the artistic. Instead they are square and firm, those of a man who is fond of both physical and mental activity and who has great endurance. His thumb, while well placed, is rather heavy, and indicates fixity of opinions, fortunately tempered by logic as shown in the second phalange, with will power and intelligently directed perseverance shown in the nail phalange. Holman-Black is tenacious in holding to his opinions, persistent in following any work or pleasure that attracts him. The wide stretch between his thumb and fingers and between the fingers shows his tendency to overdo in behalf of others, and with the long nail phalanges of his fingers, indicates a highly developed conscientious quality which is characteristic of the man as an artist as well as a war worker.

Before meeting Marie, Grand Duchess of Russia, I had been told that she had beautifully formed hands, equalling those depicted by the great artists. Her hands are beautiful, but when I welcomed her at my hotel, and she shook hands with me I was surprised to receive a firm pressure, which gave an impression of great mental and physical poise—they are not hands which were made only to be seen; they do things.

The smooth, satiny skin of her palms indicates with the most delicate tracings of the capillaries, a love and desire for physical comfort. Her left thumb is stiff, and the mount of Jupiter under her forefinger is very high; inborn pride and love of power make her natural reaction to people one of aloofness. But her right thumb is much more flexible: she has responded to the emergencies of her life, and has become friendly. In this she has been aided by great intuition shown plainly in the whorl on the mount of the Moon. The drooping of the head line in both hands, together with the finely grained skin, are signs of a highly sensitized receptive nature. She unconsciously, or half consciously, absorbs and reflects whatever experience life brings to her, and gains strength and knowledge with which to arm herself for future experiences. This reaction is that of expediency. Within her last citadel of defence she cherishes what she believes her imperishable self. Unconsciously she has held to the memorable cry of the defenders of Verdun, "On ne passera pas."

The long first phalange of her second finger with its rounded tip shows the buoyancy that keeps this inner self alive against all odds of fate. She is a brilliant woman, as the forked head line indicates. The pointed tip of her first finger shows quickness of perception, and the gift of expression shown in the tip of the fourth finger denotes power as a speaker and writer. She has inspiration in her smooth fingers, and the flare of the fourth finger from her hand shows a natural love for the dramatic side of life with a desire for a rapid succession of events. She can indulge in self pity and despondency, the drooping of the head line into the mount of the Moon in her left hand shows this, but her natural buoyancy and desire for results enable her to sweep all this away and to go on. Under her third finger are decided lines of ability. As a stranger within our

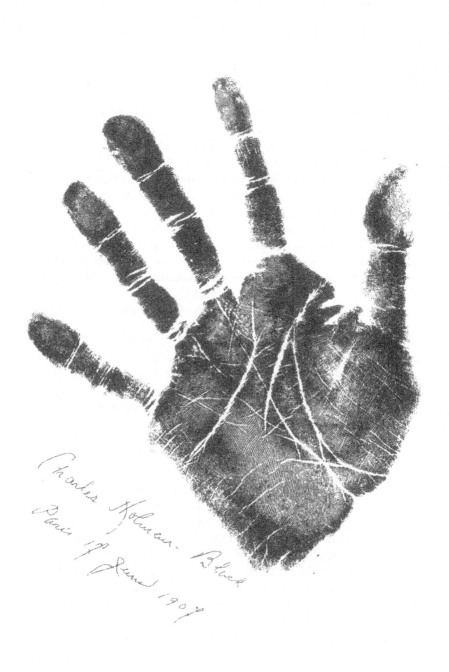

Charles Holman- Black
Paris 1er June 1907

Charles Norman-Black
17 June 1907

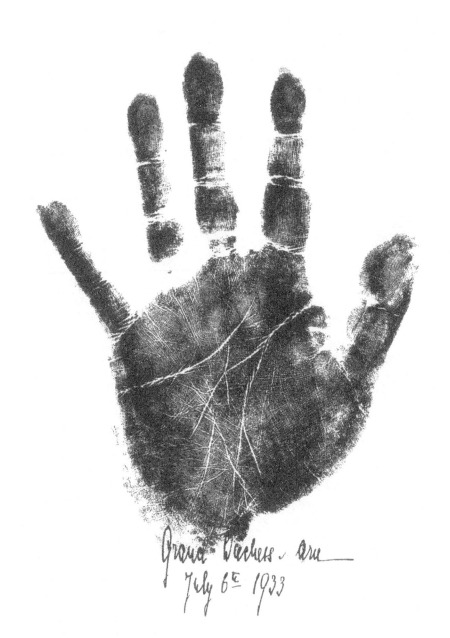

Grand Duchess Anne
July 6th 1933

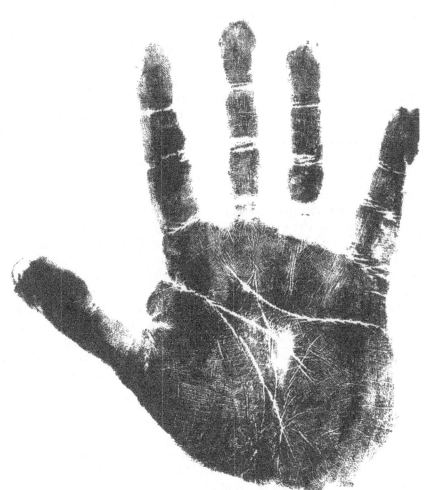

Grand Duchess Marie
July 6ᵗ 1933

gates, Marie, Grand Duchess of Russia, brings considerable gifts and a desire for friendliness.

I am often asked whether the lines of the hands change with the passing of years. The science of palmistry accepts the left hand as denoting the potential qualities of the individual, the right hand as made by the individual himself, with the reverse being true of left-handed persons. I have before me the impressions of the hands of Quill Jones, the famous collector and foremost authority on Oriental rugs and antiques, objets d'art, etc. The first impression is dated May, 1897, and is followed by others dated 1898, 1900, 1901, 1905, 1906, and 1933. The impressions of the hands make a fascinating record of a remarkable life. Quill Jones has searched in strange places for the rugs he prizes and the hands tell of hardship and danger from many possible sources, pestilence, war, famine, bandits, and accident. All of the lines are bound by squares, known as "squares of preservation," or fainter lines running along the life lines, lines of re-enforcement.

Between 1905 and 1929 Quill Jones made ten extended trips to India, China, Persia. On the eighth he covered thirty thousand miles, and on the ninth trip he was gone two years and traveled forty-three thousand miles by water, horse, camel and auto, coming face to face with revolution, starvation, all the horrors of the war-ridden invaded countries of Russia, Persia, Mesopotamia, Palestine, Turkey, and the little known but fascinating Yemen land in lower Arabia. He came back unscathed. How? Look at his thumb. His will, evidenced in the nail phalange is powerful and determined when he decided his goal. It dominates the phalange of logic, the second phalange. The curve of the second phalange shows tact and mental brilliancy. Both thumbs are flexible, Quill Jones has all the charm of a good mixer.

The decided development of the second joints of his fingers indicates a love of law and order as applied to personal belongings, and, with the thickness of the third phalanges, a personal neatness and a liking for luxury and beauty in his surroundings. Quill Jones has in addition, strong mystical tendencies, shown in the whorls on the mount of the Moon and the whorls on the mount of Apollo, indicative of his sixth sense, and what is known as "the ring of Solomon" under the finger of Jupiter, disclosing an aptitude in understanding occult forces. This mystical tendency enhances his treasures; to him they represent not only their actual material attraction, but the history of the people who made and possessed them. In the jars from Mesopotamia brought from beneath countless layers of earth and stained with the oil carried in the passing of centuries, is something of the soul of man through those centuries. His love of his objects of art is not only that of color and line, but of this intangible quality sensed by the mystic, but not by the materialist.

In Quill Jones' firm palms are indications of the strength and endurance that enabled him to undertake and come through such hazards.

His first finger shows ambition and executive ability, while his second finger has the rare spatulate tip of the lover of discovery, especially if that discovery means physical activity and adventure. The whorl at the base, with the shape and length of the second phalange of this finger, shows his prudence, a love of animals and an uncanny gift for managing them. Animals will be friendly to a man who possesses such a mark, and, unless they are frightened, the wild beasts of the desert will not harm him.

To give a complete reading of these unusual hands would take the whole of this chapter. In the left hand he has decided marking of two possibilities, one in some expression of art, and the other a vent for his physical restlessness, as explorer and discoverer. In the right hand is foreshadowed another possibility, along another phase of work: notice the line coming from the head line, a sign of intellectual activity, probably in writing.

It has been some years since I met Ishbel, Countess of Aberdeen, and was entertained at her home, Dollis Hill House, just outside London. Then, as now, she was much in the public eye. She was an officer in the International Council of Women, afterwards its President. When her husband, the Earl of Aberdeen, was Viceroy of Ireland she worked hard in promoting the work of lace making, weaving, and similar crafts in the hope of improving the lot of Irish women.

Her hands are soft, and broad under the fingers; she is a mental rather than a physical worker. The resiliency of her palms, showing an active interest in many fields, is accentuated by the wide stretch between the fingers, a sign of independence in thought and action. Her flexible thumbs tell of her adaptability to people, surroundings and responsibilities. The length of the first finger discloses her executive ability, the fulness and length of the third phalange a liking for power, and the tendency to use her authority according to her personal point of view. While her head line shows mental concentration and intelligence, the rather narrow space between head line and heart line reveals that Lady Aberdeen can be fixed in her ideas, although she is generous in giving her time and strength as is indicated in the flare of her thumbs from her hands.

She has the smooth fingers of the woman who dislikes detail to the point of making snap judgments in her anxiety to avoid infinitesimals.

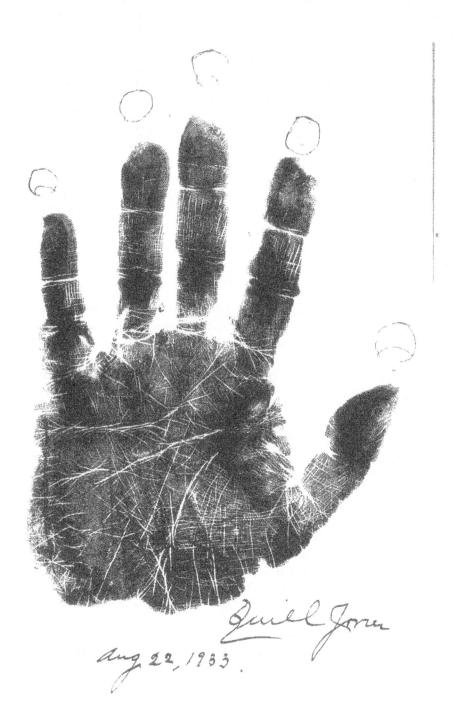

aug 22, 1933.

Quill Jones
aug. 22, 1933.

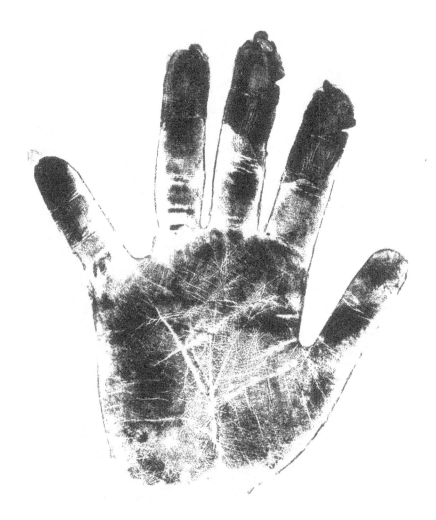

Ishbel Aberdeen

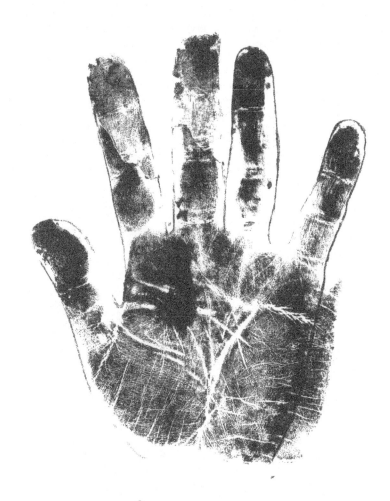

Countess of Aberdeen
Aug 3 1903

The fulness of the third phalanges of all of her fingers indicates the comfort lover who wants the niceties of life. But with her adaptability and the high mount of upper Mars rising between the heart line and the head line on the percussion of the palm, there is indicated courage, not only in meeting limitations in personal comfort, but in accepting the personal tragedies and adversities that have been her portion. She carries on with her chin up, smiling.

CPSIA information can be obtained at www.ICGtesting.com
Printed in the USA
BVOW08*1328150216

436773BV00001B/1/P

9 781163 216668